"LUMINOUS . . . Nuanced and passionate, her book achieves what many travel writers can only aspire to: the sense of being both inside and outside of a culture at the same time and the profound feeling that this journey has indeed led her to someplace she always wanted to go." —*Booklist*

"A LOVELY BOOK . . . It offers both the most balanced view of Japan I have encountered and a gripping personal journey. Strong and delicate, it resembles the Japanese people Cathy Davidson describes." —Marilyn French, author of *The Women's Room*

"DAVIDSON IS A DROLL GUIDE AND A QUESTING SOUL. Her observations of Japanese women, and of the nighttime 'Floating World' of bars . . . are particularly sympathetic and astute. In traveling halfway around the world, Davidson discovers how to abide with herself." —*Elle*

"BEAUTIFULLY WRITTEN . . . *36 Views of Mount Fuji* is not a travel book in the usual sense. . . . It is a book about a much deeper process, the way in which another culture can infiltrate us and make us different people. . . . It opened my eyes to the beauty of another culture and also made me appreciate aspects of my own." —*Raleigh News and Observer*

CATHY N. DAVIDSON is a professor of English at Duke University. She is the author or editor of more than a dozen books, including *The Book of Love: Writers and Their Love Letters*, and her articles have appeared in *Ms.*, *Vogue*, *The Women's Review of Books*, and other publications. She lives in Durham, North Carolina.

"THIS BOOK IS HONEST AND EVEN-HANDED, respecting the complexity of the mystery that is Japan. . . . It is a book that should be read by anyone serious about learning more of this fascinating country."   —*Lincoln Journal-Star*

"DELIGHTFUL . . . Reads like a wonderful, intimate letter from a friend. . . . Davidson's book is brimming with understated emotion . . . and insightfully plumbs the spiritual dimensions of both cultures."   —*Virginian-Pilot and Ledger-Star*

"Empathy infuses Davidson's reactions to the Japanese and lifts this graceful, balanced account of her experiences in their country above the ordinary. . . . Her charmingly drawn word-pictures resonate."   —*Publishers Weekly*

"SUPERB . . . A JEWEL . . . *36 Views of Mount Fuji* is several books in one, and each one is a delight. . . . Davidson writes in the higher tradition of elegant memoirs—gracefully, thought-fully, humorously."   —*Trenton Times* (New Jersey)

"Parts of this very personal American teacher's Japanese memoir, like the delicate chapter about her Nigawa neighbors' reactions to a Christmas season death in her husband's family, had us crying. . . . Trust us. Try it."   —*New York Daily News*

"TOP DRAWER . . . grows like a novel and takes on unusual richness as it keeps reinvesting itself in earlier scenes and people."   —*Kirkus Reviews*

Also by Cathy N. Davidson

*The Book of Love: Writers and
Their Love Letters
Revolution and the Word: The
Rise of the Novel in America
The Experimental Fictions of
Ambrose Bierce*

Edited by Cathy N. Davidson

*Reading in America: Literature
and Social History
The Lost Tradition: Mothers and
Daughters in Literature*
(with E. M. Broner)

CATHY N. DAVIDSON

36

VIEWS

of

MOUNT

FUJI

On finding myself in Japan

A PLUME BOOK

PLUME
Published by the Penguin Group
Penguin Books USA Inc., 375 Hudson Street, New York, New York 10014, U.S.A.
Penguin Books Ltd, 27 Wrights Lane, London W8 5TZ, England
Penguin Books Australia Ltd, Ringwood, Victoria, Australia
Penguin Books Canada Ltd, 10 Alcorn Avenue, Toronto, Ontario, Canada M4V 3B2
Penguin Books (N.Z.) Ltd, 182–190 Wairau Road, Auckland 10, New Zealand

Penguin Books Ltd, Registered Offices: Harmondsworth, Middlesex, England

Published by Plume, an imprint of Dutton Signet,
a division of Penguin Books USA Inc.
Previously published in a Dutton edition.

First Plume Printing, October, 1994
10 9 8 7 6 5 4

℗ REGISTERED TRADEMARK—MARCA REGISTRADA

The Library of Congress has catalogued the Dutton edition as follows:
Davidson, Cathy N.
    36 views of Mount Fuji : on finding myself in Japan / Cathy N.
Davidson.
        p.   cm.
    ISBN 0-525-93707-2
        0-452-27240-8 (pbk.)
    1. Japan—Description and travel—1945–   2. Japan—Civilization—1945–
3. Davidson, Cathy N.   Journeys—Japan.   I. Title.   II. Title: Thirty-six views of
Mount Fuji.   III. Title: 36 Views of Mt. Fuji.
DS811.D332   1993
915.204'48—dc20   93–17162
                                                                                CIP

Printed in the United States of America
Original hardcover design by Steven N. Stathakis

This book is for many people:

Ted, Charles and Susan
Karina, Bruce and Ross
Maryvonne and Ichirō

and other Japanese friends who,
though pseudonymous here,
inspired every page.

CONTENTS

CONTENTS

A NOTE ON JAPANESE NAMES

In Japan, the genderless suffix -*san* is appended to names as a token of respect. It is roughly the equivalent of *Mr., Ms., Mrs.,* or *Miss.* Many of my Japanese friends compromise between formal Japanese address and the informality of English by calling me "Cathy-san," and I call a number of my friends by their first names, "Kiyomi-san" or "Tomoe-san." Some Japanese who have spent time in the West drop the -*san* suffix entirely. I have rendered these levels of formality (and Westernization) in this book situationally, mainly according to the terms I would have used in Japan. Also, I have given the family name last here (although in Japan it would go first).

In my phonetic transcription of Japanese words and phrases (*rōmaji*), I have used a macron to indicate long vowel sounds except in the case of a long *i* (which is indicated by a repeated letter, as in *hazukashii*). I have also followed the usual practice in English-language publications of omitting the macron in common Japanese place names such as Osaka or Kyoto.

A "Glossary of Japanese Words and Expressions" can be found at the back of this book.

ACKNOWLEDGMENTS

I took ten years to *begin* this book, always held back by joint commitments to specificity and privacy. It seemed urgent (never more so than at the present) to write about actual Japanese women and men, not the stereotypical ones regularly featured in renderings of that country. But I feared a personal account might be embarrassing to the individual Japanese who inspired it. After four visits to Japan and more than a decade of close contact with the Japanese, I still do not know the borders of shame.

My solution was to create "composite" characters, thus allowing me to report actual events but to blur details in order to preserve the anonymity of the people involved. With a few exceptions (such as Maryvonne and Ichirō Okamoto), the residents of Japan are pseudonymous here. Their stories have been put together from the common elements in numerous other stories; the basic facts of their lives have been so altered that I hope even they will find themselves unrecognizable. In particular, "Professor Sano" represents many people who served as guides through Japanese life. Similarly, specific places, such as "Kansai Women's University," are composites. By telling my story in this way, I hope I have not presumed on either the privacy or the generosity of the many people who helped make my time in Japan so rewarding. I thank them all for their kindness and their candor.

The process of building a Japanese-inspired house forced me to think on both practical and profound levels about what Japan has meant in my life. Much of this book was written in a tatami room designed by Dail Dixon and built by Greg Pruitt and Bob Jenkins. Jonathan Kidder made the little Japanese *koi* pond where I begin most mornings. Edith and Lee Calhoun showed me that a Japanese house really could exist in rural North Carolina.

Several individuals were kind enough to answer innumerable questions and to correct mistakes on all or part of this manuscript. Rebecca Jennison, Seiki Kinjō, Dana D. Nelson, Oliver Statler, Kimiko Yagi, and Kazuko Watanabe each read one or two chapters and provided invaluable information and advice. Setsu Kawata helped with the glossary, while Cynthia Davis and Caren Irr checked facts and proofread various versions of the manuscript. Jan Freeman and Alice Kessler-Harris offered generous and perceptive critiques of the entire book, as did Ted Fowler, who read with attention, care, and wisdom far beyond anything I could have hoped for. Their advice was always appreciated (if not always followed).

My writing group—Alice Kaplan, Jane Tompkins, and Marianna Torgovnick—pushed me, constantly, to make this book mine. I didn't know what that meant when I began, but I am grateful that they did. My appreciation of them, as colleagues and as friends, never ceases.

The members of the Danceries, a Japanese group that specializes in medieval French music, were kind enough to invite my husband and me to join them on their tour of France in the summer of 1992, when I was completing this book. Despite an arduous concert schedule, they took the time to participate in long discussions of the nuances of various Japanese words and concepts. I especially thank them for a beautiful night spent in a café in Dijon, sipping *kir* under the stars and reminiscing about Oki.

LIST OF
ILLUSTRATIONS

All illustrations come from Katsushika Hokusai's *Thirty-Six Views of Mount Fuji.* Courtesy of the Honolulu Academy of Arts.

LIST OF ILLUSTRATIONS

36

VIEWS

of

MOUNT

FUJI

PREFACE

The title of my book, *Thirty-Six Views of Mount Fuji*, comes from the series of woodblock prints done by Katsushika Hokusai (1760–1849) near the end of his long life. In these brilliantly colored prints, as well as in a black-and-white sequel that he called *One Hundred Views of Mount Fuji*, Hokusai portrays the different, even contradictory, aspects of Japanese life. There is tremendous variety and vitality in both series—aristocratic courtiers, humble workers, carefree picnickers, devout pilgrims. The only constant is Mount Fuji, symbol of that which is permanent or unchanging in Japan. Hokusai does nothing to reconcile contradictions, but the presence of the mountain suggests that all of the views, taken together, make up Japan. In one woodcut, a weary traveler pauses for refreshment and is surprised to find Fuji reflected in his tiny sake cup. In another, boatmen row madly to escape a fearful storm, too concerned with survival to notice Fuji, calm in its indifference, beautifully framed within the curl of a towering wave.

My version of *Thirty-Six Views of Mount Fuji* focuses on individual encounters, intimate moments, and small revelations that helped me make sense of Japan. If a theme underlies the memories in this book, it is what I learned from the rituals, celebrations, customs, and traditions through which the Japanese cope with life—both its joys and its pains. More than that, my Japanese experiences prompted me to come to terms with painful events in my own life, events whose emotional impact followed me all the way across the Pacific or whose consequences brought me home again.

In the largest sense, celebration and mourning have spiritual dimensions, dimensions also present in Hokusai's Fuji prints. For all his exuberant zest for life, Hokusai was a holy man. In old age, he returned repeatedly to the subject of Mount Fuji, seeking to communicate something of what the mountain represents in symbolic or metaphysical terms. One meaning of *Fuji* is "not two" or "peerless one," that which is constant—one—in the midst of life's changes. Another reading of *Fuji* is "not death," "undying." In an almost literal way, Mount Fuji is the soul of Japan.

Not until my fourth trip to Japan did I see Mount Fuji for myself. On the first, in 1980, I was in Japan as part of a faculty exchange program, teaching English for a year to Japanese students at Kansai Women's University. Some of my students invited me on an outing to climb Mount Fuji during the brief period in summer when the mountain is officially open. That year's rainy season seemed interminable, and, with reluctance, we canceled our trip because of continuing bad weather. On various excursions to Tokyo by plane or train, I watched anxiously from the window, hoping for a glimpse of the majestic mountain. Shrouded in clouds every time, it withheld its secrets.

In January of 1983, my second time in Japan, I missed Fuji four times, twice by plane and twice by *shinkansen* (bullet train), and I began to feel jinxed. "It's good that you still haven't seen

Fuji-san," Professor Sano, my department head at Kansai Women's University, assured me as we bid one another good-bye at the airport. "It means you have a reason to come back to Japan again."

Yet when I did return, for another year of teaching, in 1987–88, I declined an invitation to join the hundreds of thousands of Japanese who make the pilgrimage up Fuji each summer and went instead to Oki, a remote island between Japan and Korea. Saddened by the recent deaths of several friends and by my grandmother's lingering final illness, I needed the solace of Oki. I spent days snorkeling off the coral reefs, looking at beautiful seascapes through my diving mask, and evenings talking and laughing again among friends.

I finally had my view of Mount Fuji late in 1990, ten years after my first *Oshōgatsu* (New Year's) in Japan. I was looking forward to two carefree months in Japan without teaching or other responsibilities. Yet it turned out that on this fourth visit several of my friends were facing crises of their own. I tried to comfort them with what American consolations I had to offer—talk that went late into the night and the occasional un-Japanese hug. En route to Tokyo to visit one friend, I saw Fuji from my train window. The disembodied voice of the conductor came over the P.A. system. It was a seductive voice—the kind that begins like molasses and ends with a whisper—and everyone in the train car, both men and women, seemed to sit expectantly, waiting for the conductor to purr the name of each stop. As we came abreast of Mount Fuji, he told us in a tragic voice that it was too rainy today to see Fuji-san, directly to our left. Then his murmur changed to a gasp of wonder: *"Subarashii!"* he exclaimed (Spectacular!). For one moment, the leaden clouds parted and there stood Mount Fuji, snowcapped and gleaming.

The scene was an update of Hokusai: dark storm clouds perfectly framing Mount Fuji, admired by travelers pressed against the window of a bullet train hurtling toward Tokyo. In another second, the clouds closed back over the mountain and all was gray again. We turned to each other then, as if to reassure ourselves that we had really seen what we had seen. We bowed to one another;

several people came forward to shake my hand. *"Subarashii,"* we repeated, in whispers.

I'm convinced that moments like the one on the bullet train to Tokyo illuminate a culture as much as do larger historical or social events. Sometimes it's the odd or even quirky encounter that is most revealing, like clouds parting to show the mountain hidden within. The idiosyncratic, the piece that doesn't quite fit, is often what makes one understand the dimensions of the puzzle, as Hokusai must have known when he included forty-six views of Mount Fuji in his famous series. If the artist threw in more than the thirty-six he promised in his title, who's to complain of the unexpected bounty? After four visits to Japan, I've come to see this oddity—an acquiescence to the incongruous—as "typically" Japanese.

In some of Hokusai's woodcuts of Mount Fuji, the mountain is seemingly not pictured at all. The events in these pictures take place on the mountain itself, reinforcing the basic Buddhist (and quintessentially Japanese) idea that the person closest to a subject or event can never really see it. Sometimes it is the person passing through and at a remove who has the clearest view. As an American writing about Japan, I'm hoping that Hokusai is right.

1

SEEING AND
BEING SEEN

I dreamt Japan long before I went there. Moss gardens, straw-mat rooms, wooden bridges arching in the moonlight, paper lanterns with the fire glowing inside. Whenever I paged through photography books of traditional Japan, I found myself gasping with appreciation. Three rocks, a gnarled pine tree, raked white sand: awe. Pictures of Windsor Castle or the fountains of Versailles have never left me breathless.

But what struck me as we drove away from Osaka International Airport was the unattractiveness of the scene. Forget rocks and raked sand! Neon everywhere, billboards as far as the eye could see, concrete apartment blocks dingy with pollution. Even the details radiated a sense of urbanization run amok. Whereas other affluent nations bury power lines and strive for at least some

sense of visual harmony, Japan seemed to be clotted with the ca-
bles and wires of modern life. Looking out the car window at gray
buildings with rusting metal roofs, the power lines crisscrossing
bizarrely overhead, I was reminded of some grim old photograph
of a nineteenth-century immigrant ghetto, zapped by late-
twentieth-century electronic overload.

My husband, Ted, and I were in Japan to teach English.
Michigan State University, where I taught at the time, had established a faculty exchange program with Kansai Women's University. A Japanese professor would teach my courses at MSU while I
taught hers at KWU. Ted took an unpaid leave from his liberal
arts college in the States and accepted part-time jobs at both
KWU and a larger, coed university in a nearby town. It had all
happened fast—a note in the faculty mailboxes one winter day inviting applications, a few hasty lessons in conversational Japanese,
and then, in March, we were there.

"Is it what you were expecting?" Professor Sano, the department head at KWU, asked as we drove from the airport to
Nigawa, the suburb where we would be living for the next year.

I knew that Japan wouldn't look like the picture books but
I was surprised at how different it really was. I joked that I had
thought the streets of Japan would be paved with gold.

He laughed and said that many Americans had that reaction.
Then, nodding at the passing scene, a particularly drab stretch of
warehouse-like buildings, he added more soberly, "We Japanese
like to say that we have a great sense of beauty and no sense of ugliness. You'll find a lot of Japan is like that."

The beauty is still there, he explained; one just has to look
for it. What happens outside, in the world, is chaotic, contingent,
filled with speed and accident. But, as we would later see, bleak
stretches of urban sprawl are punctuated by exquisite Buddhist
temples set off from the city, sometimes by stark clay walls or
elaborate wooden gates, a separate peace within the chaos. On national holidays, Japanese go to these temples en masse to recharge,
and they become as packed as a rush-hour subway train. We'd see
the same thing soon in cherry-viewing season, he said, when every-

one sets aside the tragedies or just the predictable dailiness of life to picnic and party beneath the fragile blossoms.

He described one of his favorite places, a busy intersection in a nondescript area of Kyoto where a simple carved stone Buddha, much beloved by the residents, smiles enigmatically amid the carbon monoxide and the car horns.

Professor Sano dropped us off at the Western-style home of an American couple who taught at Kansai Women's University, a kind of halfway house between the two cultures, where we spent our first night in Japan. The next day the couple showed us around the local grocery store, explained how the train system worked, and delivered us to our apartment building in Nigawa, an affluent suburb between Kobe and Osaka, about half an hour by train from either. They told us that, before the War, Nigawa was a sleepy resort town, with *ryokan* (inns) and country villas, and long before that a stop for pilgrims on their way to Kabuto-yama Daishi, a Shingon Buddhist temple built in the ninth century on the helmet-shaped mountain a few miles beyond Nigawa. Carrying our suitcases up the three flights of stairs to our apartment, we heard the low, somber gong of the temple bell mingled with suburban sounds of commuter trains and mopeds.

We lived on the top floor of a "mansion," the Japanese term for a modern ferro-concrete apartment complex. Kansai Women's University owned our apartment and two others on the floor, each a 2DK—two rooms plus a galley kitchen, with a dining area large enough for a table and four chairs. The Western-style living room was furnished with small brown tweed couches and a coffee table. The bedroom was more traditional, with tatami (green-gold straw mats) on the floor and walls covered in a rough ocher paper that recalled the clay walls of a tea house. We had been asked if we wanted a double bed and declined in favor of the traditional futons. A bed would have filled the entire room. With futons, what was a bedroom by night became, with the futons folded away, a study where I worked on the floor, Japanese-style, breathing in the incomparable fragrance of rice straw.

A few days after our arrival, I set out for my first official visit to Kansai Women's University. Our American colleagues had drawn us a map of Nigawa that included two different routes to the university—a direct one along well-marked streets lined with apartment buildings and expensive suburban houses and a more circuitous scenic route past the last thatch-roof building in Nigawa, by a few remaining old *kura* (storehouses), over a small stream, and then up a path that led through a rice paddy at the very top of a hill. On clear days, they said, we'd be able to see Osaka. Beyond the smokestacks, factories, and oil tankers, we'd even glimpse the fabled Inland Sea.

Of course I took the scenic route, noticing, with anticipation, that the cherry trees arching over one part of my walk were in bud. On campus, a few early trees were already in bloom. The students were blooming, too, hundreds and hundreds of them, looking fresh and lovely.

In the English Department office, I met various new colleagues, most of them Japanese but also a few *gaijin* (foreigners), from the United States and the United Kingdom. I heard again how happy everyone was that I was able to come for the year. The auto industry in 1980 was suffering its worst crisis in history, and anti-Japanese feelings ran high in Michigan. I liked to think of myself and the Japanese exchange professor as minor goodwill ambassadors.

As my new colleagues hurried off in the general bustle of starting another school year, I stayed behind in the main office, sipping a cup of green tea that one of the secretaries had offered me. I browsed through the mail that had accumulated in my box, mostly institutional memos about commencement, class lists, and other official matters. There were a number of notices in Japanese that the secretary told me not to bother about and then a brief note in both English and Japanese announcing that "everyone should please try to have the health examination before the beginning of classes."

I was puzzled. We didn't get memos at Michigan State that told us "please try" to do things. And what kind of health examination? My doctor had given me a complete physical before I left the United States, but I wasn't sure whether that counted or not. I'd been told I would be covered for the year by Japan's national health plan and supposed that this physical was part of the plan. I also suspected that the vague wording in the memo might be an example of *tatemae,* the form of a polite suggestion masking the substance *(honne)* of an explicit order. I'd read about this Japanese habit of indirect expression in all the travel guides.

"I guess I should take this health exam, shouldn't I?" I asked one of the secretaries who spoke excellent English.

She nodded agreement and told me that it was being given right now in the auditorium in the next building. I could just follow all the young women who were walking in that direction. I thanked her, bowed, and headed off for my first all-Japanese experience.

The room was filled with students, most of them from the high school and junior high that are also part of KWU. As far as I could see, there was only one other faculty member present. I wasn't at all sure what to do, but took heart when I noticed that the youngest girls, probably away from home for the first time, seemed every bit as bewildered as I. I smiled at them and drew startled, wide-eyed expressions in return. It occurred to me that some of them had probably never been this close to a foreigner before. I bowed. They bowed. We waited in line together and were handed plastic slippers and hospital gowns as well as small baskets for our clothes and shoes. We then waited in another line to enter a room where, presumably, we would have our medical examinations. A tiny girl, smaller than her friends, gazed up at me with a look somewhere between excitement and fear. I introduced myself to her in formal Japanese, just as I had learned in my first lesson in conversational Japanese. She broke into giggles, then bowed and solemnly introduced herself to me, her friends still giggling behind hands held to their mouths.

My determination to act confident and congenial wavered as

soon as I entered the next room and realized that there were no private changing areas, no discreet doctor's cubicles. I was going to have to slip into my hospital gown out in the open, in a room filled with curious Japanese schoolgirls. Still worse, as I unfolded the gown I saw that it was intended to fit a Japanese junior high girl, not a tall *gaijin* woman.

I'd read about the Japanese virtue *gaman* (perseverance, endurance). In the *gaman* spirit, I decided I'd get through this as best I could. I started to take off my blouse and skirt, then noticed that the Japanese were disrobing differently. Somehow they managed to get out of their clothes and into the hospital gown without revealing an inch of extra flesh. It was impressive to watch: a flurry of arms and *voila!* The gown on, the clothes off, the underwear zipping out from underneath to go folded neatly, with everything else, into the mesh basket. Maybe it was a skill learned long ago in cramped living quarters or something you practiced before taking a communal Japanese bath. My American body didn't know how to do that Houdini bit with the underwear, especially with some two hundred pairs of eyes taking in my failure.

I felt my *gaman* slipping.

I had an unusually brief interview with the doctor. He knew as much English as I knew Japanese. When he pantomimed that I should open wide, I volunteered *"Ahhh!"* the way I would in America, and he almost fell off his chair.

"Why you *do* that?" he asked, sounding both hurt and offended.

I learned later that the whole process is quieter in Japan. With visible relief, the doctor waved me on to yet another line.

This was for chest X rays. Two young men with fashionably permed hair, probably in their early twenties, had the dream job of administering the X rays to hundreds of nubile schoolgirls. And to me. Once again it became clear that my prior education had been incomplete. The girls went up to the X-ray machine, pressed against it, then opened their hospital gowns, with nary a hint of indiscretion. I could tell by anxious glances in my direction that they expected I would again embarrass myself and them when it came my turn. I *studied* their method. After I executed it with fair success, the two students in line behind me actually applauded. I strode out of the X-ray room, dignity intact.

"*Gambatte kudasai!*" (Persevere! Do your best! Good luck!), one of these young women said to me a few moments later as I stood in the auditorium, unsure of what to do next. Then, in excellent English, she added, "It's almost over. Only one more thing to do." She brought me a clear plastic cup from a cart I'd overlooked near the door. "You go there"—she pointed to the lavatories—"then take it to the nurse at the front of the room. That's it!"

Even as I thanked her for her help, I foresaw, with despair, what was going to come next. The medicine I was taking for a minor bladder infection happens to turn my urine an exquisite azure color, reminiscent of the sky in old Japanese prints.

"*Aoi! Aoi!*" (Blue! Blue!), I heard whispered as I walked through the packed auditorium in my minigown and carrying the plastic cup. The well-bred young students of Kansai Women's University made like hooligans, popping in and out of various lines, attempting to get a look for themselves, then joining in the chorus "*Aoi! Aoi!*" Never had I been the subject of such wonder and awe.

"You know, you didn't really have to take that physical," one of my new colleagues, an American, said when I slunk back into the English Department office a few days later. "Nobody does."

"You've heard?" I asked her.

"Cathy, this is Japan. Of course I heard—we all did. Get used to it. This is a village of 120 million people. There isn't much you can do here without everybody finding out."

She thought the whole thing was hilarious. I realized, with a sinking feeling, that just about anyone I would meet over the next few weeks would have heard about the *aoi* incident. So much for making a good first impression!

I asked why the department secretary hadn't told me that I didn't have to take the physical. My colleague explained that, especially at a place like KWU, one of Japan's most elite women's colleges, status and politeness mean a lot and it is very awkward for a secretary to tell a *sensei* (teacher) what to do or not do.

She told me about a visiting foreign teacher who, on a train platform, had asked one of his students, "This is the train to Osaka, isn't it?" and had been told yes, even though it wasn't. It would have been rude to tell him that he was mistaken. If he had asked, "Excuse me, please. Could you tell me which is the train to Osaka?" he would have been answered very differently. My situation was much the same. I was a *sensei* and the secretary would have felt presumptuous telling me that I had been wrong to assume I had to take the physical. Nor could she tell me the notice did not mean what it said. It was an official notice; the university was doing its job by providing annual physicals; the students obeyed the requirement but most of the faculty just threw the notice away. "It's like ignoring the 55 mph speed limit on highways back in America," my colleague said.

"You haven't made my job any easier," one of the foreign teachers at KWU's junior high kidded me a few weeks later. "My Japanese students come here already convinced that the Japanese brain is different than ours, that their tongue has a different shape, that their blood is stronger. I can't tell you how many oral reports I've heard this term about how Japanese and *gaijin* look and act so different because *gaijin* have blue pee."

≈

It was a funny way to enter a new culture, but it didn't feel funny at the time. I was in Japan to see, to experience, to learn, to understand. I wanted to be a good tourist, receptive to new experiences, new sights and sounds. It never occurred to me, until the moment I donned my hospital gown, that I would *become* one of the sights—examined, not just the examiner.

I'm not sure I'd call it a baptism by fire, but the health exam taught me that no matter how hard I might try to understand this new culture, to fit in as gracefully as possible, at times I was going to fail. There would be many more embarrassing or painful moments, misunderstandings, conflicts, confusion, frustration. Since I am not a person whose anxiety diminishes at the prospect of certain failure, I gave myself a pep talk. A nation that could tolerate ugliness without losing its appreciation for beauty would probably be a pretty forgiving place. Think gardens in the urban chaos, I told myself. Think Buddhas amid the car horns.

Walking back home to the apartment in Nigawa, past the last thatch building, under cherry trees aching to bloom, I realized that I was seeing Japan but I was also seeing myself again, inside out, viewed as well as viewing. This, I thought, is what it means to be a foreigner. Conspicuous, ardent, cowed, I began my year in Japan.

2

FOREIGNERS

Once we accepted the idea that we were foreigners, Ted and I resolved to avoid all other foreigners, a resolution shared by many North Americans living in another country for the first time. We wanted our Japanese experience pure, untainted. Then we began meeting interesting people who didn't happen to be Japanese and decided we had better drop our purist notions. Where else would we have come across someone like Maryvonne, a French painter influenced by Japanese art whose Japanese husband, Ichirō, is a lutist who performs medieval French music? Or Becky, an English teacher and new mother, who makes serene ink drawings inspired by Zen calligraphy and works with Japanese feminists for more equitable treatment of women, both in Japan and internationally? And Sally, who married Toshi before she spoke Japanese or he En-

glish. At one of the funniest parties I've ever attended, she pantomimed the way Toshi had acted out the need for birth control on
the first night they spent together.

"I thought of all the American men who *know* the word for
'condom' but never bother to use one," Sally joked, "and decided,
then and there, I'd better marry this guy!"

To the Japanese we may all be *gaijin,* but Ted and I early began to distinguish those foreigners who had preserved a sense of
wonder (which doesn't mean unthinking approval) in their adopted
land from others we called the *'gaijin-gaijin'—foreign* foreigners.
They chose to stick to themselves, to create their own separate
community, as distinct as possible from the rest of Japan.

It's not hard to do this in urban Japan. Most cities have one
or two grocery stores that specialize in the foreign trade and stock
Western foods, from Mars bars and Cheerios to frozen butterball
turkeys and T-bone steaks. English-language newspapers and magazines are widely available, including a number published in Japan. There are guides in English that list local doctors and dentists
who speak English or that provide advice on more esoteric matters
such as how to get a driver's license without knowing any Japanese. There are English-language schools and churches as well as
support groups for foreign women married to Japanese men and
clubs that allow Japanese visitors only when they are the guests of
a regular member. A *gaijin-gaijin* can live in Japan for years without ever learning the language or coming into more than superfi-
cial contact with the Japanese.

We had our first encounter with the *gaijin-gaijin* a few weeks
after our arrival. In one of the local English-language magazines,
we saw an announcement for a group called the Kansai Foreign
Travelers. It was run by a Mr. Tanaka, a middle-aged Japanese
who, we found out later, had been given an education by Americans after the War and so, as a payback, spent one day each month
taking foreigners to interesting places they would not normally
find on their own. We sent Mr. Tanaka the stamped, self-addressed
envelope requested in the notice, and he mailed us back personal-
ized instructions for our excursion: Saturday morning take the lo-

cal 8:01 train to Nishinomiya. Transfer to the Kobe line and catch the 8:20 express train. Get off at . . .

Worried that at least one of these trains might be late, Ted and I left early and ended up waiting at the other end, along with a few other *gaijin* also newly arrived in the country. Mr. Tanaka and a group of long-term residents of Kobe all arrived half an hour later, on the 10:13 train, exactly according to Mr. Tanaka's instructions.

Our day in Tatsuno, an old samurai village noted for its sake and its *soba* (buckwheat noodles), did not get off to a good start. The group from Kobe grumbled as a spring shower turned into a downpour. One woman wondered out loud why Mr. Tanaka couldn't have picked a nicer day. A man responded that there was no such thing as a nice day in Japan and warned that it would only get worse. "Wait till summer," he said. "John Steinbeck compared it to breathing warm blood." From the weather they went on to other things they disliked about Japan.

We were too busy admiring the town to let their griping bother us. Tatsuno was like a stage set, clay walls and weathered-wood houses, groves of bamboo arching low in the leafy rain, wisps of fog clinging to the hillsides close around us.

"I feel like I'm in a Kurosawa film!" Ted exclaimed.

For the first time since our arrival, we had found the Japan of our imaginings, and we slowed down to take it all in.

"Where is everybody?" I asked after a time, startled to discover we were alone. At some point the rest of our group must have made a different turn down one of Tatsuno's winding, mazelike streets.

"I think we're lost," Ted said, smiling.

I pulled out our instruction sheet on which was printed the name of the *ryokan* where we were all to have lunch. In simple Japanese, I asked a local shopkeeper where the inn might be. He was so surprised at encountering two *gaijin* that he could barely respond. He pointed, then turned and hurried through a dark doorway at the back of his little shop.

We walked in the direction he indicated but didn't find our

ryokan. We asked for help again, this time from two giggling high school girls happy to have a chance to practice their English. They led us through the narrow streets to the tall wooden gate of the *ryokan.* Pleased with the success of their venture with English, they skipped away from us, arms linked in the rain.

We were wet, hungry—and ecstatic. A hostess helped us remove our wet shoes and raincoats in the *genkan* (entry). She gave us slippers to wear down a long hall that led to a tatami room where the others from the tour knelt or sat cross-legged on the floor at low tables, drinking warmed local sake served by women in kimono, eating *soba* noodles made at the inn. We were charmed, but the English conversation was still about what was wrong with Japan.

"Look at this table!" one large man was saying. "I can't even kneel at it. You'd think by now they would have realized that there are taller people in this world, too!"

"You'd *think* by now they'd realize it's more comfortable to use chairs," another griped.

As each dish came from the kitchen, a self-appointed food policeman in the group held up something in his chopsticks and asked Mr. Tanaka what it was. After Mr. Tanaka answered, the food inspector would sometimes take a tentative bite or sometimes simply drop the item back onto the lacquer tray on which it had been served. As he declined yet another course, someone else told of a friend who had had his company ship over a year's supply of canned foods so that he could avoid eating stuff like this.

The rest of the afternoon passed this way, the grumbling a bonding among the *gaijin-gaijin.* On the train ride home, Mr. Tanaka sat stone-faced, as if he could not hear the complaining around him. I tried to imagine what he might be thinking but he gave no sign of his feelings for these foreigners who derided his country. When we reached our stop, Ted and I thanked Mr. Tanaka profusely for bringing us to Tatsuno, the most beautiful place we had seen so far. He nodded simply and waved good-bye through the train window.

We went a second time and a third with the Kansai Foreign

Travelers. The places were fascinating but we finally wrote Mr. Tanaka a letter of apology saying we had to drop out of the group because of scheduling conflicts. The real reason was we couldn't stand the *gaijin-gaijin.* We felt implicated by their unceasing barrage of anti-Japanese talk.

Yet it was from the foreigners on Mr. Tanaka's tours that I learned about the contradictory ways in which many Westerners view Japan. It was curious to me that they all disliked Japan intensely—but they disliked it for seemingly opposite reasons. Some were disappointed that Japan wasn't more Americanized. They complained that you couldn't get a decent burger anywhere except at one of the McDonald's just starting to spring up in and around Kobe. Others wanted Japan to be less developed, more exotic, and spoke wistfully of earlier postings to Nepal or Sri Lanka, fondly remembering places where, on strong American dollars, they had had live-in cooks, full-time gardeners, chauffeurs, maids. These *gaijin-gaijin* resented Japan's affluence *and* its discomfort, having to live in cramped quarters with none of the amenities accorded Western businessmen in Third World countries. For them, Japan was already just like America, only worse.

All these contradictory attitudes about Japan are partly right. From an American perspective, Japan can seem like a more extreme version of the United States: busier (more people per square yard), more workaholic (one of the longest workweeks in the world). Yet the corollary—that Japan somehow got that way by "copying America"—is dead wrong. Japan *is* different. Philosophically and socially, it's one of the least "Americanized" non-Western countries, despite its rampant modernization. The Japanese value system has been little changed by extensive borrowing from the West.

I think this is one reason why Americans are so often thrown by Japan. It looks familiar but, an inch below the surface, it isn't anything like the West at all. We don't even have a category for Japan's economic system: virulently anticommunist, Japan also has an active socialist opposition party (formerly chaired by a woman, Takako Doi). The Liberal Democratic Party (LDP), Japan's ruling party since World War II, has engineered a planned economy that carefully regulates and subsidizes business and R&D. The ideal (far from realized) is a middle-class state. There's national health and child care, competitive wages for such white-collar workers as public school teachers and civil servants, and relatively low salaries for top-level executives, including CEOs of the nation's largest firms. The gap between rich and poor is considerably smaller than in the United States. The Japanese like to say that they learned these economic principles by going to American business schools in the fifties.

One hundred years of diligent missionary activity, however, has scarcely made a dent in Japan's religious traditions. Most Japanese practice both Buddhism and Shintoism (an eclecticism Westerners tend to find baffling). Less than 2 percent of Japan's population is Christian, the lowest conversion rate on earth, and many of those who nominally convert do so because "I'm Christian" is an accepted shorthand in Japan for "I choose to be different." One of the most radical Japanese activists I've encountered is a Christian; I know several feminists who became Christians to "explain" their decision to be single parents or not to have families at all. This too is very Japanese: to employ some crucial feature of Western culture (Christianity) partly for a Japanese purpose (to signal difference).

I even met a man called "Kūpā" (after Gary Cooper) who dresses in a cowboy shirt, leather vest, Wranglers, rodeo belt buckle, western boots, a Stetson, and heaps of beaded and turquoise Indian jewelry. Kūpā wears his silver hair to his shoulders, Buffalo Bill—style. "He's married to a Catholic," his friends say by way of explanation. Kūpā, incidentally, speaks not a word of English and considers himself a typical Japanese.

I like people like Kūpā. I have several friends, in both countries, who, by most standards, are distinctly off-center. Or, rather, who have their own center. *All* of Japan feels that way to me, not only because it's not my culture, but also because the Japanese who seek me out are themselves in search of difference. More to the point, when I'm in Japan, I'm a *gaijin,* necessarily off-center, and comfortable that way. Although I'm not a classic loner, I prize the solitary, independent part of myself and revel in the ease with which I can attain that status in Japan.

Like most foreigners, I'm pretty good at adapting to new situations (or I wouldn't enjoy traveling in the first place) but I'm also a bit of a misfit (or I would never have wanted to leave home). The Japanese I like best share my ambivalent desires. A recent survey showed that 40 percent of Japanese have no desire for contact with foreigners. Americans might not be so candid about their xenophobia, but the majority of Americans probably don't yearn to hang out with Japanese either. Because I'm a *gaijin,* I attract people who like to negotiate cultural differences but who are willing to accept a certain distance. Every friendship I make in Japan is grounded in the unalterable recognition that, however often I may return to Japan, I will always be going home.

There's an intensity in relationships based on anticipated absence. Communication, imperfect and fleeting, seems all the more significant, even momentous. I think of Mr. Takeshita, the *maître d'hôtel* at Crillon, our favorite French restaurant in Osaka. On each visit, he made a point of conversing with us, in some makeshift combination of his poor English and our poorer Japanese. He gave us his *meishi* (personal business card) and requested ours, and one day, to our surprise, telephoned our house and invited us, in carefully rehearsed English, to come with him to some of his favorite restaurants in Osaka. We spent the night at mom-and-pop places, laughing, joking, riffling through conversation dictionaries we'd each brought, pantomiming when language failed. On our last visit to Crillon that year, he told us that he was taking an English course and studying hard so that he could write to us. We have corresponded now—in some nether-language between English and Japanese—for several years:

Dear Mr. Ted and Mrs. Cathy,
What is your goal in the future? My lifework's target is run a business at foreign countries. The world is starving from hunger. I'd like to make a contribute to the so-

ciety. My age is thirty-five years old now. I'd like to implement till fourty-five years old.

I can't even imagine what mistakes I make when I attempt to write back in Japanese.

But mistakes aren't the point. Being a foreigner, especially in a country where you are not fluent in the language, has an odd filtering effect. Ordinary, everyday language all around you becomes a kind of white noise, murmur without meaning, almost soothing in its inconsequentiality. When communication does occur, it seems to have *more* meaning (even when you can't figure out exactly what's going on). I feel the urgency with which Takeshita-san tries to express life goals far beyond the reach of his English vocabulary and the childlike joy when cultural and linguistic gaps are miraculously bridged. Understanding across such barriers comes like revelation.

Intensity, novelty, urgency, surprise: that's what it means, to me, to be a *gaijin.* In Japan I am foreign territory, slightly forbidden, hard to categorize. An eccentric American who has lived in Japan since the Occupation likes to say that only when he's back in America does he realize that he's just another crotchety old man. In Japan, he has a role, *henna gaijin* (crazy foreigner), and he plays it happily to the hilt.

I'm not always sure what my role is when I'm in Japan. Some of my Japanese friends say that when they're with me they find it easier to break rules and they feel they can do so without incurring immediate censure. The very fact of their being with a foreigner puts them outside the realm of ordinary conduct and responses. They become generic, "A Japanese with a Foreigner," and so feel less self-conscious because others seem less conscious of them too. For them, I exist as a friend but also as an excuse to be Not Japanese, ironic since I'm with them because they *are* Japanese.

Japan also allows me to be Not American, to feel and act in ways I might hesitate to do in America. During a summer spent in the Oki islands with the Danceries, the medieval music group conducted by Ichirō and managed by his wife, Maryvonne, I waited with my friends for the island's only bus to pick us up at a remote stop during a torrential downpour. No one was sure the bus would make its run out to the far end of the island this late in the afternoon and in such terrible weather. The other Japanese waiting at the stop weren't particularly happy to be stranded with three Japanese musicians and two *gaijin* women. We did seem pretty strange. My friends were wearing two and three sweaters and had beach towels draped around their shoulders for extra warmth. My umbrella had blown inside out, its spokes jutting alarmingly into the dark afternoon. My plastic slicker had snagged and torn. While we waited, we passed the time with a chorus of "Singing in the Rain." Already soaked to the skin, I stepped outside the little bus shelter and did a rendition of Gene Kelly's famous dance number, tapping through the puddles, kicking up my soggy heels.

"I think we're frightening these people," Maryvonne, who's lived in Japan for twenty years, suddenly whispered.

I was surprised to see that the other Japanese at the bus stop—on this isolated spit of land on an isolated island in the middle of a fierce thunderstorm—really did look as if they were sharing the bus shelter with a band of lunatics.

"*Gomen nasai.*" I and my friends bowed to them in deep apology, then worked hard not to burst out laughing again.

"Do you think they would have been as frightened if I were a Japanese instead of a *gaijin* dancing in the rain?" I asked Ichirō later, back in dry clothes at our hotel.

"I think only a *gaijin* would have tap-danced in the rain," he teased.

"But I did it *because* I'm a *gaijin*. Back in America, I would have waited quietly and respectfully with the other passengers, like a good Japanese!"

It's a comment I've thought about a lot since then. At times when I'm in Japan, I feel freer than I do in America, more irresponsible, because it is assumed that, as a foreigner, I am strange. I cannot completely conform in this culture that prizes conformity so I might as well act as freely as I wish. This is the heady sensation that most travelers relish, the freedom that comes from feeling unaccounted for and unaccountable.

It would be misleading, though, to suggest I like Japan because I'm freer there. Often being a foreigner in Japan is extremely constricting. Frequently I am the object of attention, simply by virtue of being different, and sometimes I want nothing more than to hide, to blend in, to be less conspicuous, more Japanese. Like other *gaijin* (and particularly white Americans), I often find myself cast in the role of model or guide, with even my slightest actions scrutinized. Instead of being off-center, I am, in this respect, too much the center, too much the one observed.

For all the sensitivity to contingency and the vaunted relativism of its Buddhist origins—perhaps *because* of those relativist origins—collective behavior in Japan is governed by elaborate rules, beyond contingency and preference. One of the most venerable proverbs in Japan is *"Mochi wa mochiya"*: "For rice cakes, go to the rice cake maker." In other words, if you want something, go to an expert, and don't do a thing unless you plan on doing it right.

I board the train on a rainy day and as I start to put away my collapsible umbrella I notice that the people across the aisle are watching me with horrified expressions. I look around, and see that others are also staring censoriously. I can't locate the source of this collective disapproval but I feel it. Only after the next stop, when the new passengers begin to fold up their umbrellas, neatly, impeccably, every angle and fold in precise relationship to every other, do I realize what has caused the consternation. I unsnap the fastener and attempt to refold my umbrella the right way. There are now smiles all around me, the kind of beaming approval that one normally bestows upon a two-year-old just learning to master chopsticks. Even now, back in America, I find it impossible to just roll up an umbrella and jam it into its cover.

By my second or third month in Japan, Maryvonne, who usually wears jeans, started teasing me about my "KWU uniform," my prim dresses and skirts, stockings, restrained accessories. Without fully realizing it, I had begun dressing more and more like my women colleagues and my students at Kansai Women's University.

"It's getting to you, isn't it?" Maryvonne said one day, over tea. "It's because people here expect you to be 'an American' all the time. You feel on display."

That's exactly how I felt. Often someone about to visit America would come up to me on the street or in a restaurant and request an impromptu lesson in how they should act abroad. On a crowded train platform in Kobe, a woman stopped me and wanted me to show her the precise place and angle at which, as an American, I carry my shoulder bag. Another time, a mother watched as I tied a shoe that had come undone and then immediately turned to her child and had him retie his shoes just as I had tied mine.

"Don't you think it's because *they* are the ones who feel like foreigners?" Maryvonne wondered when I again complained about feeling like a walking museum exhibit on modern Western life.

During the last one hundred years, virtually every aspect of Japanese life has been superficially Westernized beyond recognition. Things we think of as simple or "natural"—carrying a purse, tying shoes—have all been borrowed from the West. An older, "pure" Japan exists now only on the samurai shows popular on Japanese television. Gone is the world in which a kimono sleeve held all one needed and where one wore high wooden sandals, *geta,* efficiently designed to carry one above the mud of the street and to be slipped off easily before entering a dwelling.

Americans in Japan often become role models because the West has penetrated every material aspect of Japan but has not displaced Japanese values. Despite the Japanese addiction to baseball or Kentucky Fried Chicken or rock music, we remain as incomprehensible to them as they sometimes appear to us.

Ted and I are having dinner one evening at Crillon. The restaurant is on the top floor of an elegant building in Osaka, and, in the glowing crimson of the city sunset, even the dingy riverways look lovely. From this distance, the bridges resemble those on the Seine in Paris.

Seated across from us is a middle-aged Japanese couple, obviously husband and wife. In itself, this is a relatively unusual sight. Most public socializing after marriage is between same-sex business associates or old school friends.

These two seem as nervous as newlyweds. We notice that they are watching us intently and are working up the courage to speak to us. Soon, the wife turns to our table, bows deeply, apologizes for her intrusion into our evening, and then explains that she and her husband are about to visit America. They wonder if we would be so kind as to watch how they eat their Western-style soup. They have been practicing, she says, but they're not quite sure they have it right.

Traditionally, Japanese soup is sipped (not spooned) from rimless bowls. Noodles or other ingredients are fished out with chopsticks, often accompanied by a loud slurping noise (an expected bit of etiquette that few Westerners fully master). The Western soup bowl apparently can be a formidable obstacle to first-time Japanese tourists, who are convinced that there has to be more to it than just scooping up the soup with a spoon.

I already knew that the Japanese expect Western table manners to have strict and formal rules. In a magazine I once leafed through at the doctor's office in Nigawa, I came across an article with photographs of the proper resting place for silverware during the course of a Western meal. Some of the photos (which looked virtually identical to my eyes) were marked through with a large, ominous red X. Resting your fork on your plate even five degrees from the place where it should be was a clear faux pas.

The middle-aged couple in Crillon had obviously been reading articles like this. Hands in their laps, both husband and wife address the soup bowl, bowing. Simultaneously, each then raises a left hand to gently grip the rim of the soup bowl at precisely the same place (let's say, the 8 o'clock position on the rim). They next pick up the soup spoon like a pencil, check each other for the right curve of the uplifted pinky, then make the first dip into the soup bowl, carefully sweeping the spoon away from them. Beads of sweat appear on the gentleman's upper lip. We hasten to assure them both that they are doing it just right.

"*Omedetō!*" (Congratulations!), we nod our approval as if they have each just earned a black belt in soupmanship.

We go back to our own meal, aware that we are still being watched. We find ourselves consuming our own soup with a care never exercised before or since. As we finish, the woman asks another question. When one tips the bowl away in order to take up the last spoonful, just what is the correct angle for the bowl? We have lived in Japan long enough to know that saying it doesn't matter a fig is no answer at all.

"Twenty degrees," Ted says definitively. They insist on treating us to an after-dinner cordial to thank us for our counsel.

"Where will you be visiting in the U.S.?" we ask before we leave.

"Disneyland," they smile back.

Midway through my first year in Japan, in 1980, something strange happened. It was as if I couldn't cope with the contradictions of life as a foreigner and so became convinced I was Japanese.

After six months living in a Japanese apartment complex in a town with only one or two other foreign families, teaching Japanese students with Japanese colleagues, I got to a point where I was certain, on some profound emotional level, that everyone else knew I was Japanese too. I couldn't get over the way other foreigners would nod familiarly to me or address me in English as we passed on the street. (How did they know?) It surprised me when young Japanese children out in the countryside would point at me and exclaim, "*Gaijin!*" More than once I looked, too, to see the foreigner.

My friends and family reported that in photos I sent home I was looking more and more Japanese all the time. Since I am

5' 7" with brownish red hair and brownish green eyes, this came as quite a surprise to them. To me, it seemed perfectly natural.

"I went through that stage too," Maryvonne observed. Maryvonne paints haunting abstract landscapes reminiscent of both O'Keeffe and Hokusai. She is from Dijon, France, but has lived in Japan so long with her husband and son that sometimes the Japanese cannot figure out who or what she is. She looks French, but she speaks impeccable, idiomatic Japanese, something a *gaijin* supposedly cannot do, so frequently taxi drivers or shopkeepers will ask her if she's Japanese. Yet when she's on tour in France with the Danceries, the French compliment her on the excellence of her French, as if she has somehow become Japanese by osmosis from all of the other Japanese in the group. I love the way Maryvonne takes delight in such crosscultural confusion.

"You'll get over it," she pats me on the back. "Believe me, you are *not* Japanese."

One day in a restroom in Osaka's elegant Mitsukoshi department store, I look up into the mirror after washing my hands and see myself surrounded by Japanese schoolgirls. They are wearing their school uniforms, black jumpers with white blouses and neat black bows at the neck. Their hair is shoulder-length and straight (perms are not allowed until after graduation, at which point many teenagers—male as well as female—get one, a rite of passage). I look in the mirror at the sea of glossy blue-black hair, pale faces, shining dark eyes. I look at my own reflection: a red turtleneck under a purple suede bomber jacket, auburn hair, a complexion that tends to the rosy. Frozen by the gaze in the mirror, I look like a Kodachrome person let loose in a black-and-white snapshot.

3

AFTER
SCHOOL

When I asked one of my neighbors why the Japanese school year begins in spring, she told me it's so mothers can send off their children as cherry blossoms fall from the branches. What a poignant sight! The kids in their dark uniforms and heavy black leather school backpacks march off to school under fragile white-pink blossoms. An annual ritual of initiation, school marks the entrance into Japanese life.

Nothing could be more abrupt than the transition from childhood to school. For the first four or five years after they are born, Japanese children are allowed virtually limitless freedoms. As infants or toddlers, they are not subjected to feeding and sleeping schedules or other Western versions of early discipline and control. They eat when they are hungry, sleep when they are tired. One rarely encounters a crying child or infant since it is considered a mother's business to make sure all of her child's whims are anticipated and fulfilled. In rare instances where some kind of discipline might be required, it is done with a stern look, with affection ever so briefly withdrawn. It's unusual for a young child to be spanked or even scolded. By all reports, child abuse is rare.

A child-centered culture with one of the lowest birthrates in the world, Japan prizes its young children. Even in the poorest sections of Osaka, I've seen toddlers dressed up in expensive fantasy clothes like little dolls or huggable stuffed animals. They are the object of constant physical attention and exhibit a joyous self-confidence.

Then school begins.

Mother, *okāsan,* is replaced by *sensei,* arbiter of right and wrong, the ultimate authority figure. The world of affection, approval, and love is replaced by the world of order, work, and entrance exams.

Within a month or two after our arrival in Japan, Ted and I could guess pretty accurately which kids were preschoolers and which had already started Japanese elementary school. What we noticed wasn't a size or developmental difference so much as a changed body language, a look in the eyes. Sometimes there was a new seriousness, the supple posture of childhood exchanged for squared shoulders and a stiff spine. Sometimes the look was almost tragic, as if the child were waiting, desperate and bewildered, to be rescued from a terrible mistake.

It is 10:30 on a Thursday night. My friend Kazue-san and I are coming home from Kobe. We will probably have to stand since the late-night trains are always packed with *sarariiman,* Japanese for "salary man" or businessman. Also on the train are schoolchildren, boys and some girls, heading home from after-hours cram schools.

In the morning when the trains are also packed, I try to avoid standing near any men since they are notorious for using the anonymity of the crowd to snatch a feel of a bottom or a breast. At night, I needn't worry. Most of the red-faced men are too spent from overwork and alcohol to be a problem. Tonight, as we wait for the train, a *sarariiman* moves out of his place in line to retch a little more discreetly a couple of feet away. A few places behind us, another man struggles not to be sick.

"It's disgraceful," my friend Kazue-san says, in low tones. *"Hazukashii"* (I am ashamed).

We talk about the pressures on businessmen, how they're expected to go out after work, often to company-owned bars, where they may or may not talk directly about business but where they will lubricate the relationships that allow business to flourish. No one likes this system. The law courts are starting to hear more and more cases about *karōshi,* death from overwork. Widows are suing the companies for death benefits, demanding compensation for the loss of husbands worked into an early grave.

I know something about this firsthand. A dear friend, someone we met years ago when he was an exchange student in the States, recently quit a top-level executive position with Sony in Tokyo in order to move back to his hometown in northern Japan and open a *yakitori-ya,* a traditional grilled chicken restaurant.

"I knew if I stayed at Sony," Matsuo told us, "I would have been an alcoholic or maybe even dead before I was forty."

He told us how he and his wife have to work hard at their small business but at least now he can survive without drinking himself into a stupor every night. When we asked why Japanese businessmen drink so much, Matsuo looked sad.

"This was my life in Tokyo: I woke up each dawn, traveled two hours to work, did my job, then was required to do company drinking in our company bar. It's impolite not to keep up with the others, so I always drank too much. That was my life. Commute. Work. Drink. When I was drunk, I didn't think about the next day and the next. I could act silly and childish. Perhaps the whiskey was necessary."

The English-language newspapers in Japan are filled with articles and editorials about alcoholism, partly because so many foreigners are shocked by the widespread spectacle of public drunkenness. The phenomenon is not only tolerated but actually encouraged by Japanese companies since it is thought to ease the pressures of daily life. As long as one stays within certain limits (drunk driving is not tolerated), one can be as foolish or outrageous as one likes when drunk. At least in principle, after-work inebriation is specifically designated (indeed, almost *institutionalized*) as a time for "frankly" expressing opinions and feelings to coworkers and even to a superior. One can get a reduced sentence for committing certain crimes under the influence of alcohol. Like children, drunks aren't judged by the normally rigid standards of right and wrong. That, I think, is key: when drunk, a man becomes a child again. There's even a new brand of sake called Mother's Milk, packaged in a bottle that resembles a female breast and with the slogan "Mother's Milk helps keep you warm and happy."

Perhaps because of its deep associations with childhood, drunken behavior is usually more infantile than aggressive. I've encountered only a few mean drunks in Japan, but I've witnessed hundreds of instances of unseemly or just plain silly behavior. I've seen high-ranking executives play patty-cake for hours with bar hostesses. I've watched a group of prominent doctors pass an evening singing nonsense nursery songs in childlike, falsetto voices, with hostesses cooing and fretting at them in baby talk like indulgent mothers. At a company party the president crawled between the tables on his hands and knees. He wore a folded napkin on his head like a baby bonnet. He stopped at each table, put his hands up like paws, and begged with panting tongue to be fed some little treat, like a lapdog. His employees would pat him on the head and he'd move on to the next table. If I hadn't been present, I'm not sure that anyone would have been particularly embarrassed for him. He was drunk, after all, and that's how men act when they are drunk. Like children.

On the train from Kobe, the real children do not act like children. I feel sorry for the besotted, exhausted businessmen, but it is the schoolkids on the train who break my heart. There are at least two dozen of them in this car alone, some as young as seven or eight and others of high school age. I know that most of them have been up since dawn, commuting to school. After school, if there was time, they went home for a hasty supper before *juku*, the special independent schools set up all over Japan, designed to teach students advanced skills or subjects they don't learn in regular school or, increasingly, to help them cram for the all-important entrance exams.

The nearest equivalent to *juku* in America are the cram courses set up to prepare college graduates to take the law boards or the standardized exams for medical school. In Japan these after-school cram courses can last ten or twelve years. Some kids only attend them for intensive study in one or two subjects, but others enroll in the full course, several hours a day, five or even six days a week, often all year round. During the summer I spent on Oki, a group of twenty junior high students came to our government-run inn to participate in a two-week *juku* in mathematics. Here they were, children surrounded by the ocean, and they spent six hours a day sitting at long tables in the cafeteria. The teacher lectured and they took notes from nine to noon every day. After a brief lunch, the lectures resumed until about four or five P.M. The only real break in the day was a leisurely bath before dinner. After dinner, they disappeared into their rooms, studying silently until midnight for the next day's lessons. Never once during their time on Oki did these children enter the turquoise sea.

I know some recent graduates of Japan's most prestigious universities who never went to *juku*. But they are the exception. For most of the affluent or the upwardly mobile, there's little choice. There are *juku* to help four-year-olds pass entrance exams for elite kindergartens. There are even *juku* to help kids pass entrance exams to get into prestigious *juku*. Sometimes children commute long distances from home to school, from school to *juku*. When they finally do get back home at night, they must study and do homework, both for school and for *juku*.

On a seat near us on the train, two grade-schoolers heading home from *juku* silently play a version of cat's cradle. Although they neither laugh nor talk, it passes the time on the thirty-minute ride.

Across the aisle, two other children slump forward, asleep. They are maybe eight or nine years old, and they lean into one another for most of the ride and then wake up instantly, simultaneously, as the train pulls into a station in an affluent suburb. One of them quietly stands up, bows to the other, and then gets off alone at his stop. He waves good-bye through the window.

After the friend leaves, the little boy on the train reaches into his book bag and brings forth a *bentō,* a traditional Japanese boxed lunch. He leans forward over the *bentō* and begins eating surreptitiously. It is highly improper to eat in public in Japan, especially on a train, and everything in the boy's posture signals that he knows he's violating a taboo. He doesn't take the time to chew or to pause between bites. He hunches down and pokes at the food with his chopsticks in darting motions, like some shore bird going after a fish.

"*Kawaisō!*" (How pitiful!), I whisper to Kazue-san.

"Yes," she answers, in English. "It's awful. We didn't have such *juku* cram schools when I was a child."

When he finishes his supper, the boy tucks the lunch box back into a shopping bag and closes his eyes.

He wears navy blue short pants and a little navy blue jacket with bright gold buttons. Snoring on the train seat next to him is a *sarariiman* in the standard navy blue suit, a gold company pin in his lapel. Under the bright lights in the train, both boy and man look pale, lifeless.

As I leave the car, I see that the little boy is now fast asleep. His head rests carelessly on the slumbering body of the unknown *sarariiman* beside him.

Americans anxious about Japanese success and American debt often attribute both to our respective educational systems. Our schools are failing, we hear. Japanese kids are doing better on all the standardized tests. Our children just aren't equipped to deal with modern life. The Japanese are winning the trade wars because they've won the education war.

I agree that the American educational system is in need of major reform, and there are many important things we can learn from early childhood education in Japan. Elementary schoolchildren have active exercise and play periods in Japan between subjects, every forty or forty-five minutes, allowing them to move their bodies and also refocus their attention for the next lesson. In the early grades, cooperation not competition is stressed, and children work together to solve problems in small groups or squads *(han),* with the brighter children helping and encouraging the slower ones. The successful *han* depends on cooperation among students with a range of talents, so that the same child who might be slow in one area (such as mathematics) can help the group in others (perhaps art or reading). Japan has no real concept of learning disability; all children are told that, with hard work, they can do better. Mistakes are welcomed by teachers since it is from mistakes that we learn how to do things right, a very different attitude than the American notion that a mistake means failure and stands as an emblem of irrevocable (even genetic) deficiencies.

But the same *han* that can be so nurturing can turn into a censorious and even tyrannical peer group over the years, exerting tremendous pressures toward conformity. Because everything is standardized, slower children fall further and further behind while good students often grow bored in the classroom. It's common for junior high school students to say that after-school *juku* is more important and interesting than regular school. On all levels, the pressure intensifies in the later grades, as every aspect of education is shaped to the entrance exams. These pressures can be utterly debilitating, and most Japanese today dislike the present educational system, a product of the recent economic miracle, they say, not its cause.

Every year that I've been in Japan, from 1980 to the present, some agency or another has released a survey indicating how dissatisfied the Japanese are with the education their children receive.

Any symposium on the need for reform draws hundreds of people. No one wants to inflict this pressure on children. Yet the same surveys indicate that few parents act individually against the system. Few are willing to encourage their own children not to study so hard, not to attend *juku,* to enjoy their childhood. Who can take such a risk? As every parent knows, major Japanese companies hire according to the prestige of the college attended, and the only way to get into college is by passing an entrance exam. Although there have been some national scandals involving rich parents who donated money to private medical schools in an attempt to ensure their son's acceptance, there is no Japanese equivalent to the widespread American practice of permitting lower entrance standards for the children of alumni (especially generous or prominent alumni). When the son of the president of a private university in our area of Japan failed the school's entrance exam, he was denied admittance, something that would happen at few equivalent American universities.

The Japanese system is, in this sense, impartial, something the Japanese are justifiably proud of. But it is also relentless, and the effects of the system are apparent throughout Japan. Teenage depression, alcohol abuse, and even suicide are all attributed to the pressures of the exam system. More and more students engage in *tōkō kyohi,* resistance to school, even if it means destroying their chances for economic success. A lifetime of low-level employment is a high price to pay for slacking off in junior high.

The Ministry of Education has issued various reports suggesting things have to change. Yet collective, national education reform seems mostly a pipe dream. Even the most tender mother realizes that by not pushing her child, she may be sealing his or her fate, and, if the child should fail, it is considered the mother's fault. Like it or not, the typical Japanese mother falls into the role of the *kyōiku mama,* the much-maligned "education mom" whose life is focused on the academic success of her children. Not surprisingly, family violence is rising. Newspapers recount incidents of teenage boys beating up mothers who put pressure on them to do well in school. There are also grim reports (perhaps apocryphal) of an increase in mother-son incest, rapes, as well as mothers having sex with their sons to help relieve the boys' tension. Such lurid stories are no doubt exaggerated, yet their prevalence in the popular media suggests the depth of Japanese misgivings about the present situation.

The arduousness of Japanese education is only one source of complaint. What many people object to even more is that education, especially in the later grades, often focuses more on obeying *sensei,* yielding to authority, and memorizing endless bits of information (some of it nonsensical) than on really knowing or learning.

A good example of the mechanical nature of Japanese testing—and therefore Japanese education—is language teaching. Since Japanese *kanji* have little intrinsic relationship to spoken sounds, every *kanji* character must be memorized individually. The basic *kanji* are now taught in the schools grade by grade, 46 characters in the first grade, approximately 100 in the second, and so on until 1,850 of the most common *kanji* have been mastered. They are not taught conceptually or etymologically but in the (hypothetical) order of frequency in which they are used in ordinary Japanese. Since a *kanji* can be made up of as many as nineteen or twenty strokes, memorizing each character requires considerable mental effort. By tradition, one must write them following a prescribed stroke order as well, something also to be memorized.

When I first went to Japan in 1980, many Westerners were still predicting that the Japanese would never be the economic equal of the United States because of this "cumbersome" and "unwieldy" writing system. Commentators emphasized the wasted time it took for Japanese to master the basic characters required for minimal literacy. By 1990, when I was last there, all economic indicators showed that Japan had surpassed the United States, and commentators were now saying it was *because* of the Japanese writing system. The new rationale was that from early childhood on, the Japanese learn that even a tiny mistake impedes communication. Unlike sloppy American children, Japanese children strive for perfection and precision, since both are required to communicate with *kanji.*

But if these same commentators had noticed the way English is taught in Japan, they would have seen that memorization and meticulousness are valued in themselves, not just as components of a difficult writing system. Starting in middle school, Japanese students study English and they study it much as they do *kanji.* Everything is memorized, but what is tested is not fluency in English. Although phonics and a syllabic alphabet should, theoretically, make English an easier language to learn than Japanese, the schools concentrate on the oddities in our language, the elements that make English a perfect subject for high school and college entrance exams. Every arcane Latin-based grammatical rule; our irregular spelling; odd nuances of odd words; strange idioms (many of which I've heard only in Japan); idiosyncratic English constructions—and there are thousands of these—all must be mastered by the would-be successful Japanese student. At Kansai Women's University I was warned early not to even try to teach grammar because these students, who had passed tough exams to get into this prestigious women's university, knew rules and sub-subrules that I would never even have heard of, despite a Ph.D. in English.

One thing is clear: English is not taught in Japan for communication purposes or to implement some broader ideal of internationalism. The typical high school graduate can't begin to actually speak English and probably has never heard it spoken correctly in the classroom. English instruction reinforces the Japanese tendency toward precision, persistent and determined labor, rote memorization, and, I'm convinced, xenophobia. Studying English prompts in many Japanese a lifelong aversion to the language. More times than I can count, I've asked a simple question in pretty decent Japanese to someone at a train station or on the street.

"No Engrish! No Engrish!" is the immediate response. The person's panic-stricken face communicates instantly that more is at work here than lack of understanding. Most Japanese have had six years to work up a healthy distaste for our language.

≋

When Ted and I enrolled in an introductory Japanese course at a language institute near our apartment, we somehow thought that, as foreigners, we'd be exempt from the Japanese educational system. Over the Japanese green tea that preceded our first official private language session, we told our *sensei* that we had taken only a few weeks of informal Japanese language lessons before coming to Japan, and, since we planned to be here only a year, we were interested in a crash course in survival Japanese.

Sensei nodded thoughtfully as we made these remarks, then ushered us into the small classroom across from where we had had our tea. She bid us kneel in front of Japanese-style writing desks. She assumed her position at the front of the room.

"The basic rule for stroke order when writing the *kanji* characters," our first lesson began, "is that you proceed from top to bottom, and left to right. When two or more strokes cross, make sure to draw the horizontal strokes before the perpendicular ones, although in some cases such as *den* (rice field) or *o* (king), the perpendicular stroke must precede the horizontal."

"Would it please be possible to concentrate on oral Japanese?" I ask, trying to sound as deferential as I can.

"Yes, I don't think we'll have time to do both written and oral Japanese," Ted backs me up.

"This is a mistake foreigners always make," our *sensei* says definitively. "They think that it will be faster if they just learn to speak. Actually, the reverse is true. If you start with writing on the very first day, the speaking comes much faster."

For the next two hours, Ted and I sit like humble schoolchildren, copying onto our papers the *kanji* characters that *sensei* draws on the blackboard. We make sure our horizontal strokes precede our perpendicular.

For me, the class is a revelation. I had never really looked at

Japanese characters before and I find that I love them. I love the way each character has a discrete meaning—often many discrete meanings—and I love their beauty and economy. As I page through my orange *kanji* book, I start to see relationships between the simpler and the more advanced characters and feel as if I am tapping into some wonderful, secret world. That afternoon I rush out to the local stationery store and buy *fude* (writing brushes) and ink. I practice the first fifteen *kanji* we are to have memorized by next week along with *hiragana,* one of the two phonetic alphabets. *Hiragana* interests me less—its principles are more familiar—but the *kanji* feel like magic.

From another book, written entirely in *hiragana,* I study the week's basic sentence patterns: "This is a pen." "Is this a pen?" I'm not learning anything that would be particularly useful in an ordinary, everyday conversation, but at the end of one week, I can write fifteen *kanji* and I can ask, *"Where* is the pen?" and answer with the relational words—*kono, sono, ano*—crucial to Japanese discourse: The pen is here near me, the speaker. The pen is nearer to you, the listener. The pen is over there, far from both of us.

I spend three or four hours a day learning *kanji,* a couple more hours each day getting ready for my teaching at Kansai Women's University. Outside, on the path to Kabuto-yama Daishi, the ancient temple near our house, cherry blossoms are falling. In Kyoto, an hour away, cherry blossoms line the Philosopher's Walk. I kneel at the coffee table in our apartment, my legs folded beneath me, writing out the *kanji* for *getsu, ka, sui*—moon, fire, water.

"We have to make a choice," Ted says finally. "Either we're going to take that language course or we're going to see Japan this year. I don't see any way that we have time to do both."

We opt for Japan but, stubbornly, I insist that I will spend my travel time learning *kanji* my own way. Everywhere I go, I carry a pencil and blank flash cards. I write down new *kanji* announcing the names of stops we see in train and subway stations. When I get home at night, I bring out my *kanji* book and find the characters. I learn the different pronunciations (Chinese and Japanese) and see what other compound words use the same basic characters. These I also memorize through association with my travels. On every new trip, I look out the train window, seeking more instances of "my" *kanji.*

By the end of our stay, I can recognize two hundred *kanji* without hesitation and can guess the meaning of roughly a hundred more. This still isn't enough to read a simple menu, much less a newspaper, but occasionally I can make out a few items or decipher a street sign or a person's name. I've worked very hard at this and I'm inordinately proud of my accomplishment.

"Welcome to third grade!" Professor Sano, the department head at KWU, teases me.

After we stop regular language lessons, I make a deal with the son of one of my Japanese friends. I tell Kenji I will speak English to him if he will answer me back in Japanese. He's just entered middle school, and his mother hopes this will help him learn English. He's having a hard time of it.

He speaks in rapid Japanese to his mother, who translates. She wonders if, before we get started on English conversation, I might be willing to look over his homework. Although he can barely write even the simplest English, this week his assignment is to fill in the blanks in some very long sentences that turn on the difference between *who* and *whom, that* and *which.* "The boy to whom I gave the dictionary lives next to the girl who goes to the school that is located by the bookstore that sells comic books about which my mother, who is old-fashioned, has a low opinion."

Whatever happened to "See Spot run"?

Kenji has ten of these ridiculous sentences, and there's no way I can explain to him that English usage blurs these distinctions all the time. Kenji knows there's a right way and a wrong way and stays up every night until almost midnight studying such English sentences, trying to divine the rules that make sense of it all.

When I try to talk to him in English, he looks at me wide-eyed.

"What will you do this summer on your vacation?" I begin, saying each word clearly and distinctly.

"*Wakarimasen, wakarimasen!*" he waves his hands in the air (I don't understand, I don't understand!).

We go back to *who* and *whom, that* and *which.* He has an English test tomorrow.

≈

What Kenji and all other Japanese schoolchildren learn from the very first day that they start off in their new uniforms under the falling cherry blossoms is that life is order and order emanates from an authority figure. *Sensei* embodies wisdom and provides the hierarchical structure that makes Japan work. In a collective, communitarian culture, order is essential. It is essential to such notions as national and even company loyalty, the basis for the lifetime employment system in Japan (a system which, in theory, is open to all but, in fact, is limited mostly to employees in the larger corporations). It is essential to a planned economy—what a friend calls socialism with a raging capitalist face. In Japan, the entrepreneurial millionaire isn't the ideal. On the contrary, the Japanese like to boast that in national surveys almost 90 percent of the respondents describe themselves as middle class. Income redistribution through taxes is far more rigorous than in the United States, with rates starting as low as 10 percent and going up to 70 percent. Similarly, full employment is the Japanese economic and social ideal, in contrast to our capitalist system, which is predicated on the notion that a 4 or 5 percent unemployment rate is desirable to keep a competitive edge.

Order, authoritarianism, and communitarianism are essential to peaceful coexistence in a world where people live in tiny, crowded spaces, in apartment blocks that go on for miles. From preschool onward, they've been part of a school system that teaches them to live and work collectively, to get the tiniest detail absolutely right, and to take responsibility for their own actions within a context that requires group consciousness. "I will do my best" is a favorite Japanese expression, and, in Japan, one's best must be very, very good.

Yet there are gaps. The vomit dotting the train platforms at night is a reminder of one gap. Drinking is one respite from the pressure as are the other escapes of Japan's infamous "Floating World," a world of bars, prostitution, live sex shows, gambling. Pornography is another escape. It's ubiquitous—on the front pages of newspapers, in graphic (and often extremely violent) comic books, all read openly on the trains and in other public places, mostly by men and boys but also by schoolgirls, mothers, and sometimes grandmothers, too. *Rape Man* and other popular comics frequently portray child sexual abuse and torture. Pornographic movie houses often specialize in films depicting violence against women. Yet the incidence of rape is far lower in Japan than in the United States, even taking into account both sexism and Japanese reluctance to report personal injury. There are also grotesquely violent nonsexual movies, senseless and explicit, again a seeming contradiction in a nation with one of the lowest rates of violent crime in the world. Tearjerkers are also commonplace since a movie house is one of the few places in Japan where it is permissible to cry in public. More than once I've walked by a theatre racked by the collective sobs of its customers, male and female. Japan is a pressure cooker with built-in escape valves.

Three periods in Japanese life are set off and separate from the grind of everyday existence. Early childhood is freest, followed closely by old age, which is envisioned as a second childhood and another time when one is allowed to break rules. On one's sixtieth birthday *(kanreki)*, when one has gone "full circle" according to the East Asian zodiac, one becomes a child again, donning a red vest, symbolic of the *akachan* (the baby; literally, little red one).

The third period of freedom in Japanese life is during college. The majority of those who attend college enjoy a four-year vacation between the end of study for the grueling entrance exams and the beginning of life as a *sarariiman* or, for women, an OL (office lady), a brief period of menial corporate labor typically followed by marriage and child-rearing (often combined with a full- or part-time job). There are notable exceptions (especially in the sciences or for those at top-ranked universities seeking the very best jobs at the best companies), but most Japanese college students enjoy a break from the normally frenetic pace of Japanese life.

This arrangement is quintessentially Japanese: one spends one's entire childhood studying to get into college; one's place and level of employment are determined, in large part, by where one went to college; but college itself can be inconsequential. In a process culture, the point is the study; the goal diminishes as soon as it's achieved. More materially, employers feel that character—the evidence that one is able and willing to study hard and pass the college entrance exams—is the important thing. Anyone who has passed an exam to get into an important university is dedicated enough to do well for the firm. The rest is job training, best taught by the company. When more sophisticated research and development skills are desired, companies send their most promising employees to the United States for a year or two of intense graduate or professional study.

At Japanese universities, clubs, parties, class outings, and other forms of socializing regularly take precedence over classes. College is a place to meet friends, many of whom will be useful business connections for the rest of one's life. School friendships persist and are the focus for just about the only socializing one does outside of one's workplace. To refer to someone as "my classmate" is to bestow upon them a very special status, almost as distinctive as a family member. College even provides one of the few instances in Japanese life of cross-gender, platonic friendships. I know an outspoken feminist in Japan who has been treated relatively generously by the press largely because she is a graduate of one of Japan's foremost national universities. Her school chums may disagree with her politics but they treat her respectfully and make sure their colleagues do, too.

Other than a few cultural or intellectual events, such as the speakers so prevalent on U.S. university campuses, there is remarkably little intellectual life for the typical Japanese undergraduate. Since most students seldom go to class, there is also little intellectual exchange. When Ted taught conversational English at an average, coed university, he found that very few students regularly attended class and that a number of the teachers in the same building often didn't show up either. Ted didn't even receive a class list until the day of the final exam and was surprised to learn that he had some forty students, not the eight or ten he had taught during the yearlong term. With the class lists, he also received an explanation of the university's grading system, including one grade that turned out to be very useful. Roughly translated, the grade means: student did not attend class, did not pass (or take) the final exam, but does not fail the course.

This four-year vacation is institutionalized throughout Japan. We've participated in several conversations with Japanese professors who reflect nostalgically on their own carefree college years. Often they engage in a kind of one-downsmanship, bragging about how little they did academically. At least conversationally, there seems to be an almost inverse relationship between status and work: the better the university, the more one is allowed to play. After four carefree years, one enters the Company, where the daily round of obedient toil begins again.

One day, on the way home from the local market, I crossed one of the small bridges over the river that runs through our section of Nigawa. Sitting cross-legged in the middle of the bridge was a high school boy in uniform. As I got closer, I could see that the boy was quietly tearing pages out of a schoolbook and throwing them into the water. It was late in winter, around the time of "examination hell," the entrance tests that determine if a student will get into college. The river, which is usually little more than a trickle, was swollen from recent rain to a depth of maybe two or three feet, and was racing angrily over the rocks, down toward the sea. I had no way of knowing how long the boy had been on the bridge, but it seemed as if he must have made his way through two or three books already. Everywhere there were pages from the boy's books—floating whitely on the churning brown water, clinging soggily to the riverbanks, hundreds and hundreds of pages.

The boy didn't look up when I passed by. He didn't seem to look at anybody or anything except the river. He kept tearing pages, tossing them onto the water, the expression on his face perfectly blank.

As I was about to turn the corner to my house, I paused and looked back at the boy on the bridge. Two women were with him now. One of them, perhaps his mother, tugged at him, urging him to stand up. The other woman was gathering up his remaining schoolbooks and loading them into a small cart, the kind Japanese women use to carry their groceries. I was too far away to hear their voices, but I watched their anxious pantomime as first one woman, then both, began pulling at the boy's arms, his jacket. The sun was setting behind the clouds. The boy continued to stare at the muddy river that might wash his school lessons away.

4

FROM
THE BEST
FAMILIES

In some ways Kansai Women's University is an exception to many of the rules about college life in Japan. A private university with rigorous admissions standards, KWU was founded by American missionaries who were alumna of one of the Seven Sisters schools and is also modeled on the liberal arts ideals of prestigious American women's colleges. The women who go to KWU study hard, American-style, during their four years of college. They are brilliant students from, we were told, "the best families," typically the daughters of professional people. Many are on their way to being wives and mothers of future business leaders and statesmen, the country's elite. Some cherish hopes of being business and civic leaders themselves.

Many of the English majors at KWU are fluent in English.

Often they have spent time abroad, sometimes only a few months but sometimes as much as six or eight years. Many of their courses are conducted entirely in English, whether taught by Japanese teachers of English or by native English speakers.

Unlike many Japanese students, KWU students do not enter college with the anticipation of a four-year vacation. On the contrary, for KWU students, their college years may be the busiest time in their lives. They take over fifteen courses each semester and can spend thirty to forty hours a week in the classroom. After class, their time is filled with other lessons: tea ceremony, *koto* (Japanese harp), *ikebana* (flower arrangement), piano or violin, tennis, French, aerobics, Chinese cooking, French cooking, and kimono dressing (no easy task, especially learning to wrap and tie the twelve-foot-long *obi* sash). All of these accomplishments become part of the young woman's "dossier" as she and her family set out to find her the perfect life partner, through an adaptation of the ancient custom of *omiai,* the formal meeting between the couple, parents, and go-between preparatory to arranged marriage. Nearly 85 percent of upper-class Japanese still go through at least a loose form of *omiai,* and KWU students are no exception. It is almost a truism that the English majors at KWU make perfect, cosmopolitan wives, able to function effortlessly in any environment, East or West.

Yet despite the exceptional intelligence of the KWU students, they did not perform in the classroom with anything like the articulateness and liveliness of my American students. Twelve years of a more passive educational system, coupled with a basic Japanese idea that one should not show off in front of one's peers, made it difficult to elicit the kind of classroom discussion that I prize in my American students.

The only way I found to break through this pattern of passive learning was by using Japanese group consciousness and "team spirit," as they say, to an American end. I divided my classes into rows and asked each row to pick a group leader. I'd ask a question ("What does the image of the wall suggest to you in Robert Frost's 'Mending Wall'?") and have the rows work in teams to see who could come up with the best answer. In my advanced classes, I asked that all discussion in the group be conducted in English. I'd give them a time limit, two or three minutes.

At first, there were faint murmurings, barely audible even within the row, and self-conscious answers from the team leader. But as I encouraged them to be more freewheeling and gave them permission to do something they weren't used to doing in the classroom, hesitant whispers gave way to a flurry of excited discussion. They would argue strenuously in their group and then the team captain would report what the group had come up with. I've seldom encountered more insightful, sensitive responses to poetry.

By the end of the year, students were coming up with their own team questions and answering them. Sometimes, on their own, they would challenge one another, never in a combative or even competitive way, but with seriousness, as if this discussion of modern American poetry really mattered.

It was exhilarating. Once given a mechanism by which they could adapt American-style dialogue to their Japanese group patterns, these Japanese overachievers were spectacularly articulate.

≋

There was only one course in which Professor Sano, my department head, thought I might have trouble. I was assigned to teach Oral English for Non-English Majors, the B class, and Professor Sano made a point of warning me that these students would be very different from my English majors. Few, if any, would have had any contact with English except through the traditional Japanese educational system. Intelligent young women, they still would have learned English the way my young friend Kenji had— lots of "who" and "whom," virtually nothing resembling practical conversational English. Most never would have heard a native speaker of English, except in Hollywood movies.

The "English" taught in their Japanese schoolrooms was actually *katakana*, the Japanese syllabary for foreign words, a way of transliterating all foreign sounds into the forty-six basic Japanese sound patterns: *r* becomes *l*, *v* becomes *b*, each consonant (except *n*) must be followed by a vowel. *Rocket* is *rokketo* (pronounced "locketo"), *ventillator* is *benchirētā*, and, the classic example, *blacklist* is the six-syllable *burakku-risuto*.

Perhaps because I was struggling so hard to learn even the most rudimentary Japanese, I was eager to teach these students English. My dislike of the traditional Japanese way of teaching English also made me feel almost a missionary zeal upon entering my Oral English course at KWU. I'd never taken any courses in the field of TOESL, Teaching of English as a Second Language, but I certainly knew from colleagues that the way English is taught in the Japanese schools is exactly the *wrong* way to encourage people to really communicate in a new language.

I tried a different tack, beginning with the conscious demotion of *sensei*. Unlike many language teachers who refuse to speak anything but the language being taught, I delighted in speaking to the students in my execrable Japanese. Partly this was selfish; I practiced more Japanese in beginner's Oral English class than anywhere else. But it was also pedagogical. I figured if they realized that *sensei* wasn't ashamed to make mistakes, they certainly didn't have a right to be—a way of using the Japanese proclivity for authoritarianism and punctiliousness against itself. To show what I expected on the first formal presentation, a requirement in all of the Oral English sections, I initially prepared the same assignment—in Japanese. At first I thought I'd intentionally throw in a few mistakes, but quickly realized my Japanese was quite bad enough on its own without my having to invent errors.

I came up with a whopper. It is the kind of mistake often made by native English-speakers, who have a hard time differentiating between repeated consonants. Mine, I found out later, was already a famous mistake; it happened when an American introduced the oldest and most revered woman in the Japanese parliament on national television. The American meant to say that this legislator was not only "very distinguished" but also "very feminine" *(onna-rashii)*. She ended up saying the legislator was both distinguished and *onara shi* (which means, roughly, to cut a fart).

"That double *n* is hard for foreigners," I said when one of my students started to giggle. "We can't really hear the difference between *onna ra* and *onara.*"

The students were now all laughing, but in polite Japanese-girl fashion, a hand covering the mouth.

"Wait!" I shouted in my sternest voice. "This is Oral English class!"

The laughter stopped. They looked ashamed.

"No, no. In this class, you must *laugh* in English. Think about it. You've all seen American movies. How do you laugh in English?"

I could see a gleam in Miss Shimura's eye, and I called on her: "Would an American woman ever put her hand over her mouth when she laughed, Miss Shimura?"

"No, *sensei*—I mean, teacher."

"Show me. Laugh like an American movie star."

Miss Shimura kept her hands plastered at her side. She threw back her head. She opened her mouth as far as it would go. She made a deep, staccato sound at the back of her throat. *Hanh. Hanh. Hanh.*

We all laughed hysterically.

"Hands down!" I shouted again. "This is Oral English!"

They put their hands at their sides and imitated Miss Shimura's American head-back, open-mouth plosive laugh.

"What about the body?" I asked.

I parodied a Japanese laugh, pulling my arms in to my sides, bowing my head and shoulders forward, putting a hand coyly to my mouth.

Again they laughed. This time it was American-style.

"Oral English is about bodies too, not just words." I smiled.

Miss Kato raised her hand.

"Hai?" (Yes?).

"Americans also laugh like this." She put her head back,

opened her mouth, and rocked her upper body from side to side, her shoulders heaving and dodging, like Santa Claus.

There were gleeful shouts of "Yes! Yes!" and again a roomful of American-style laughter. It would start to die down, then someone would catch her friend doing the funny American laugh, and she'd break into hysterics again, the hand going to her mouth, me pointing, her correcting herself with the Santa Claus laughter. I continued to laugh Japanese-style, which made them laugh even louder, bouncier. We were off and running, laughing in each other's languages.

I'm convinced shame kills language learning faster than anything, even more so in Japan, where shame lurks so close to the surface of every social interaction. The laughing routine was a childish exercise, but then all language learning is childish, inherently infantilizing, a giving up and a giving in, a loss of control. Learning a language means returning to a state of near idiocy.

And honesty. Language learning is so consuming, there's no energy left over for invention. Ask someone to tell you their height and weight in a beginning foreign language class, and you'll likely get a much more reliable answer than the one on her driver's license.

This quickly became the case in beginners Oral English, where I learned aspects of Japanese life that the sophisticated, cosmopolitan students in the advanced classes at KWU would not have revealed, under normal circumstances, to a *gaijin*. My beginners talked in English the way they might talk in Japanese, among friends. They didn't know enough about Western culture to anticipate what we might consider strange or exotic, controversial or even reprehensible. Consequently, they spoke without excessive censoring, something I never experienced later on, when I taught an Advanced Oral English class.

My advanced students often dodged my questions with polite evasions. "The Japanese myth of racial homogeneity is as erroneous as the American myth of the melting pot" offered a student who had spent several years in the States. I had thought my opening question, "What is racism?", would provoke a heated debate that would lead us around, by the end of the class period, to addressing each country's particular brand of racism. Typically, Japanese are happy to discuss American racism but blind to the equivalent prejudice in their own country. The student's pointed answer effectively short-circuited the lesson I had hoped to make that day by anticipating what my own point of view might be. The rest of the class period was filled with platitudes and bored and knowing nods. The students in the advanced class knew exactly where to fudge.

After summer break, I require students in beginning Oral English for Non-Majors to give a brief presentation on what they've done over the vacation. It's designed to be simple, to ease them back into the term. They've been in Oral English since April, the beginning of the Japanese school year. They have had six weeks off for the summer, and now must return to classes for three more weeks before the grueling end-of-semester exams in late September.

I call on the first student.

"I was constipated most of the way to Nikko," a lovely young woman in a Kenzo flower-print jumper begins her talk.

I set my face like a Japanese mask, careful to express no emotion, and steal glances around the room. No one seems even remotely surprised at this beginning except me, and I know that it is absolutely mandatory that I act as if this is the most ordinary opening in the world.

"I was with the tennis club, and my *sensei* made sure I ate *konnyaku* for my constipation."

At this point she gets flustered. She is obviously embarrassed.

"It's okay," I jump in hastily, searching for my most soothing and encouraging Japanese. "You're doing very well. Please go on."

"It's just," she stammers, also in Japanese, "I don't know the English for *konnyaku*. Do you know?"

I assure her that there's no American equivalent. *Konnyaku* is a glutinous substance, made from the root of a plant that seems to grow only in Japan. In America, I tell her, most people eat bran to cure constipation or we take over-the-counter medicines such as Ex Lax.

"Ecks Racks," she repeats solemnly, then breaks into giggles (American-style). So does everyone.

The word sounds so funny. It becomes the class joke for the next few weeks. If anyone forgets a word in English, someone else inevitably whispers to a friend, loud enough for the rest of us to hear, "Ecks Racks!"

Three or four other speeches that morning give blow-by-blow reports of near gastrointestinal crises and how they were averted, usually by the wise intervention of some *sensei.*

What surprises me most about the morning is how embarrassed *I* am, although I think I've concealed it pretty well. These students would wilt with shame if they had any inkling that this is not something we would talk about in America, and I find myself in a quandary. They trust me to tell them about Western culture, but I know that if I tell them it's not considered polite to talk about one's bowel movements in Western society, it will destroy the easy camaraderie I've worked so hard to foster this year. But if I don't tell them, I'm violating a trust.

I decide to resolve this by keeping a list of things they bring up that wouldn't be acceptable in the West. All semester I've been working to correct certain Japanese misconceptions and stereotypes, especially their idea that English is a completely logical and direct language, and that Americans always say exactly what they mean, regardless of social status or power relationships. Often my students say things that sound very rude because they've been taught that English lacks the politeness levels of Japanese. These are topics we discuss all the time, so it will work just fine to devote the last week of the semester to lecturing, in my comical Japanese, about misconceptions and cultural differences that I've discovered during my year in Japan. I can tell them about how surprised I was the first time I used a public restroom that turned out to be coed or about bathing Japanese-style with a group of women I barely knew or having a male colleague slip around a corner on the way home from a party. I started to follow, then realized he was taking a quick pee. I know I can act out my own surprise, making my Westerner's prudishness about bodily functions seem funny but also relevant. This is as close as I can come to having my pedagogical cake and eating it too.

From my beginning non-English majors in Oral English, I learn a great deal about Japan, including the rituals and superstitions that have not been effaced by the rampant capitalism of modern, urban Japanese life. They tell of phone numbers one can call for horoscopes, fortunes, curses, cures. Rituals for marriages, pregnancies, births, divorces. A kind of Japanese voodoo that takes place in the forest on a certain kind of night. Number symbolism. Lucky and unlucky days, lucky and unlucky years, lucky and unlucky directions ("Never sleep with your head to the North, the way the dead are buried"). Blood-type matchmaking. Tengu, the wicked long-nosed trickster goblin. Kappa, the amphibious river imp. Tanuki, the raccoonlike creature with the money bag and enormous testicles, a symbol of plenty. Dragons, supernatural foxes, thunder gods, long-life noodles, boiled eels for stamina on hot summer days, chewy *mochi* rice cakes for strength and endurance on the New Year, the ashes of a burnt *imori* (salamander) served to someone you want to make fall in love with you. They talk seriously about prejudice and injustice toward the *burakumin* (Japan's untouchable caste), the Ainu (the indigenous people, now almost extinct), and Koreans (who must take Japanese names before being allowed citizenship or who are denied citizenship even two or three generations after their family immigrated to Japan and who must carry alien registration papers with their thumbprint, like foreigners). They talk of burial customs, going to the crematorium with the long chopsticks to pick out the vertebra that goes in the urn in the family altar at home.

When they talk of *omiai* and arranged marriage, one woman starts to cry. Her friends comfort her. It's the only time I've ever seen someone express personal sorrow in a Japanese classroom. Several students insist that they will never marry an eldest son, because they do not want to be responsible for taking care of his aged parents. Two say they will never have children because they do not want their children to hate them the way they hated their mothers all through school. One young woman says if she marries, it will be to a foreigner because she knows from the movies that foreign husbands help around the house. Another protests that she wouldn't want to marry a *gaijin,* because she doesn't want a *gokiburi teishu* (a cockroach husband), some man scurrying around underfoot in her kitchen. Funny or serious, they talk with candor. And, mostly, they talk. In English.

≈≈≈

"There was so much laughing going on in the next room this semester, I checked the schedule," sniffs one of the part-time teachers. "It's your Oral English class. My students are getting jealous. All we hear from your room is laughter. Is anyone learning anything at all in there?"

I've had conversations before with this woman, none of them pleasant. She teaches at one of the more conventional Japanese universities and comes to Kansai Women's University only one day a week. I've heard her say more than once that she's been here so long that now "she's more Japanese than the Japanese."

We're sitting and talking together over our *bentō* boxes, eating our lunch in the faculty room. I tell her, proudly, that my students are learning to speak English very well, and, maybe more important, they are learning to speak freely and confidently.

"And you think that's a good thing?" she asks rhetorically. "They graduate and get to be OLs for a while. Then they're married off to some jerk of a *sarariiman.* But it's okay, you've taught them how to 'speak freely.' "

I am not liking this woman. I am not liking the insinuation in her voice or the smirk on her face. But I can't ignore her comment. I've thought about it myself, many times, especially on the train to and from the university, as I watch the faces of older Japanese women and think about where and how my students will fit in.

Most of these KWU students will graduate and they will, indeed, work as OLs for a few years before marriage, smiling politely and serving tea for busy male executives in Japanese firms. The closest they will come to real "business" might be working the Xerox machine or the paper shredder. Since only about a quarter of the population at four-year colleges in Japan is female (compared to well over half in the United States), there are lots of women available to work after the completion of secondary school. OLs are perpetually replenishable, an eternally young group of women. Most quit—or are fired—once they are married or after they become pregnant.

The KWU women are the crème de la crème of Japanese female students. Some well might advance further in corporate life than the OLs. A few might even achieve their dreams. One of my students wants to be a composer. Another wants to be an international news correspondent. Still others want to be doctors, lawyers. The odds are stacked against them, but the very fact that they are here shows that they are good at overcoming odds.

"My dream is to be a housewife and a mother," one of my Oral English students said in class one day. "But when I am a mother, I will give my children a *choice* of whether or not they want to go to *juku*. I will help to improve Japanese society by allowing my children to be free."

To be free. It's a phrase I've heard a lot this year, and I suspect some of this is just student grandstanding to please the *gaijin* teacher. Some of it is probably wishful thinking. Many of these smart, polished young women will become thoroughly conventional upper-middle-class housewives and mothers. It's hard for me to understand the point of all their study, all their years of deprivation, all those hours in *juku* cramming for "examination hell," just so one day they, too, can become "education moms," sending their young sons and daughters off under the falling cherry blossoms, the whole cycle beginning again with a new generation.

"We are told Japanese workers are better than American,"

one of my students says in an assignment about the work ethic. "We are told this so that we keep working—hard, harder, and hardest. Even as children, we're told to work hard. We Japanese work ourselves to death."

She is as startled as the rest of us by the burning quality of her speech. Her accent isn't perfect and her vocabulary has its limits but her eloquence is unmistakable. We have heard her. She returns to her seat, flushed with attention.

When I take the train home to my apartment in Nigawa that afternoon, I can't help noticing that the only men on the train are elderly, retired. The train is filled with mothers coming home from shopping and with schoolchildren in uniform, finished with one more day of regular school and now on their way to *juku*.

I find myself asking the big question, the dangerous question. What am I really doing here? My students are having fun, they're learning English, but what is my role here? I have learned a lot teaching at Kansai Women's University, and I know my students have learned things too. I don't think it's romanticizing to say we've touched one another, shown each other glimpses of one another's culture. Is that enough?

I can tell sometimes, as I look out over the classroom, that something like love is happening in there. It scares me. My students are convinced I look like a Western movie star. If I wear my shoulder-length hair up in a twist on a hot day, I can predict that at least a dozen of them will have their hair in a twist the next week. If I roll my jacket sleeves, they will roll theirs. My Oral English class has fun imitating my American slang, especially my habits of saying "Oh wow!" They have fun telling me their culture's secrets. They have fun making jokes and laughing and speaking English, hair in a twist, jacket sleeves rolled.

Maybe that's my function. Not very consequential but perhaps necessary. "Visiting Foreign Teacher" is the official title on my visa. The students call me *"sensei,"* but I'm not like other *sensei* in the Japanese scheme of things. I am exotic and I am temporary. My embittered colleague might be right. In the sum total of their existence, it doesn't matter greatly that their English has improved. At my most cynical, I think of myself as a diversion, a respite from frenetic Japanese life, the pedagogical equivalent of the *sarariiman*'s whiskey.

But I don't think you can be a teacher unless you believe in the possibility of change. When I'm feeling optimistic, I like to think I give my Japanese students the same thing I try to give my American students back home: a space in which to speak and be heard.

Sometimes I look at middle-aged women in Japan and I'm filled with awe. Often they *look* middle-aged—not engaged in the frantic and self-defeating American quest to look forever young—and often they look happy. Their children grown, many become adventurous. For some, it's ballroom dancing or traditional Japanese *koto,* hobbies given up during the busy child-rearing years. For others, it's running for local government or working for school reform or in the peace or environmental movements. KWU recently started accepting "returning women"—older women, including mothers whose children are grown—into its graduate program, and the success rate, both in school and for subsequent employment, has been impressive.

That's what I think about when I teach the brilliant young women of Kansai Women's University. I think about their future, and hope that someday, soon or late, they will stop and hear the sound of their own voices and remember their young fire.

5

TYPICAL
JAPANESE
WOMEN

Unlike my American students, the students at Kansai Women's University rarely visited me during my office hours. Then one day a local newspaper reporter interviewed me for a column in which resident *gaijin* answered the question, "What is your impression of the typical Japanese woman?"

Her question stopped me cold. Before I came to Japan, I probably could have answered without hesitation. I had the same preconceptions that most Westerners have about Japanese women—submissive housewives, flirtatious geisha, accommodating prostitutes of the legendary "Floating World." After living and teaching in Japan for a few months, I couldn't begin to characterize the Japanese women I'd met. I was impressed, in general,

by their strength and independence, but I didn't know how to answer a question about "the typical Japanese woman."

"Is there one?" I finally asked helplessly.

I told the reporter that I now knew what was *not* typical (I'd
seen only two geisha), but I didn't have a clue about who the typical Japanese woman might be.

"I guess I'll have to spend the rest of my year trying to find
her!" I joked.

I don't know how this comment translated into the newspaper article that appeared sometime later, but I was told that I was
described as a "feministo" who had come to Japan partly to learn
more about Japanese women. Apparently that was the magic
phrase. Suddenly students began showing up during my office
hours, as if my words in the newspaper had been an invitation to
them. I had said publicly that I was interested in learning more
about Japanese women, and they were there to tell me. And because I was an outsider, they could discuss personal matters with
me and ask my advice without compromising their own lives.

≈≈≈

Most of them come to talk about possible jobs. I am a typical Japanese woman of my generation, they say. I don't want what my
mother wanted. I don't want to be an Office Lady. I don't just
want to marry some *sarariiman.* I want to be a translator, a
journalist, a writer, an international correspondent, a professor.

"I would like to translate Fumiko Enchi into English so foreigners can come to appreciate the beauty of her work," one student proclaims. I try to tell her that the best translators usually
translate from a foreign language into their native language.

"But no foreigner could understand Enchi-san in the original,
I think," my student insists. "She is too Japanese."

Too Japanese. We arrange for her to show me five or ten
pages of her translation the next week. The language is perfectly
grammatical—but as dull as a high school English theme. I sug-

gest again that she might want to try translating one of her favorite American authors into Japanese.

"No, *sensei*," she is emphatic. "We Japanese already translate hundreds of Western writers into Japanese. I want Americans to see what excellent women writers we have."

She looks down at her translation. "I will work harder. I will do my best."

Other students come with vaguer yearnings. "How did you begin your career?" one asks, then later, "How should *I* begin mine?"

They want me to tell them how to do it, what to do, where to go. They want *my* life—it looks fun, easy, glamorous.

"You and Mr. Davidson are a very happy couple," several of them say, using almost exactly the same phrase. I'm sure it's something they've discussed. They are in fantasyland, also confiding that they think Ted looks exactly like James Dean and I like the young Audrey Hepburn. No American would dream of making these comparisons.

I don't have a clue how to break through their romanticism, and I know even less about how they might lead their lives.

"I hate the man my family wants me to marry," confides a stunningly beautiful young woman with iridescent eyes and a heart-shaped face. I've noticed that she has started to gain weight, and during the course of our conversation I realize her weight gain is strategic. She tells me how her parents arranged a marriage for her long ago, to the son of her father's business partner. Being modern parents, they hope the marriage will make their daughter happy, but her desires are not the real issue here. She knows her parents will never forgive her if she refuses to marry the young man, so she eats and eats, hoping to make herself so fat that the man will call off the match himself.

She carries her weight voluptuously, becoming more attractive with each new pound. She is in despair when she comes to me for advice, yet how can I suggest what course she might follow? I can't even guess what it will mean for her—what the *consequences* might be—if she refuses him.

"I'm an outsider," I tell her. "I don't know enough about your culture to be giving advice. Perhaps you should talk about this with one of your Japanese professors."

She doesn't take my suggestion. Whenever I pass her, she is busily eating pizza, rice balls, pastries.

"I want to study in the States for a year," one brilliant student says during her office visit. "Could you please help me with the scholarship forms?"

I am eager to help. This one I can do.

≈

Not everyone talks to me. One young woman sits, wraithlike, in the back of my Survey of American Literature classroom. She looks anorectic, cheeks hollow, eyes burning and blank. Sometimes she just sits and stares at me the whole class. There are over seventy students in this course, so I only occasionally call on them to answer questions in teams, but on one such occasion the student leaves the room. Another young woman in her row quickly comes forward to apologize on her behalf, explaining that her friend has another appointment that day but is too embarrassed to talk to me about it in English.

I'm required to keep attendance records at KWU. I've thought that she has been absent a lot, but one day I realize that she's there, in the classroom, but simply does not answer when I call, "Miss Saitō." When I ask a second time, looking straight at her, she turns away from me and gazes out the window.

One day she stands, through our entire class, staring out our second-floor window. Another day she sits absorbed in picking at her hands. I try not to notice but find my eyes continually shifting in her direction, watching as she first peels flesh away from her fingers and then takes out a small knife to cut the peels away. Blood drips onto the desk.

As casually as possible, I finish up the lecture and dismiss the students early. I hurry down the corridor to the English office for help. Two colleagues are deep in conversation. I excuse myself and interrupt to tell them about the woman in my classroom with the pocketknife.

"It must be Miss Saitō?" the senior *sensei* observes, without getting up. When I nod that it is, she insists that Miss Saitō will be okay.

"We're watching her," she continues. "We've talked with the family. Thank you for telling us. You need not feel she is your responsibility."

"Will she hurt herself? Will she hurt someone else?" I am trying to sound calm even though I am very upset. A young woman has sat in my classroom peeling her fingers like carrots and I'm being told it's not my responsibility.

"I'm very sorry you had to have such a disturbing experience, but please try not to worry about this," the older teacher says, turning back to the younger one and resuming, in Japanese, their discussion.

I learn later that day, from one of the resident foreign teachers, that Ms. Saitō's family is trying to blame KWU for their daughter's problems. Clearly she is having some kind of mental breakdown but the family doesn't want to admit this or seek professional help unless it's absolutely unavoidable because a record of psychiatric problems will hurt her chances on the marriage market. She is going through *omiai* now, a few years earlier than usual, because the family would like to marry her off before she gets any worse. And if she does have a full mental collapse, the family wants it to be while she's at KWU: school pressure is one of the few acceptable reasons (more or less) for a breakdown. The university, on the other hand, is hoping she'll last until the next week, the beginning of summer vacation, so the family will finally be required to take some responsibility for their daughter.

She comes in late for class the next week. It is a miserably hot and humid day, the last day before summer vacation, and the air conditioner is going full blast. The first thing she does is march to the back of the classroom and turn it off. She refuses to sit. She just stands there in the last row looking defiant.

"Nippongo tsukatte kudasaii!" Ms. Saitō shouts at me on that last day of class, demanding that I speak Japanese.

"Excuse me," I say, trying to sound kind although I'm sure anxiety is evident in my voice. "Is there something I can do for you?"

"Nippongo tsukatte kudasaii!" she shouts again.

I repeat my question in Japanese, how may I help you?

She turns her back on me.

I decide that perhaps I should just ignore this and resume my lecture. I turn to the board to write some English words but hear footsteps rushing up behind me. I turn immediately to see her coming toward me, her face contorted in rage.

She pushes past me, the sleeve of her blouse brushing my arm. Aggression without violence. The tension in the room is unbearable. No one breathes. Ms. Saitō picks up a piece of chalk and shouts, *"Nippongo, Nippongo, Nippongo,"* marking an X through every English word on the board, then races out of my classroom.

"Gomen nasai," I turn back to my class, bowing deeply. I am very sorry, I say in *Nippongo*. I tell them I'll see them again in September, after the summer break is over. I tell them I'm sorry we have to part on such an unhappy note but that I hope they have a very nice vacation. I work to hold back my emotions.

One of my students jumps up and bows deeply. *"Gomen nasai,"* she apologizes back to me. All of the students stand, bow, and apologize to me, then start to gather their books in silence.

I gather mine too and head into the English department office, where I report what has just happened. Again there are apologies, but it is clear no one wants to hear about this.

"Ms. Saitō is seeing a doctor now. Perhaps she'll be given some medicines and will be better soon," one colleague observes. "If you feel the situation in your classroom was intolerable," she continues, carefully measuring her words, "then we could take official action. But it will soon be summer vacation."

Translation from indirect Japanese discourse: We will be really pissed if you make a fuss about this now, when we are almost home-free.

I know this kind of thing doesn't happen just in Japan. At KWU, the issue is responsibility. The school doesn't want to be scapegoated by the family. I've seen a similar scene played out, with different motives, at an American Ivy League university where the disturbed son of a rich alumnus was treated with kid gloves in order not to jeopardize future contributions from the family. I'm sure there are rough equivalents everywhere. But this larger perspective doesn't soothe. It happened here, in my classroom, and I feel devastated. During my office hours that day, I lay my head in the crook of my elbow and close my eyes. I want to weep for that young woman, I want to weep for all of these young women who come with problems I cannot solve, and I want to weep for myself.

There is a small rap on my office door. It's a delegation of students, the women from the same row as Ms. Saitō, her "team."

We exchange polite bows, and I invite them to sit down. They busy themselves clearing books and papers off the chairs, then arranging the chairs in a tight row in my small office. Every gesture they make exudes solicitation. They ask if I have summer plans; they express a hope that Mr. Davidson and I will go somewhere cool, away from the humid summer weather in this area of Japan.

Then the team leader speaks.

"Saitō-san's condition has nothing to do with you," she says kindly. "It's not personal. We all wish you to know this."

The young woman stands after she says this and makes a deep bow. All the other students stand and bow. I get up and bow back.

I am moved by their thoughtfulness. Of course I am taking this personally. I find myself fighting back tears as I thank them for coming.

There is another ritual of farewell, more bows, more wishes for a happy summer vacation.

"Please do not blame yourself," the team leader again reassures me, as she is about to slip out of the room, "Kazuko-chan is acting this way in all the classes with *gaijin* teachers."

All of the *gaijin* teachers.

Is this possible? To break down selectively, only in front of those outside the system, those who cannot do too much permanent damage? Or is the breakdown specific, *because* of us foreigners?

"May I ask why this is happening?"

The students speak among themselves in rapid Japanese. I pick up more than they realize—Ms. Saitō feels under too much pressure; she has a sense that the *gaijin* teachers look down on her because she's Japanese; she is unhappy and confused. The words *"muzukashii"* (difficult, complicated) and *"gaijin"* keep coming up over and over, in tandem. They are trying to figure out a tactful way to tell me that *gaijin* make Ms. Saitō nervous without making it sound as if they are blaming me for her breakdown.

"Perhaps she has developed some kind of a complex," the team leader says presently. "We Japanese sometimes feel inferior to foreigners. *Gomen nasai,*" she says, bowing deeply.

"Gomen nasai," I say too.

On the way down the hill from KWU to the train I think about all these students. Roughly the same age, brilliant and studious, from affluent families mostly in the Kansai region of western Japan, there is nothing "typical" about any of them. They are as different and unique as any of my students in the United States.

"Sensei, sensei!" a voice cries out excitedly. It's my beautiful student. She is sitting on a quiet bench, eating an eclair. "I'm not sure but I think perhaps he's not so interested anymore!"

I'm at a loss for words. Do I congratulate her on this odd accomplishment? Do I fear for her chances of making another match? Do I worry that she has alienated herself from her family? It occurs to me that I wouldn't know how to react to a parallel situation in America either. I tell her, whatever may happen, I hope that she will be very happy, a lame comment but the best I can manage today.

"Have a nice vacation, please, *sensei!*" she calls out cheerfully, turning back to her eclair.

≈

"*I* am the typical Japanese woman," my neighbor, Mrs. Okano, insists a few mornings after the newspaper interview comes out. It's been at least two or three weeks since we've seen each other. I'm coming back from shopping and she's at the foot of the apartment stairway waiting, she tells me, for the mail carrier.

"I'm serious," my neighbor says, "if you want to know anything about typical Japanese women, you can ask me."

Ted calls Mrs. Okano "the mayor" of Maison Shōwa, our apartment complex. She's there at the mailboxes at eleven o'clock most mornings, exchanging gossip, news, and information with the other women in fifties-style housedresses and slip-on plastic street sandals. I am the outsider in this group, the only foreign woman in Maison Shōwa, but she makes a point of including me in their conversations. She tells me when a neighbor has twins, an event for Maison Shōwa, and is delighted when I respond that I have stepsisters who are twins. She says she will make sure to tell the neighbor and perhaps we can talk together sometime about twins, in America and in Japan. ("Do you know," she asks me, "that twins are twice as common in America? Some scientists think it is because of our diet. Maybe too much soy sauce," she jokes.) Often, Mrs. Okano passes along more mundane information: she warns me of an upcoming earthquake drill one day and, another time, tells me that a woman from NHK (the national public television station) will be by to collect a "voluntary but required" user fee.

Twice she's invited me into her apartment for afternoon tea. It's a 2DK just like ours but seems smaller. It is crammed with furniture, including several large, freestanding wardrobes that hold clothes for herself and her husband, their two children, and Mr. Okano's mother, who has just moved in with them. Their housing situation is not atypical, even for this affluent suburb. I have gathered that Mr. Okano is an executive at a major corporation; they drive an Audi and own state-of-the-art electronic equipment. But housing costs are astronomical here. A new apartment in the Kansai area can be hard to find and often requires exorbitant "key money," sometimes up to a year's rent paid in cash in advance. Mrs. Okano occasionally hints that they will be moving soon but always abruptly switches to some more immediate topic, so we never discuss the new home.

I've never seen her husband or children. From our conversations, I've learned that her son is in junior high and her daughter in high school. Both are enrolled in *juku* five nights a week.

"It's necessary" is all she says, putting an end to any further questions I might have about her children spending so much time in school, studying so hard. "Besides," she laughs self-consciously, gesturing around the crowded living room, "at *juku* they can stretch their legs."

Over tea, she tells me I am the first *gaijin* she's ever had in her apartment. She taught high school English briefly before she got married but this is the first chance she's had to practice her English in years. She is one of the few Japanese in our apartment complex to put out a Japanese flag on national holidays, so I assume her politics must be fairly conservative, but it's not a subject we discuss. We talk about our town, Japan, children, America, and anything else that happens to come up. Since neither of us is fluent in the other's language, we spend a lot of time riffling through dictionaries, gesturing, pointing. We speak a strange language, somewhere between English and Japanese, and sometimes find ourselves frustrated that we each know exactly the same words in each other's language.

"Interesting," she'll say.

"*Omoshiroii,*" I respond.

"*Muzukashii,*" I'll say.

"That's difficult, complicated," she'll translate.

She's been to tea in my apartment too and has told all of the neighbors how I hang old kimonos on my walls like art and use *soba* to make spaghetti. We have learned from one another, enjoyed each other's company.

"Why do you consider yourself 'typical'?" I ask her.

"Because I am," she laughs. "There's nothing unusual about me at all!"

"I think it's unusual," I say admiringly, "for someone to admit she is typical. Most people think they are pretty special."

"Oh, maybe in America," she laughs. "But in Japan, every woman thinks that she is typical."

As we are laughing, the mailwoman zooms up on her red motorbike. Mrs. Okano excuses herself and goes out to meet her.

She reminds the mailwoman that she will be moving today and that from now on her mail should be delivered to her new address.

"You're moving *today?*" I ask, surprised at how disappointed I feel.

"Gomen nasai, gomen nasai," she apologizes, realizing that I'm outside the information loop. Probably everyone else at Maison Shōwa has known for weeks.

I tell her I'm sorry to hear that she is moving, but that I hope she will enjoy her new apartment.

"It's a *house,*" she says, unable to conceal her pride.

She is expecting the movers this afternoon but insists on inviting me in so she can give me a copy of a map she has neatly drawn, marking the way to her new house.

"Now you can come visit me," she beams, handing it to me. "I gave my husband a map this morning so he can find his way to our new house tonight after work." She says this casually, as we start to make our formal good-bye bows.

"I don't understand. You mean, he doesn't remember the way?"

"He's never been there."

"I don't understand," I repeat, this time in Japanese. "He's never been there?"

Now she's confused by my confusion, and repeats again, in her best English, that she's drawn him a map because he's never been to the house itself.

"Excuse me, please," I say, upping the politeness level of my

71

Japanese. "I do not understand how he could have bought a house without seeing it?"

"He didn't buy the house, *I* did."

"And he never saw it before you bought it?"

"Of course not. That's woman's work. I told you I'm a typical Japanese woman. Isn't this how women do it in America?"

Mrs. Okano is shocked when I tell her that few American married women make major financial decisions without consulting their husbands and that I don't know any married woman who would go out and buy a house on her own. There might be some, but I don't know any.

"Really?" She's as incredulous as I am.

"Never."

"What about a car?" she asks me.

I shake my head no.

"Appliances—refrigerator, television?"

"Not usually."

"Furniture?"

"Probably not. Most American husbands would be mad, I think, to come home and discover their wife had just bought a new couch or dining room set without consulting them."

"I thought all American women work, earn their own money?" She knows me well enough to know I wouldn't lie about this but she's finding the whole conversation bizarre.

"It's true many American women work outside the home," I begin again, slowly. "But even the ones who earn their own money often consult their husbands about big purchases."

"This is what Americans call 'women's lib'?" Mrs. Okano laughs out loud, then covers her mouth with her hand. She apologizes for her rudeness, but cannot stop laughing.

By noon, everyone in our apartment complex will have heard about how the poor *gaijin* woman works full-time as a college teacher, but wouldn't even buy a measly sofa without first asking her husband's permission.

"*Kawaisō!*" she says finally, exchanging her laughter for the ritual expression of sympathy (How pathetic, how pitiful!). Mrs.

Okano reaches out and pats my arm encouragingly, as if I'm a small child badly in need of comforting.

"No wonder you like Japan so much!" she says.

≋

It took a while before I came to realize that, at least so far as money goes, Mrs. Okano might actually be a typical Japanese woman. I doubt that very many Japanese women would buy a house without some input from a husband, but everything I've seen and read suggests that women do make many of the major and minor purchases for the family. Japanese feminist groups rightly caution that having primary budgeting and consumer responsibility is not the same thing as having one's own salary, yet few Westerners are aware that Japanese women have any kind of domestic power at all. In publications produced by Japanese women's groups, I have also read the surprising figure that 70 percent of married women with teenage children now work outside the home, but that even women who do not work for wages are usually the ones who decide how much a family saves or spends. My parting conversation with Mrs. Okano gave new meaning to what I had read about Japanese women being the secret force behind the nation's stunning economic success.

Many Japanese companies actually pay a man's wages directly into his wife's bank account. I've heard male professors joke about how they only give speeches around the country on the condition that they be paid discreetly and directly, a way of getting their hands on some cash their wives don't know about and can't control. Many Japanese wives handle all the family income and give their husbands allowances. Men frequently complain among themselves about their stingy wives. It's a familiar topic of comedy on television, the hardworking *sarariiman* whose wife won't let him have enough money to go out drinking or to play *pachinko,* the pinball game that's a national obsession. In fact, the beauty of the company bar is that one's tab is usually picked up by the company or deducted directly from one's salary, before it lands in the wife's account.

You would not know from observing popular culture that women are Japan's primary consumers, however. Most Japanese ads cater to male fantasies, as if men were the potential customers who had to be persuaded.

"But isn't that typical in Japan?" one of my friends responded when I asked her about this. "We women pretend that men have all the power—and then we go about our own lives. As long as the men *feel* they are in control, we can do what we like."

The difference between the appearance of submissiveness and the reality of control is something Ted noticed almost immediately, especially since he kept meeting foreign men with Japanese girlfriends or wives. Not all *gaijin* fell into this category, certainly, but Ted joked that there were some *gaijin* men who looked cocksure when they were dating Japanese women, happily anticipating the Western fantasy of the totally deferential Oriental wife. Yet there was a perplexed look of lost illusions that unmistakably marked those who had learned, too well, that there could be an iron will and enormous capability behind the demure smile of the "submissive" Japanese wife.

"She has me teaching full-time at one university and part-time at four others," a colleague confided to Ted one day. "And now that the second baby's on the way, she's looking for a bigger place. I guess I'll have to find another part-time job."

Yet the stereotype of the submissive Oriental woman never goes away. Every English-language publication in Japan is filled with desperate personal ads, like this one from an English-language magazine published in Kobe:

OBEDIENCE. An American man who is sensitive but strict seeks a woman of a delicate and docile nature who is interested in exploring the full range of the meaning of this word. What do you think of the ancient Chinese statement "He who rules, truly serves and she who serves, truly rules"? All who are interested should write to . . .

The pathetic author of this advertisement was partly right; in Japan, the person who has the power frequently *is* the one who acts the most powerless. This appearance of submission may be one way that Japanese women survive in a system that, by tradition and law, grants men a superior position. Again I think of Mrs. Okano. I doubt that she would find any contradiction between selecting and arranging the financing for a house that in our suburb could easily cost a million dollars, and making sure she's always there, rice cooker at the ready, when her husband comes home from work or from after-work barhopping. In our conversations, she always refers to her husband with the old-fashioned term *teishu:* "My Master."

If she's really typical, Mrs. Okano also spends part of her day reading financial reports and phoning her broker. Women actively participate in the Nikkei, the Japanese stock market, and Japan's astonishing 20 percent savings rate (one of its biggest weapons in the current trade wars) is due almost entirely to the pecuniary habits of Japanese women.

My friend Sally told us about the first time she and her husband, Toshi, prepared to go on vacation. Toshi asked how much money she had saved from their salaries. She was shocked because, as a product of middle-class American suburbia, she had thought it was her duty to spend their money and had assumed he was the one minding their budget. They had some major cultural and marital readjusting to do when they realized that each had expected the other to put the brakes on their spending and neither had. They were flat broke.

Toshi, a direct descendent of a famous *samurai* clan, explained that a *samurai*'s clothes did not even have pockets. No *samurai* would deign to carry money; that was women's work.

"This is why boys do so poorly in math," Toshi noted. "If there weren't lower math standards for boys than girls, our best national universities would be filled with women."

75

Other Japanese friends confirmed this. Boys in Japan often have math anxiety. There are special *juku* courses to overcome this fear.

When a study done in America in 1980 "proved" that girls have lower math scores than boys due to lower testosterone levels, I made Xerox copies of the *Time* magazine article and brought it into my Rhetoric class at Kansai Women's University. I asked them to read the article first, and then to write an in-class essay about it.

It's one of the few times where my students began to laugh spontaneously, without my making it clear that they were "allowed" to do so.

"*Gomen nasai!*" one of my students said, working hard to control her mirth. "We know this article isn't supposed to be funny but it is. We all help our brothers with arithmetic."

≈≈≈

"So are *you* typical Japanese women?" I joked with the women I sat with on the train to Shirahama, a seaside resort town to which I'd been invited on a retreat by members of the Japanese Women's Studies Society. These feminists and social activists were passing my interview back and forth among them, commenting on the article, teasing me about it Japanese-style. The nail that sticks up gets hammered down, goes an old Japanese proverb. A little bit of fame and you can expect ribbing from your friends.

"Oh, yes, we're even more typical than *typical* Japanese women," Kazue-san joked.

"But *how* are you typical?" I asked.

They told me.

"We do not spend our lives entertaining our husbands' business associates," Atsumi-san said emphatically. "Isn't that what typical middle-class American women have to do?"

"Yes," Itami-san seconded the comment. "I would hate it if I were considered some asset to a husband's career."

She talked about what's called "railroad marriage" in Japan, in which married people live independent and distinct lives, with their own friendships and their own work and social lives, but have certain ties—such as children, a shared household, parental responsibilities, and, sometimes, love—that keep the marriage together. The divorce rate in Japan is much lower than in the States, partly because divorce itself is almost impossible to obtain without mutual consent and partly because the Japanese don't share the Western romantic notion that marriage should fulfill all one's emotional needs.

"Sometimes it sounds strange to me in American movies," Kazue-san said, "when an American woman will say, 'My husband is my best friend.' My best friend *is* my best friend!"

Another woman, Uenoyama-san, felt that it was their expectation of good, government-subsidized child care that made them typical Japanese women. She explained that there were problems with the Japanese system, and women's groups were working to correct them but mothers in Japan could at least count on minimum national safety and health standards, with child care fees graduated according to one's ability to pay.

"I think typical Japanese women care about maternity leave, too," Sakamoto-san added, patting her stomach. "By law, my job will be waiting for me after I have my baby—and my university will pay my salary for the six months I'm on leave."

She said she didn't understand how American women could accept the fact that their nation had a worse infant and maternal mortality rate than many Third World countries. "A typical Japanese woman wouldn't put up with that," she insisted.

Our conversation had begun about "typical Japanese women," but my new friends had turned it into a discussion of differences between "typical" American and Japanese women. American women weren't coming out ahead. For the rest of the long train ride to Shirahama, we talked about rape (official statistics indicate there are about ten times more reported rapes in America than Japan); domestic violence (again, higher in America); and birth control. I learned that the pill was outlawed in Japan after studies showed dangerous side effects for women. The condom is the most popular form of contraception, followed by legal, safe abortion.

"But at least American women face a better situation in the job market than we do," one of the women said, trying to help me save face. "Japanese women comprise 40 percent of the labor force—but we only earn 51 percent of what men make."

I pointed out that the 1980 figure for America was only around 59 percent, not much higher.

There was a long silence.

"Perhaps on our retreat we can talk about some of these issues," I suggested. "I'd like to hear how Japanese feminists deal with these problems so I can tell women back in America."

"Good!" Akiko-san laughed. "Now that we are on an equal footing we can talk about the serious problems faced by typical women—in America *and* Japan."

≈

Of course there *are* serious problems in Japan, all the ones we read about over and over in the American press. We know that it is almost impossible for women to succeed above a certain level in even the most progressive Japanese company; only 10 percent of Japanese working women occupy management positions (compared to almost 45 percent in the United States). As in America, women are woefully underrepresented in government. We know that there's no real concept of monogamy for married men and that the legal basis for marriage is totally patriarchal: a woman is erased from her family's registry upon marriage and entered into her husband's, another reason why divorce is so difficult and why it is difficult for a woman to keep her own family name after marriage. A daughter is not an asset in any real, permanent sense since she is expected to marry and become part of her husband's family. I've heard that in Nagano, where families scour the mountains for the wild *matsutake* (large mushrooms that sell for up to fifty dollars apiece), young daughters are not allowed to go mushroom hunting with the rest of the family since after marriage they might be pressured to reveal their family's secret mushroom-hunting grounds to their in-laws, their *new* family.

All these issues are attracting the attention of Japanese women, not only organized feminists but "typical" women of all political persuasions. I met Japanese feminists who were protesting the exploitation of the *Japa-yuki,* women from other countries— mostly Filipina, Thai, and Korean—brought to Japan with promises of legitimate employment and then forced into prostitution. These same feminists also opposed discrimination against Korean nationals and *burakumin* and other outcastes.

"But you're forgetting something," observed a Korean feminist at one of their meetings. "Sometimes *our* men are forced to make a living as pimps by Japanese society."

Because ethnic Koreans and *burakumin* cannot assimilate easily into mainstream Japanese culture (there are detective agencies that specialize in investigating a prospective spouse's background to make sure that no Korean or *burakumin* blood "taints" the family line), their economic prospects are severely limited. Of necessity, some become involved in organized crime to survive.

Other Japanese feminists are lobbying for more equitable working conditions for women. But this turns out to be another heated issue, far more complicated than I originally suspected. Many Japanese women don't *want* to work the long hours required of the *sarariiman.* They do not want merely to imitate Japanese men. They want to change the entire system of labor in the culture, hoping to make it better for men and more open to women.

It's something we discussed in my Oral English class.

"I would like to have a job," one of my students said, to a chorus of nods from her peers, "but I do not want to be a salary man—or a salary woman!"

Many Japanese insist that gender roles are changing very fast, maybe too fast. People are alarmed that women are putting off marriage longer and longer. Japan has one of the latest average female marriage ages of any country in the world, and in a 1992 survey a full 14 percent of women insisted they never want to marry. Once married, many Japanese women are declining to have children or refusing to have more than one. The birthrate currently is 1.53 children per woman, not even close to "replacement" level. It's almost a national biological strike, and the government is now doing everything it can to coax young women to marry and have children again: from tax incentives to advertising to changing sexist laws to pressuring businesses to improve maternity leave and to provide other benefits for women.

Since Japan has one of the world's lowest birthrates and the highest life expectancy, there is much anxiety about the future. Who will support all those aging Japanese? You can see in popular culture evidence of the "baby strike" and other aspects of changing gender roles. One of the fastest-growing categories of magazines is the men's fashion magazine. Almost precisely parallel to *Seventeen* or *Glamour,* magazines such as *Fine Boys* or *Gainer* are pitched to young men desperate to catch a wife. These magazines regularly feature comparative photos of men in outfits that look virtually identical. It turns out that one is a knockoff; the other, the real thing. Arrows point to collar, cuffs, belt loops, and in the margins there are comments on why these details are indisputably superior in the Armani original than in the cheap copy—and why any marriage-age woman will be able to detect the poor imitation in an instant (and will reject you because of it).

There are before-and-after haircut photos (with fashion hints about which haircut is most flattering to which kind of face); before-and-after clothes makeovers; advice to the lovelorn; and surveys that feature young women expressing their opinions about what they really like in a man. One representative article describes a young woman's dates with four men who do their best to wine, dine, and please her. The woman then reports which is her favorite date and why. The winner is the young man who not only bought her dinner at an elegant restaurant but also took her on a computerized, virtual reality space walk.

"Very imaginative—not like a *sarariiman* at all," one of my students observes in response to this article. "I don't know if I would marry such a man, because I'm not so interested in marriage now, but I might be willing to date him."

≈

As soon as I arrive in Shirahama with the members of the Japanese Women's Studies Society, I realize that this is not going to be a typical three-day vacation by the sea. Instead of being shown to my room, I'm shown to *our* room, a gigantic tatami room. Except when we're at the beach, I'm told, this is where we will be meeting during the day and sleeping at night, all fifteen of us. Now we need to hurry to take our bath together because our dinner will be served in this room in an hour and a half.

"You've had a Japanese-style bath before, haven't you?" Kazue-san asks a little nervously as we head down the hall to the women's bath.

"Oh, of course," I shrug off her comment.

Of course I haven't, but I'm not about to give that away. I know the basics from the guidebooks: wash thoroughly *before* you get into the bath; make sure never to do anything to spoil the communal, clean bath water. I figure I can wing it on the details.

We undress in a small anteroom and fold our clothes neatly into baskets on the shelves. We walk into the bath with our tiny white terry washcloths. Along one wall is a row of faucets for washing, with drains in the sloping tiled floors. On the other side is the mosaic-tiled bath, as blue as the sea, beneath a cascade of tropical plants.

I've seen naked women before in showers in various gyms in America, but the mood in this Japanese bath is entirely different. I've never seen people more comfortable with their bodies. There are twenty-five or thirty women in the room, our group plus a group of *obāsan* (grandmothers) here on vacation from the country-side and some members of an Osaka teachers' association having an annual meeting. The oldest woman is probably close to ninety; the youngest is three. The mood is quietly happy, utterly relaxed.

We sit naked on low wooden stools, soaping ourselves with the terry washcloths, rinsing with red buckets filled from the taps and poured over the body. The conversation is lulled, languid, like the water, like the steamy air.

I finish washing my entire body and notice that most of the women from my group are still soaping a first arm. I slow down, going back again over my entire body, washing and washing, the soapy cloth, the warm water, the joking talking laughing atmosphere, the bodies. The women in my group are now washing a second arm. I slow down again, deciding I will try to do it right this time, Japanese-style, concentrating on a leg. I baby each toe, each toenail, each fold of flesh, noticing for the first time in years the small scar on the inside of my ankle, a muffler burn from a motorcycle when I was a teenager. I'm fascinated by this ritual attention to the body, so different from the brisk Western morning wake-up shower. When I finish (again) and go to shampoo my hair, I see that most of the women in my group are still scrubbing. I give up. It must take practice. I have never seen such luxuriant pampering of bodies.

The bath is a revelation for another reason. I read once that a one-hour bath has the same physiological effect as four hours of sleep. Maybe this is how the Japanese do it, I think, a ritual stop in the otherwise frenetic day.

As I watch these women soaping their bodies with such slow concentration, it is almost impossible for me to remember what they are like most of the time, raising families, working full-time, responsible for all of the household chores and the household finances, as busy as any American women I've ever met.

I tell this to my friend, Kazue-san.

"It's hard to be busy when you're naked," she says smiling. "It looks too silly!"

I find myself laughing. Everywhere around me are the bodies of typical Japanese women, every one different, every one alike.

"May I help you wash your hair?" Kazue-san asks, as I struggle to pour some water over my hair from the little red plastic bucket.

"Please let me!" interjects one of the *obāsan* who has been watching me for several minutes. She is very old, probably in her seventies or even eighties. Standing, her face comes even with mine as I sit on the tiny stool. Her body is bent over, almost parallel to the ground. Kazue-san says she's probably crippled from malnutrition during the War years and the chronic lack of calcium in the traditional Japanese diet as well as from bending to plant and harvest the rice crop every year.

"I bet she still works in the fields," Kazue-san whispers in English, and I smile back into the old woman's smiling face. Her hair is pure white, her face covered with spidery lines, but her eyes are absolutely clear, sparkling. The old woman introduces herself, bowing even more deeply. Her name is Keiko Doi. I'm too self-conscious to stand up so I introduce myself sheepishly, trying to bow as low and respectfully as I can without getting up from my little stool. The other old ladies in the bath are watching us. They seem abashed by Doi-san's forwardness, but they also look thoroughly delighted. One of the old ladies says you can never tell what Doi-san will do next. She is their ringleader, a real character.

"She has no shame!" one of the grandmothers says half critically, half affectionately of the mischievous Doi-san.

"Too old for shame!" Doi-san retorts, and the other old lady starts laughing so hard I'm afraid she might hurt herself. She pulls up a stool and sits down next to us, watching intently, still unable to stifle her laughter.

Doi-san squeezes shampoo into her hand and then rubs her palms together briskly. She's a pro. She massages the shampoo into my hair, the thick pads of her fingers making circles against my scalp. Then she lays one hand on my head, and starts clapping up and down on it with the other hand, making a sound like castanets as she works her hands over my head. It feels great. After about ten minutes, she chops with the sides of her hands over my head, my neck, and my shoulders, a kind of shiatsu massage.

I think I could die at this moment with no regrets. I feel about four years old and totally at home, this tiny grandmother massaging my back and shoulders, my scalp and forehead. "Do you like this?" she keeps asking. "Is this comfortable?"

Yes, yes.

The other old ladies are cutting up, making jokes, and Doi-san douses one of them with a bucket of water. The woman douses back, and someone else flips at Doi-san with a washcloth. Kazue-san says we've run into a group of eighty-year-old juvenile delinquents. She's never seen anything like this in her life, and she tells Doi-san, jokingly but admiringly, that she's the most outrageous old lady of them all. In English, I start calling Doi-san the "Leader of the Pack."

"Shuuush!" Doi-san admonishes us to stop talking English to one another. She hands me a cloth to put over my eyes and motions to her friends. Each fills her bucket and comes to stand in a circle around me. They take turns; one pours a full bucket over my head like a waterfall. I take a breath, then the next bucket comes. The water is exactly the right temperature.

When they finish, I just sit there for a while, feeling cleaner than I've ever felt in my life.

The old ladies can't stop laughing, and several of them are slapping Doi-san on the back, chiding her for her outrageousness, but also beamingly proud of their brazen friend.

I ask Doi-san if I may wash her hair but she refuses. Now, she commands, I must soak in the bath. It's time for me to relax.

I say that I can't take water as hot as most Japanese, and one of the strangers already in the bath motions me to a place beside her where the water, she says, is coolest. I lower myself slowly, allowing my body to adjust to the heat.

When I look around, Doi-san has disappeared. The rogue and her octogenarian gang from the countryside have all departed. A new group of bathers is coming in. They look startled at first to see me, a *gaijin*, but then go about their business. They are probably high school or junior high school girls, many of them still at the last stages of chubby adolescence, utterly unself-conscious about their nakedness.

"That was her," Kazue-san whispers, absolutely deadpan, as she slips into the water beside me.

"Who? What do you mean?" I ask, puzzled at first, then skeptical as Kazue-san smiles impishly.

"Why, the typical Japanese woman," she teases. "Doi-san. I think you finally found her."

6

NIGHT MOVES

My visa papers described me simply enough. *Sex:* Female. *Status:* Visiting Foreign Professor. Yet the word *foreign* complicated *female* in ways that I still don't fully understand. Perhaps because in 1980 most visiting foreign professors in Japan were men, the rules for how to treat a woman in my professional capacity just didn't exist. The Japanese professors I met were all friendly, but it was obvious that my male colleagues, in particular, didn't quite know what to do with me. Should they invite me out with them for the normal after-work drinking as they would a visiting male teacher, or would this be an insult to me (or, worse, to my husband)? Should they exclude me from such socializing, as Japanese women professors were routinely excluded, or would I consider that to be insulting, not to mention hopelessly sexist? What was polite, respect-able, collegial—and where were the boundaries?

Female and *foreign* didn't always go together comfortably away from the university either. My friend Hiroko-san used to insist that traveling around Japan with me was like traveling with a man—or maybe even like *being* a man. One time the two of us vis-ited a small pottery village out in the countryside. She stopped a local man in the train station and asked where we might catch a taxi. He stuttered nervously before managing to answer her—and when he did, he used the masculine form of address. As long as she was with me, Hiroko-san wasn't really female. Nor was she al-ways Japanese. Later she asked another villager directions to a par-ticular shop. He practically ran away from us, calling back over his shoulder that he was sorry he couldn't help but he didn't speak any English. Their exchange was, of course, conducted entirely in Japanese.

In professional contexts, more than one Japanese woman re-marked that I was often spoken of and to with forms of respect re-served for men in Japan. These women were broad-minded enough to be more bemused by this than resentful. When I pushed the is-sue, they also admitted that, if I was respected, it might be be-cause in some sense I didn't really count. I was from another world, beyond the pale of professional competition, outside the battle of the sexes Japanese-style. It was as if my foreignness put me in some different gender category, on one level proximate and titillating, on another androgynous and remote.

I discovered more about this category by riding the Takarazuka train. Takarazuka, the end of my own branch line, is the home of the Takarazuka Revue, an all-female theatrical com-pany that produces traditional Japanese dramas as well as Western musicals. With their masculine, clipped haircuts dyed a distinct auburn and their aggressive long-legged strides, the Takarazienne who play the *otoko-yaku,* the male roles, are especially striking. They comport themselves in ways that are unmistakably Western and are at their best as the dashing male heroes in such classics as *The Three Musketeers, The Lady of the Camellias,* or, more recently,

Me and My Girl. Hundreds of young girls gather outside the Takarazuka theatre each day, hoping to catch a glimpse of these female "men." The girls sigh and cry and scream with love like American teenyboppers at a rock concert.

On the trains, I regularly saw the Takarazienne who play the male roles, and saw, too, that they were watching me, examining how I sat, my gestures, even my facial expressions. Later, when I came to know Nomura-san, a retired Takarazienne, I asked her why some of the Takarazienne seemed to be studying me.

"That's easy," she answered with her characteristic wry smile. "We often watch Western women to understand better how to act like a man."

Dietrich, Garbo, Katharine Hepburn, Bette Davis, Joan Crawford—the standard repertoire of Western transvestites—these are the actresses that Takarazuka women emulate in order to portray romantic male leads in Western dramas.

"And young Brando," Nomura-san added, with a wink, "when he was still pretty."

Many foreign women visiting in Japan have had the same experience I have had when entertained in elegant Japanese restaurants. On two or three different occasions, I became the focus of the smiling, seductive attentions of a hostess or a geisha. She flirted and attempted to engage me in repartee as she would a man.

"It's not what you think," I whispered one night to a lesbian friend, a visiting writer who was the occasion's guest of honor, when a geisha started making eyes at her.

Later, at a kabuki performance I attended with the same visiting writer and my friend Hiroko-san, I found myself at a loss when the writer asked me to explain the hordes of women outside—from young girls to aged grandmothers—all swooning over Tamasaburo, the stunningly beautiful actor renowned for playing *onnagata,* the stylized female role in kabuki drama.

"Japanese sexuality is a mystery to me," I answered lamely, in response to her question about the country's tradition of professional cross-dressing and the ardor it excites in ostensibly straight, heterosexual men and women in the audience.

"It may be a mystery but you sure like it, Cathy-san!" Hiroko-san chided me. She and I had been to both the Takarazuka Revue and kabuki and often watched sumo wrestling together on television. There were times when we giggled like schoolgirls over the handsome performers in all three.

"I can understand your fascination for the women who play men and the men who play women," the American writer teased, only half-jokingly, "but one of those overstuffed sumo wrestlers? How could you, Cathy?"

She would not believe me when I tried to explain that I (along with about 120 million Japanese) thought sumo star Chiyonofuji was one of the world's most handsome men.

The unexpected and unpredictable are always titillating (for me, at any rate). And it is partly the element of surprise that makes Japan so appealing—so *sexy*—for me. I like the excitement that comes from living in a country where I'm regularly at sea about what's really going on. Situations that would be mundane or irritating in America become interesting because they both are and are not recognizable. More than once I've been baffled by Japanese male attentiveness, uncertain whether I'm on the receiving end of politeness or a proposition. In America I would sense a come-on immediately, but in Japan there are rituals of compliment and deferral—almost like flirtation—that I've seen men engage in among themselves. I've seen it with women, too, a jockeying among politeness levels and status codes that require a more intimate knowledge of Japan than I possess.

Not knowing such rules adds intensity and suspense to the simplest interaction. I think this rubs off on the Japanese too. They can play the role of guide, an interpreter of their culture. Or they can invent rules, make up "Japan" as they go along. This is one pleasure and danger of being a traveler: one never really knows how much to trust one's guide. When a friend was a visiting professor in Denmark, one of her students told her how he had once sent two unusually arrogant Englishmen off to a fancy restaurant with a Danish phrase that, he assured them, meant, "We have a reservation." What he had really taught them to announce to the maître d' was "I am not a pencil."

My most complicated experience of being guided—or misguided—came after I participated with some Japanese academics and journalists on a panel assessing the role of internationalism in Japan. One of the speakers, a Japanese professor, asked if I might be free later that evening to sample some of Osaka's more unusual restaurants, small establishments in the entertainment district that he frequented but that foreigners rarely visited. I immediately agreed, delighted to have the chance to see a new side of Japan. When I met Professor Itō at the designated time and place, I was surprised to see that he and I were the only two setting out for this night on the town.

I had assumed he was inviting the other panelists as well and at first I hesitated. This struck me as one of those existential moments in the life of a happily married woman. On the one hand, Professor Itō was a handsome man, dapper almost to a fault, with a permanent twinkle in his eye. On the other, I had no reason to believe he was offering me any more or less than he had said, a chance to savor his favorite Osaka haunts. Besides, I was dying with curiosity about the entertainment district, the fabled Floating World that I'd read about in virtually every book on Japan written by Western men. These accounts almost always detail the author's liberatory experiences in the unrepressed world of the entertainment districts. Topless, bottomless, live sex, the full array of mysterious Oriental sexual tricks that no Western woman (we're told) can ever master, and all for the asking, guilt-free, in a Floating World happily untouched by either puritanism or feminism.

I had assumed I would be forbidden access to this part of Japan, and now Professor Itō was there, looking every inch the scholar, offering me an opportunity to enter this world, as voyeur, as spy.

"It's too bad Mr. Davidson isn't here tonight," Professor Itō was saying with a decorous bow. "Perhaps some other time all three of us can go. But in the meantime—"

He gestured toward the street, the bright lights of Osaka shining before us.

As we walk through the entertainment district, I try to be free-wheeling and curious, part of the gaudy, festive atmosphere around us. It isn't working. Embarrassment wells up as we pass one bill-board after another covered with photographs of naked women, many of them *gaijin* with pneumatic breasts and tight buttocks. The men we pass on the street look me over, as if I too might be available for the asking. It's hot out tonight but I find myself pulling my jacket tighter around me.

Professor Itō walks close beside me, protective and even gal-lant. He makes a joke about these "awful places," alleviating my anxiety that he might be planning to take me to some topless joint. He turns down a small side alley where the scene is quieter, with fewer glaring neon signs and nude photo displays. Here there are several *nomiya* (small drinking establishments), with charming red paper lanterns out front. Professor Itō tells me about "ladder drinking," a Japanese version of a pub crawl, and I hasten to ex-plain that I'm not a very heavy drinker. He laughs, insisting that won't be necessary, and tells me he has three or four places he would particularly like me to see. On just about any night he can count on running into someone he knows at any of these haunts. They are small and intimate, and he assures me that spending time there is equivalent to enjoying an evening in someone's living room in America. He explains that the elaborate system of bars and restaurants in the entertainment district is partly to com-pensate for the limited space for entertaining in tiny Japanese apartments.

Also, I think, to compensate for the lack of couples-style en-tertaining. There are both men and women in the entertainment district, but it's unusual to see them arriving or leaving together. In this world, men walk, singly or in groups, and women beckon—actually or, more often, pictorially, from the voluptuous photographs. Procurers—possibly pimps?—rush out, making promises about the quality of the entertainment within.

Professor Itō guides me past another gaudy striptease place and a show promising live sex, and into a small, quiet shop constructed of dark, aged wood. It feels safe to me, cozy, especially after the glitz outside. There seems to be no sign, only a *noren* (curtain) indicating that it is open. We stay a while, have some sake and a little snack, then leave for another shop that seems identical to the first, and then go on to still another.

Each place has five to ten seats arranged around a small bar. Each serves sake, beer, and some kind of food specialty: eels cooked inside tofu, whale blubber, boiled things that I cannot identify. Each time Professor Itō orders something, the other customers protest that "foreigners won't eat that!" I love most Japanese food anyway, but tonight I'm determined to prove that their stereotypes about foreigners aren't true. I try whatever I'm offered. At one of Professor Itō's haunts I am presented with three sparrowlike birds served whole in what looks very much like their nest. Later someone tells me that it *was* a nest. I've learned not to ask.

I'm surprised to discover that almost all these places are run by women. Typically, a smiling, attractive middle-aged or even elderly *"mama-san"* is the restaurant's proprietor. Professor Itō says many of these women actually own the restaurants but sometimes they manage them for someone else. The temperament of the *mama-san* establishes the mood in each restaurant, a mood as distinctive as the food. One *mama-san* is boisterous and bawdy, another cheerfully ebullient, and a third almost morose. Some *mama-san* are former geisha and retain the geisha's verbal and social skills. Some are former entertainers or bar hostesses. Some perhaps are mistresses, set up in business by a wealthy lover. This is Japan's demimonde.

I'm especially intrigued by the role of the *mama-san*. Her role is rarely described in detail when foreign men write about the *mizu shōbai,* the Floating World outside respectability that flows through and touches all of Japanese culture. This is always described as a man's world, although I have heard of bars frequented by married women where the hosts are all handsome young men whose job it is to flirt with and pamper their female customers, all at the same exorbitant prices hostesses charge in high-class bars (fifty dollars for fetching some peanuts, one hundred for coquettishly popping them into your mouth). I've even read an article based on interviews with these young men in which they protest how crudely and callously they are sometimes treated by the female customers who regard them solely as sex objects. But host bars are definitely the exception, not the rule. The Floating World exists mostly for male pleasure. The restaurants I visit with Professor Itō are filled with Japanese men. Except for the *mama-san,* except for me.

In this world of men, *mama-san* is in control. She manages her customers expertly, often through a bantering kind of flirtation, the chief idiom of the night. She flirts with me too, effortlessly. At every one of these bars Professor Itō is careful to introduce me with my full, formal title. He tells the other customers (his friends by virtue of their patronizing the same spot) that, although I might look like a student, I am really a professor at a Big Ten university in the United States ("Big Ten!" his listeners observe admiringly, if a bit mistakenly, a reminder that in Japan everything is ranked).

"*Hontō da!*" they exclaim, or, sometimes, in Osaka dialect, "*Honma ya!*", untranslatable expressions of wonder and belief, roughly equivalent to "Wow!" I am an academic in the tow of another academic but I realize, unmistakably, that tonight I am some kind of rare specimen on display, like a whooping crane or a snow leopard. I am Professor Itō's coup, A-Female-*Gaijin*-Professor-at-a-Big-Ten-American-University-Who-Is-Not-Afraid-to-Eat-Weird-Japanese-Food-in-Japanese-Restaurants-with-a-Man-She-Scarcely-Knows. I am the offering he is making to his other world, his after-work world of the entertainment district where, in a handful of intimate and special places, he is known and always welcome.

Once my status is ascertained, the conversation quickly reverts to repartee. At a bar Professor Itō says is his favorite, a slightly threadbare but fastidious-looking man asks me with a straight face to repeat after him a short poem. I can tell by the facial expressions and various exclamations of the other patrons that they are puzzled by his request. But this man, whose English is very good, knows exactly which Japanese sounds are difficult for English speakers, our equivalent to the Japanese confusion of *r* and *l*. The men laugh uproariously when I repeat the brief poem, and Professor Itō, laughing too, explains that I've managed to turn a classical allusion to twilight—"the veils of evening"—into an extended boast about my insatiable desire. I decide to be a good sport and join in this laughter, but, as the color rises in my cheeks, I am aware of how much I'm *willing* myself to laugh. Professor Itō notices my discomfort and in his best *sensei* voice explains how the mistake involves several complicated puns turning on my mispronunciation of the word *boshoku* (dusk) as *bōshoku* (ravenous gluttony or, in context, lust). I nod like a student. The man who started this apologizes, assuring me that he meant no harm, then quickly asks his pals to repeat after him an English sentence which turns on a series of hilarious confusions of *rice* and *lice*. Professor Itō, the man, and I are all in on this joke, and now it is the other men at the bar who aren't sure what they've said that's so funny. The tension has shifted. Professor Itō translates for the others. There is more laughter, more sake. I've passed some kind of test, showing that I can laugh at myself, a virtue esteemed in after-hours Japan, but I feel as if I've also managed to save face, a virtue I'm finding more and more important as the night progresses.

"Sometimes, very silly," the *mama-san* whispers to me, in Japanese, filling my sake cup. It's the kind of sentence that has no stated referent; she nods at me, winks, pats my hand, shrugs at the men. *They*—men—are very silly. I am not alone, she wants me to know that. I am in *her* bar. *Mama-san* has everything under control. I feel instantly safer. I ask if I might have some green tea and feel even better as I sip the bitter, warm liquid.

Professor Itō looks at me while I drink. He compliments me on the graceful way I've learned to hold the small Japanese teacup, with two hands, then he leans toward me, and brushes something from my cheek. He lets a finger linger ever so slightly.

"An eyelash." He answers the question I didn't ask, smiling. His teeth are small, even, white.

I smile back.

"May I take your jacket?" he says, still smiling at me. "It's warm in here. Perhaps you'd be more comfortable."

He helps slide the jacket down my arms. He hangs it out of sight, through a curtained doorway next to the bar. We're obviously staying for a while.

It turns out that the first round of pronunciation jokes is merely a warm-up for the night's real linguistic entertainment. Professor Itō tells me that one of his hobbies is *rakugo,* a form of traditional story telling that usually ends in some kind of wordplay. It demands complicated puns, archaic semantic associations, and other comic turns of phrase. As arcane as it may seem to some Westerners, *rakugo* is actually quite popular. Japan even has a prime-time *rakugo* TV show where performers in traditional garb are rewarded for special displays of verbal dexterity by receiving extra *zabuton* (floor cushions) to kneel upon. By the end of the show, the contestants are perched on piles of pillows of varying heights. Professor Itō likes to test his own verbal skills in this bar where the implicit rule seems to be that the other patrons will set him a puzzle and he will try to unravel it. Instead of mounting piles of *zabuton,* free rounds of sake flow as the night's reward.

At one point, it strikes me that I'm the only person here who doesn't know who the other participants are. They might be high school teachers (there is one reference that indicates as much) or businessmen, but I can't be sure. Everyone in the bar knows everyone else's social status, quite typical since it's difficult to communicate in hierarchical Japanese without knowing whom you are addressing. We make similar accommodations all the time in English but our rules aren't as codified or overt. From Professor Itō's gallant formal introduction, everyone knows who I am (a professor, not some *gaijin* girl picked up in the entertainment district), but I know only the names of the other people. The *mama-san* and the other patrons refer to Professor Itō as *"sensei"* so I'm guessing that Professor Itō might be the most distinguished person here. It's possible there might be some class differences among the customers. I'm particularly thrown by the man who looks shopworn, even down-and-out, but who speaks excellent English (certainly not typical among working-class Japanese).

Perhaps the challenge-and-response verbal games equalize without disturbing status disparities. What is abundantly clear to me, however, is that tonight Professor Itō's game has been given a new, titillating twist: multilingual, female, *gaijin*.

"Honorable Professor," one of the other men addresses Professor Itō in Japanese with mock solemnity, "tonight you will translate for Professor Davidson." There is laughter, a lot of nodding heads. Japanese wordplay can be extremely complex. To translate the twists, turns, and allusions of obscure language into something I can understand will require all of Professor Itō's skill, and especially because Japanese puns are not only aural but also etymological and even visual. Words are both heard and seen. Trying to think of a word, a Japanese will often wiggle a finger in the air, drawing imaginary *kanji* characters until the right one pops back into visceral, linguistic memory. The visual references that come as naturally to a Japanese as breathing can be explained only slowly and imperfectly in English. The stakes are high in this tiny bar. Ego is on the line in front of this *gaijin* lady.

Professor Itō pulls himself up tall on his bar stool. With a swallow of sake, a wiggle of forefinger in the air, he takes on all comers, vanquishing every word problem the men set for him. The *macho* aspect of this performance is palpable, making me think of that scene in Hemingway's *The Sun Also Rises* where Lady Brett participates in the festival at Pamplona, the preparation for the running of the bulls. But here there are no Hemingway heroes—bullfighters, boxers, war pilots. A professor, some guys in rumpled suits, *mama-san*, me. Instead of charging bulls, Professor Itō bravely faces a barrage of puns.

The final challenge comes from a rather seedy-looking individual with one gleaming gold tooth who suddenly blurts out a staccato sentence, maybe eight or nine words in all. There is a long pause, then exclamations of *"Hontō da!"* and *"Honma!"* as the customers savor the complexity of his pun and more laughter as they realize the task the guy with the tooth has set for the distinguished academic. Professor Itō makes a hissing sound that resembles the noise of a child trying to sip the last bit of milkshake from a glass. It is a ubiquitous sound, part of the rich subverbal Japanese vocabulary, and communicates consternation, warning: "This is going to be difficult. I might not be able to help you." Taxi drivers use it a lot.

Professor Itō requests a piece of paper from the *mama-san.* From his suit coat pocket he takes a Mont Blanc pen, leans forward, then draws two intricate *kanji* characters. As I already know, there is little relationship between the sound of Japanese and its visual representation. One *kanji* can have several meanings, but, even more to the point, because there are only a limited number of sounds in Japanese and there are nearly fifty thousand *kanji,* unless you know the context, you cannot tell which meaning a particular sound might take. *San,* for instance, can mean mountain or the number three or childbirth. The guy with the tooth has uttered a brief sentence with many possible meanings—but the point is to find the *right* comic readings, only the best puns, and to rework them into others just as clever. Professor Itō explains all of this and tells me a few of the possibilities he is considering. In each *kanji,* he says, there is a root identity or etymology, which often is quite different from the original word, just as the etymology of the English *radical* is *root.* He puns, writes out a new *kanji* for the pun, isolates its root, and then makes another pun on that. To explain the original sentence has required about fifteen minutes. All the while *mama-san* has been offering Professor Itō words of encouragement while the men at the bar have looked on and cheered him with appreciative laughter and occasional bursts of *Honma!* At a particularly difficult place, there is a group consultation accompanied by a chorus of straw-in-the-empty-glass consternation sounds. All of this energy—explaining in English the homonymic and synonymic double entendres on cognates of the ancient root meanings of words—leads, finally, to a new formulation that turns on the simple Japanese words *katai* (hard) and *chiisai* (small).

Professor Itō has solved the puzzle and everyone is cheering. All he needs to do is translate into English and he's won.

On the brink of victory, Professor Itō suddenly grows silent. In fact, he's blushing.

"*Hazukashii!*" he mutters, embarrassed. He stares down at the *kanji,* not translating, not speaking.

The man with the gold tooth starts to laugh, cackle really. He leers at me, slapping his hand against the bar, triumphant. Smirks, then wide smiles, then laughter fill the room as everyone begins to realize what's happening.

It's all been a setup. The man with the tooth counted on Professor Itō being too decorous to explain the humiliating joke to an American woman professor from a Big Ten university and he was right. Professor Itō is stopped cold at the boundary we've flitted over, back and forth, all night.

"I guess you win," he says to the man with the tooth. He doesn't look at me when he mutters an apology, *gomen nasai.*

"*Iie, iie*" (No, not at all). I touch his hand. "*Daijōbu,*" I tell him (It's okay).

This is idiot Japanese but it doesn't matter: *I know the joke.* I recognize it immediately as the retort to the Western putdown of Japanese men as being small.

"We may be shorter, but we stay harder, longer!" I shout out proudly in English, a little bemused at where I am in this "we."

Professor Itō blinks, shakes his head, then translates my punchline. There's a moment's stunned silence in the bar and then the place is up for grabs. Professor Itō collapses across the bar, exhausted, spent.

The *mama-san* holds up her hand, laughing, and we slap high-five. She offers everyone in the bar a free round of sake. They toast us as we prepare to leave, then follow us outside, bowing, applauding, and shouting invitations to me to please come again.

Out in the street, Professor Itō and I once more encounter numerous drunks and other cruising men. Everywhere there is prostitution, live sex shows, "no pants" coffee shops, topless and bottomless cabarets, breasts, legs, buttocks on display everywhere. Any woman on this street would seem to be fair game, and especially a *gaijin.* Professor Itō is about 5'5", slight but wiry, not a person one would describe as "formidable." But I note with fascination that as we leave the restaurant, he realigns his body and, even more, the muscles in his face, his eyes. No one bothers us as we walk through the busy streets. *Kamaeru,* this is called, to put oneself in a posture. It's the stance one assumes in swordsmanship, archery, or any of the traditional Japanese martial arts. It signals, "I am ready. For anything." The crowd opens up and makes way for us. No one even comments on my presence there. Without so much as touching my arm, in the territorial way that Western men will guard and claim a female companion, Professor Itō signals that I am to be left alone.

It is a bizarre night. The sexual dynamic is complicated, pervasive. I can't begin to sort out all the implications. I doubt that Professor Itō would have asked a female Japanese colleague to accompany him on such a tour. I try to imagine an equivalent evening with a male American colleague but can't. We've each enjoyed the safety net of the other's difference, and yet the night has felt like a free fall. Foreignness—our fumblings at the buttons and zippers of language—is the night's sex.

Sometime around midnight Professor Itō and I hurry back through these same Osaka side streets to catch the last trains, his to some distant part of the city, mine back to Nigawa. After the dim, woody light of the bars, the unforgiving fluorescence of Umeda Station comes as a shock. Once more, I feel exposed. Like many Japanese, my face goes scarlet when I drink sake and I realize I must look a mess. I'm surprised to notice out of the corner of my eye that Professor Itō's face is also flushed, his eyes glassy. Tactfully, we avoid direct eye contact. We bow politely to one another, and Professor Itō thanks me in very formal English for accompanying him. I thank him in stilted Japanese for keeping his promise to show me a side of Japan I'm not likely to see again.

On the train I find a seat near the doorway, next to the only other woman on board, safe from gropers. I pretend to sleep all the way to my stop but the night's *kanji* characters dance against my eyelids: hard, short.

Several months go by before I run into Professor Itō again. We're both giving papers at another conference, mine on the beginning of mass printing in America, his on an obscure English poet from another century. When I give my talk, I can feel his eyes on me and work to avoid looking in that direction. During his talk, he looks once, catches my glance, and stumbles over the next sentence.

At a small cocktail party for conference participants, we avoid one another until it starts to feel conspicuous. We address each other formally, as fellow scholars, and assure colleagues who start to introduce us that, actually, we have met once before, at another conference. I begin to thank Professor Itō again for the tour of Osaka, but a sudden change in his facial expression makes me decide not to. This isn't the place. Our colleagues are watching, listening. I quickly switch the subject, asking him something inane about eighteenth-century poetics. I notice a tiny smile play at the corner of his eyes, a gentleness, the only shift in his expression. For the next ten minutes, he bores us with a discourse on eighteenth-century poetics.

One part of me (the American part) feels something akin to disappointment, even anger, like a girl who never received the morning telephone call she'd been promised the night before. It's "very American," I know from countless conversations with my Japanese friends, this tendency to want to nail things down, define them, calculate the meaning of an experience, a moment, an act. Nonetheless, I'm annoyed at myself for not talking about that night and equally annoyed that Professor Itō avoids any acknowledgment of our admittedly tenuous relationship.

It's at this point that my Japanese aspect takes over and reads this whole scene differently. One thing I've learned to love about Japan is its freedom from the classic Western notion that a person is a stable, unchanging, continuous entity, some essential self. In Japan, behavior and even personality depend partly on context, on the rules of a given situation. That's one reason why so many of the G.I.s who came as part of the occupation forces after World War II were shocked to encounter gentle, generous Japanese. They expected the barbarous perpetrators of the rape of Nanjing, the Bataan death march or Corregidor, and were surprised to find that, as civilians, the Japanese were, in a word, civilized. It is only from a Western perspective that this is a contradiction. For the Japanese, it is the contingency and truth of life.

My Japanese self realizes that some things aren't explicable, aren't reducible to those things that, in the West, we like to partition off as "logic" or "common sense." My Japanese self sees that the woman and man who spent a night wandering the Floating World are different people, different selves, from the two professors who stand here now wearing bilingual name badges, in a sterile conference room, sipping white wine in plastic cups, nibbling chunks of cold cheddar skewered with toothpicks. After a few moments, Professor Itō and I bow to one another, then turn to mingle with the other guests, as if here, in this room, at this moment, our Night-Town walk through Osaka never happened.

7

SACRED PLACES

Charles arrived in Japan just before classes let out for summer vacation at Kansai Women's University. Charles is my stepson, Ted's son from his previous marriage. Beginning when he was only four, he lived with us for varying lengths of time each year and always for summer vacation. Ted and I had arranged our lives around his coming and his going, developing a pattern where we worked hard the other months so that our summers would be free for Charles. He had to organize his life, too, around summers spent away from his New York family and friends but also away from the neighborhood in which he lived, on the edge of Bedford-Stuyvesant, and where he learned early to defend himself against local gangs. Summer was a time for all of us to be together, to get to know one another again, to try to cram a relationship into a few months.

September was always the cruelest month. Sometimes in the airport, even after he was old enough to understand about custody laws, he looked at us as if we were traitors. After he boarded his plane, Ted and I would stand there, numb, holding hands so tight it hurt, watching through the plate-glass windows at O'Hare as the plane took him away. The drive home without him was devastating. We usually went out for dinner, a movie, a long drive in the country, anything we could think of to put off walking into his empty room.

But the summers were good. Typically, we'd load the tent and gear into the car, pick Charles up in New York, and just go, camping around the United States and Canada for the first five or six weeks and then landing at Ted's family house in Mountain View, Alberta, for the last part of the summer. Our route to Alberta was always different, always punctuated by stops that fueled Charles's particular passion that year. We made a joke of it, the way Charles always came loaded with books on some new subject. He'd read in the back of the car as we drove, filling us in on the details; at night, when he was little, we'd do the reading out loud, by lantern light in the tent. Evolution, Big Bang theory, paleontology, geology. He, too, was trying to whittle his life down to something we could manage in a few short months, something we could share: dinosaurs, rocks, bat caves, amusement parks, Indian mounds, historic forts, traditional music festivals.

In Japan, it was sacred places.

The first time Charles stepped within a temple compound he was hooked—by the silence, the serenity, a coolness in the air on the hottest summer day. He wanted to see all the temples, and, although we didn't come close to accomplishing that goal, we did visit over two hundred in two months. We bought traditional pilgrim's temple books and at each temple found the priest who could write out the name of the temple and the date and then stamp the page with the traditional red *hanko* stamp. By the end of the summer, the books drew notice from the priests, who were amazed that three *gaijin* would have made such an effort to see so many of Japan's sacred places.

Sambōin, Zuishin'in, Shisendōji, Manshūin, Shinnyōdō, Shōren'in, Tōdaiji, Kannōji: these are some of the names in our temple books, written in calligraphies too intricate for us to decipher.

≈≈

When Charles first arrived in Japan, he had a young Brando shuffle, hands in pockets, shoulders hunched, muscles taut, the walk of a sixteen-year-old who has learned how to protect himself and, more important, knows how to project the image of one able— even *eager*—to respond to any threat.

"Just try me!" his shoulders seemed to say, his jaw clenched as tight as a fist.

In every culture, body language is crucial and complex. We learn to read it so automatically that we rarely even notice it. In Japan, where it's difficult to say no to a social equal or superior and where the subject of a sentence is often left unstated, the speaker's posture, stance, and tone of voice all provide clues to what is really being said. Charles's body language was geared to communicating to street toughs. When the Japanese encountered Charles, they were often frightened. You could see it in their faces.

Relax, we told him. No one will hurt you here.

Relax: You are in a place where the worst that happens is schoolchildren shout *"Harō!"* to you on the street or they try to practice their English on you.

Within the solid walls of temple compounds in Kyoto or Nara, Charles began to relax. Ted and Charles climbed a steep hillside one hot afternoon to a temple in the town of Arashiyama and were offered tea by the priest who sat silently beside them, enjoying their admiration of the simple beauty, the quiet breeze wafting through the temple grounds high on the hill. They did not speak one another's language and, in that place, it didn't matter. Before they left, the priest wrote in their temple books.

On another day in Kyoto we sat nearly an hour on the tatami

in a tearoom overlooking an exquisite garden. It was at least fifteen degrees cooler there than out on the busy Kyoto street.

"I could live here," Charles whispered, gazing at the tea garden, a hundred shades of green—moss, leaves, lichen—amid rocks like distant mountains.

I was surprised by what I heard in Charles's voice and turned to look at him. Ted noticed it too. His shoulders had started to lose their tension. He knelt Japanese-style, his arms loose and free. The muscles in his face were relaxed, and there was a slight Buddha smile playing at the corners of his mouth. In a few weeks, he had changed, ligaments and bones realigned in some other posture, no longer urban American, not quite Japanese.

Watching Charles, I realized that Ted and I had changed too in the four months since we had come to Japan. I realized I had learned to walk through tough sections of a city like Osaka without fear. It was almost frightening to realize how easily I had lost my wary, urban ways. I'd learned to bow automatically, a simple acknowledgment to people I'd never seen before, and had come to rely on that in human relations: the mutual show of deference, one person to another. In a few months, I'd learned to rein in my usually broad and flamboyant gestures. To negotiate impossibly tiny shops filled with expensive and fragile things, I learned how to make myself small and careful, mindful of an uncontrolled body's potential to do harm.

The three of us were there together, in one of Charles's places, like summers past. But something was different. The urgency was gone, the pressure to get it all in. We knelt tall on the tatami, breath circulating through our lungs, blood pressure dropping measurably, the body at rest, the mind calm, emotions in abeyance: this moment is the world.

We felt content.

≈≈≈

In 1965, when I was sixteen, I made extra money after school by singing with folk and rock bands in the Chicago area. A group called Blood Sisters, four black women who sang a cappella in a haunting combination of blues and folk rhythms, called one day and asked if I might be able to do a three-week gig with them in a place on the Near North Side of Chicago. I knew the rules: white groups couldn't play the black clubs without someone black in the band; this group couldn't do the Near North Side without adding a white singer. I liked the women and their music and was flattered that they had asked me.

But there was a problem. We finished after midnight. The last train back to the suburb where my family was living left at around 12:30. The next one wasn't until 5 A.M. I'd take a taxi from the club to the train station, then run through the long terminal, but sometimes I got to my gate just as the train was pulling away. Since the station closed down for the night, I passed the hours until the next train at the bus station, a few blocks away. It was safe there, with an armed policeman always somewhere near.

After a few nights, the bus station started to get to me. It was too much, too close: the noise, the vomit, the panhandling winos who never lost faith that you could spare another quarter, the man who quietly walked his duck around the Loop all day, then ranted furiously to himself all night in the Greyhound station. Once I tried walking along the lakefront. It was beautiful in the moonlight, but the Vietnam War was on and there were sailors everywhere, down on leave from the Great Lakes naval base, making it a dangerous place for a girl alone. One night I decided to try a flophouse, the only accommodation I could afford that night.

It was on Maxwell Street, not far from the train station. It cost seventy-five cents for the night. There was a men's side and a women's side. A woman took me to my room, first up a rickety old elevator that stopped only at the even-numbered floors, then up a steep metal stairway, like a fire escape, to the fifth floor. Looking down through the iron grids of the stairway, I had to fight back a helpless feeling of vertigo. I still felt nauseated, both sweating and shivering, as we walked down the corridor to my room. When the woman finally stopped and unlocked a metal door to my room, I entered a small cubicle with its chain-link walls covered with a thick linoleum partition. I asked about the walls, and she said every once in a while they took out all the partitions and flushed the whole place out with a power hose. She waited until I locked myself in and then left, her feet thudding hollow on the floor. Someone in the next room shrieked at her to keep it down.

The room contained an army-style bed and a bucket, empty but reeking. I took off my jacket, laid it on the bed, walked to the bucket, and retched.

I was sick. I was frightened. Shivering under the scratchy army blanket, I was alert to the sounds around me: from every direction small moans of unknown pain, rasping breath, sleeping muttered execrations, women's snoring. I was positive that I wouldn't sleep at all that night, but I was wrong. After an hour or so, I noticed that the breathing around me had calmed and synchronized. I could no longer distinguish the sounds of the individual women beyond the thin walls of my room. It was like one person, gently asleep.

I felt myself drifting into sleep too and then, in the drowsy moment before losing consciousness, I noticed how my breathing had fallen into the same pattern as those unseen, destitute women around me. For a moment, the thought made me panic. I felt myself flail like a swimmer who has suddenly taken water into her lungs. This place, these women, were too close to my life just then—two musician friends dead from drug overdoses, another from an illegal abortion. This place was how my life felt: one breath away from disaster. And then my panic left me. I stopped fighting against sleep. The next thing I remember is locks clicking open, metal doors clanging, footsteps hollow down the hallways. Morning.

In the clean, quiet train back to the suburbs it was easy to forget the horror I felt that night and to cling to that moment of synchronized breathing. Sleeping among strangers. The train would take me to a home that was crumbling fast, my parents' marriage coming apart, my mother's mother cast as the caretaker but drinking too much and getting more violent all the time, a little brother's anger, a sister's nightmares, my overwhelming sense that it was my job to keep it all together.

Sometimes my self-pity billowed into bleak, inconsolable despair. Hard drugs were available everywhere for a musician in the sixties, and, while one part of me wanted to work hard, to save money, to escape from that life, another was tempted by the appeal of instant euphoria and forgetfulness. The night on Maxwell Street made the difference for me. Here were people incomparably worse off than I was, finding what comfort they could at seventy-five cents a night. Perhaps I knew it before, but that night was the first time I consciously remember believing that rare and special moments, moments of purity, intensity, insight—*brilliance*—can compensate for bad times, and those moments don't have to come from a hit of acid. They can come from inside. It was a relief, actually, to realize that no life is perfect, every moment safe and pure, but that a person could work at understanding the bad times, at valuing the good—and that was enough to get you through. It was an insight I needed then, and I let it wrap around me like a cashmere sweater, the warmth and softness of a saving idea, a kind of grace.

It wasn't my own idea, of course. Like many teenagers in the sixties, I was interested in Eastern philosophy, and the moment of synchronized breathing in the flophouse seemed to prove that everything we were reading about the still, calm center in the midst of *samsara*, the chaos of everyday life, was right. *AUM*, we chanted together, the meditative universal sound. *AUM*: what did it mean? A linguist once told me that *A-U-M* encompasses all of the possibilities of human sound and breath: the open-mouthed *ahh*, the puckered *ooo*, the vibrating *mmmmm* at the back of the throat.

I wanted to believe it. Desperately. Like many in my generation, I wanted to believe that peace could come from perfect breathing.

By the time Charles was sixteen, he had already read extensively in Eastern literature and philosophy, far more than I had during those turbulent years in the sixties. He liked to play Celtic music on his flute and his Irish bagpipe, and he read Lao Tse, Li Po, Tu Fu, Wang Wei. And Bashō:

> On a journey, ill,
>   and over fields all withered, dreams
>   go wandering.

While we were waiting for him to join us in Japan that summer, we wrote him about the beautiful little temple on the mountain above our house, established by Kōbō Daishi, the founder of Shingon Buddhism, a sect known for its arduousness and austerity. When he arrived, he had already read everything he could about Kōbō Daishi, one of Japan's most revered holy men. Kōbō Daishi was a genius who, as a young man, traveled to China, where he studied sacred texts and then translated them into Japanese. One of the world's great philosophers, he also accomplished many other feats, including engineering a massive dam that saved his native island of Shikoku from drought.

"Let's go to Mount Kōya," Ted said one day, poring over maps and guidebooks. Mount Kōya, founded by Kōbō Daishi in 816, is the center of Shingon Buddhism and the place where Kōbō Daishi is buried.

One of the secretaries in the English Department at KWU called ahead and made arrangements for us to stay in a small temple on the mountain, one built long after Kōbō Daishi's death. We arrived shortly before dusk and dropped off our bags at the temple. We told the woman who met us that we planned to walk to the cemetery but would be back soon.

The mountain was beautiful, cool even in the hot, humid summer, but we were disappointed that it was swarming with people and grumbled that Kōya-san felt more like the Catskills than a sacred place. Yet as we headed out of the main town site, the crowds thinned. The people we passed were all heading back into town, not out. Soon we were virtually alone as we made our way in fading light, through giant cedars and towering tombstones, to Kōya-san's innermost sanctuary, the *okunoin,* and the final resting place of Kōbō Daishi.

It's almost chill as the sun sets behind the mountain. The air is thick with the gray-green wisps of incense that cling like moss to the tombstones, the trees. "Sacred smog," Charles calls it.

The way to the innermost sanctuary is lined with tombstones. Virtually every notable figure in Japanese history has a memorial in this holy place. Many unknown souls rest here too. Today, perhaps because Charles is here, what captures my attention are not the monuments in this cemetery but the small sad stone statues of Jizō, an androgynous figure who is the patron saint of children. Hugging the ground, nestled among tree roots, huddled together near outcroppings of rock, the little figures of Jizō dot the way to Kōya-san's innermost sanctuary. Jizō feels pity for the poor, dead children who are consigned for eternity to building a tower of stones so that they might climb to paradise. Naked, they fetch and pile stones from the riverbed, but demons topple the tower before it is high enough. Jizō protects the children as well as possible, hiding them in her billowing sleeves. On earth, adults dress the statues in warm clothes and pile stones nearby, helping the children in their endless task. As we make our way toward the sanctuary, we pass dozens of the little Jizō statues wearing the hats and bibs of children who have died, sad in the shadows of the tombs of Japan's celebrated and unknown dead.

Although we've taken a side path rather than the wide thoroughfare up the center of the cemetery, even this one is well-worn. More than a million pilgrims come to Kōya-san each year. It's only a mile or so to the innermost shrine, we've been told, but since this is our first time here, we don't know exactly where we are going or what we are looking for, and it is getting dark.

Charles tells us a story. He tells us how, in the seventeenth century, haiku poet Bashō walked the whole of Japan, thousands and thousands of miles in pilgrim's straw sandals, writing travel sketches and poetry, contemplating the meaning of life in books with titles like *The Records of a Weather-Exposed Skeleton* or *The Narrow Road to the Deep North.* Bashō had been to Mount Kōya early in his life, and we decide that perhaps he had stayed at our temple. *Our* temple. We have claimed it already and have not yet spent a night.

We walk faster, aware that we'll be feeling our way back to the temple in the dark. As the light grows dimmer, the monuments feel even larger, more crowded around us, a city of the dead.

We are approaching the *okunoin.* We see the Hall of Lanterns, a large building filled with thousands and thousands of lanterns, gifts from pilgrims who have come here before us. There is another building, too, octagonal in shape, and we're not quite certain whether this is where Kōbō Daishi is buried. We pause, unsure.

A monk in saffron robes steps out of the shadows to stand beside us. His movements are so cat-quiet that he does not startle us. Perhaps he's a guide or a resident priest or just a holy man who's there when people need him. He gestures behind the Hall of Lanterns, to a small building set back and on a gentle rise, barely visible in the twilight. We bow and thank him, then walk in the direction he pointed. When we look back, he's nowhere in sight.

Without a guide, we could have missed the mausoleum, even though we've been in Japan long enough to know that the most sacred place is often the least imposing. Cedars taller than possibility bracket this sanctuary.

There is a space around it, an indescribable presence. The air swells then subsides, like breathing.

No one says a word.

At the Hall of Lanterns, we sound the temple gong, summoning the gods. We clap our hands and bow our heads. We have visited two hundred temples in Kyoto and Nara, and realize we have been practicing for this moment on Kōya-san. Tonight, gods must be listening.

We return silently down the path, the last rays of light clinging to the incense. It's like walking through clouds.

We are tired and exhilarated by the time we reach our temple, well after dark.

"I was worried about you," says the woman at the temple. She is wearing a brightly flowered *yukata,* the cotton summer kimono. "But I see from your faces that you made it to the *okunoin."*

She knows the look. We nod and mumble something polite in return, realizing we're going to have to speak again.

We remove our shoes and place them in the shoe rack in the entryway to the temple. We put on the slippers provided for us, Ted and Charles managing as best they can with the standard-size Japanese slippers. Their shoes stand out from those of the other people, all Japanese, also staying in the temple for the night.

The woman leads us down a long corridor of unvarnished cedar boards worn smooth by centuries of slippered feet. When we get to our room, she slides back the *fusuma,* the paper doors. Our bags are waiting for us. Three crisp *yukata* are neatly folded for us in the center of the room. There is time, the woman says, for a nice bath before dinner, and she points in the direction of the men's bath for Ted and Charles, the women's bath for me. Before we can thank her, she is gone, the paper *fusuma* silently closed behind us.

We take in the room. It is a perfect, traditional Japanese temple room, spare and exquisite. The only decoration is in the *tokonoma* alcove, a ceramic vase holding an *ikebana* arrangement beneath a scroll on which there is a small ink drawing of distant mountains. No furniture, only tatami on the floor and three *zabuton* on which we can kneel or sit after our bath, while dinner is served on lacquered trays, each beautiful bit of temple food in its perfect wood or ceramic dish.

When the trays are cleared away, we again walk around the temple, looking more carefully at the austerely beautiful garden of raked sand and jutting rocks outside our room. Charles says the stark, white rocks make him think of ghosts, huddling together in the moonlight, afraid of their own shadows.

There are other verandalike walkways that lead to other gardens, all of which we explore together in our *yukata* and too-small slippers. We feel like a family, with private jokes to share, a history. When we return to our room, the futon are spread on the tatami mats, ready for us to sleep. In two hours, the room has changed from living room to dining room to bedroom. The emptiness of the traditional Japanese room and its lack of a designated function are what allow it to fulfill all functions. In Buddhism, emptiness is valued most of all. Architecture, the Japanese have always known, is metaphysics.

"Doesn't it make you wonder," Charles says, "if all this prosperity in Japan is worth it? With all the building going on in Japan, aren't they destroying the one thing you *can't* build?"

We do not consider ourselves religious in any traditional sense, yet here we are, yearning for what this room, this temple, this mountain is all about. Charles says Buddhism, for him, is a lot like his flute playing—the practice is the point, not the final performance, although the performance gets better and better the more you practice. He says sometimes when he practices he can *hear* his moods—sadness, anxiety, anger—even before he can feel them. He then has to get rid of them, to deal with them, before he can make the sound right.

"That's like Buddhism too," he says, keeping his voice low so as not to disturb the people in the next room.

Ted suggests we might want to get to sleep. We will have to be up before dawn for the Buddhist ceremony. As he goes to turn off the light, Charles pats the pocket of the jeans he has folded near his head and assures us that he has his large Swiss army knife there, just in case. As much as he has loved this day, he admits that he's not at all sure he likes this, sleeping among strangers with no locks on the doors. For that matter, there aren't really doors, nothing that can be propped shut, only paper partitions separating us from the strangers in the next room. Charles is sixteen and is used to a metal apartment door with a police lock, iron grates on the windows, and now he is about to sleep in a room of paper, surrounded by strangers whispering in a language he doesn't understand. Yet, despite his comment about the knife, he is relaxed in a way that I've seldom seen before and I'm not surprised that he falls asleep almost instantly. This quiet temple on Mount Kōya is something new for him, something he didn't consider possible.

He is the same age I was during my night in the flophouse. I can barely see him in this moonlight. Under the tousle of thick blond hair, he looks like a small child again. I listen to his breathing. He and his father are inhaling and exhaling in unison with strangers sleeping in the rooms around us, the metaphor from Maxwell Street. I wait for the emotions to well up—I want to feel part of this universal breathing—but in a second I'm out like a light.

It seems like hardly any time has passed at all when the small travel alarm goes off. I set it for four A.M., just in case we missed the temple gong. Not a chance. For the first time, the temple is noisy. Groggy people pull on their warmest clothing and prepare for kneeling or sitting lotus position on the floor in an unheated mountain room. We hear them hurrying down the hallway in their slippers. Only when we push back our *fusuma* do we realize that in the neighboring room was a party of about ten or fifteen young men. They are waiting for the last members of their group to get ready so they can go together to the main part of our temple, where the service will be held. Politely, they nod to us and whisper, *"Ohayō gozaimasu!"* (Good morning!). They are openly surprised to find their neighbors for the night were three foreigners. We are amazed to see dozens and dozens of beer bottles—maybe a hundred altogether—lined up in neat rows on the floor and on a table in the hallway outside their room. There was a beer blast next door, but so quiet we couldn't hear it through the paper walls! Ted jokes that there really are some cultural differences.

Charles kneels between Ted and me at the service. Our shoulders touch. The three of us feel lucky to be here. The three of us are lucky to be here together. The chanting begins, simple, long, and incomprehensible, mesmerizing in its deep guttural drone, punctuated at intervals by the striking of a small gong. There are three priests, two young ones in plain brown and a more elaborately dressed head priest. They kneel with their backs to us. We all face an altar whose door is open but it is too dark—it is always too dark—to see the precious object inside.

We three kneel among strangers. At first, we move our lips and make a low humming sound but don't really try to participate in the Buddhist chanting. We grow more confident as it becomes clear that the Japanese in the room don't recognize the words of the ancient Buddhist sutras either. Gradually, we begin to contribute meaningless but well-intentioned murmurings in the same register, our voices harmonizing in a chant we do not understand, among people we do not know, amid the intoxication of heavy incense and dim light.

Sometimes the phrases go on so long there seems to be no place for breath. At first, we don't make it all the way to the merciful gong before gasping for breath. Gradually, we learn to conserve air. We learn to relax the muscles in our throat, jaws, even in our shoulders and back. We learn to ignore the pain in our legs. It is transient. If we focus too much on the needles pricking our feet, we lose our place in the chant, falter, and sputter for air. We stop thinking. We exist to chant. When we relax enough, breath shapes itself into sound. Our lips move less and less. As if the sound were simply emanating from our bodies, our bodies only vessels for sound. These are things we learn by trial and error. There are no instructions, no guidebook. But gradually everyone in the room seems to find a prayer, a chant, words that mean without meaning.

The priests modulate the volume and pace of the sound, louder now, then softer, then rising again, faster, slower, and then the gong, the communal intake of breath. It is almost like hypnosis, this giving over of control. It is about trust. Intensely private, it wouldn't work without the presence of strangers. There is a heady sense of freedom precisely because everything is constrained—exhausted, numb from kneeling, faint with cold and incense and rhythmic breathing. And still the chant continues. These are things I think about later. Not then, there, in the room of sound. Moonies, Mahareshi Mahesh Yogi, Hare Krishnas: part of me understands the appeal of this other Eastern world, the seductive power of powerlessness. For some, this room could be a life.

A few weeks after Charles goes back to New York, someone from the U.S. Information Agency calls and asks if I'll give a lecture at the University of the Ryukyus in Okinawa on literature and everyday life at the time of the American Revolution, the topic of a book I'm writing. Ted has an engagement the same week to lecture at the Canadian Embassy in Tokyo, so it seems like a good time for me to go off by myself to some new part of Japan. As my plane touches down in Naha, I am missing Charles, missing Ted, but resolved to enjoy myself.

Three professors from the University of the Ryukyus meet me at the airport and drive me around the island. I ask about the strange cement houses built into the hillsides. Mausoleums, I'm told. I'm shocked at so much death.

The traditional houses of the living are low to the ground, topped by red tiled roofs. Often a little ceramic guardian lion-dog, *shiisā,* sits at each end of the roof. Other houses resemble American fifties-style bungalows. They were built after the massive destruction of World War II. On the roofs of these, there are no *shiisā* to protect against typhoons. The sun is dazzling here, like the sea, but there is something sad too. This is an island of the dead, the site of horrific battles—sea, air, and land—between the Allied forces and the Japanese, and markers around the island commemorate the bloodshed.

We stop at one site and one of the professors translates the marker without reading it. A quarter of a million people died, soldiers and civilians, after eighty-two solid days of combat with the Allied forces. He adds something which may or may not be on the marker: the hundred thousand Japanese soldiers who were sent to Okinawa to fight the Allied troops considered Okinawan civilians to be "expendable" and tens of thousands of Okinawans died at Japanese hands. He says there's a history here. Okinawa has only been under Japanese rule since 1879, and Okinawans are still discriminated against in mainland Japan. It's one reason, he says, why Okinawa was ceded to the Americans, turned into a virtual military base for the United States from 1945 until 1972. "They thought we were *expendable*," he repeats the word.

After I mention my interest in local arts, a lovely, gracious professor from the university, Professor Shō, takes the day off from her busy schedule to drive me to a glassworks, to a pottery guild, and to a workshop where artisans weave fabric from dyed banana fibers. I am impressed by the beauty of the art, by the richness and distinctiveness of Okinawan culture. Professor Shō says these traditional Okinawan arts were once commonplace all over the islands in the Ryukyu chain, but now relatively few people practice them.

For lunch, I am taken to a traditional Okinawan restaurant. The tastes and textures of the food are new to me. So is some of the Japanese I hear. A professor from the University of the Ryukyus explains that many of the waitresses come from the countryside and speak only *hōgen* (dialect), known here as *Uchināguchi* (the mouth Okinawa). Despite Japanese attempts to eradicate the local dialect, it persists here side-by-side with standard Japanese. I cannot understand a word, and another professor assures me that I would have difficulty even if I were a native Japanese speaker. Okinawa has an indigenous religion, too, called simply Okinawan Religion. It's matriarchal and pantheistic, with shaman priestesses and sacred groves, an animistic religion distinct from other Chinese or Japanese religions. The Japanese have tried to replace it, too, with Buddhism and state Shinto.

I am getting the message. Okinawa may now be part of Japan, but it has a long history and heritage all its own. An Okinawan nationalist movement now advocates separation from Japan just as an earlier movement sought independence and an end to the American postwar occupation. When I ask Professor Shō about Okinawan nationalism, she says, simply, "Some people find it hard to forget the War."

At the island's main museum, we see photographs from before the War and after. I find myself working to hold back tears.

The devastation is everywhere, as in photographs of Hiroshima after the bomb was dropped. When Professor Shō steps away for a moment, one of the other professors shows me a model of the old imperial palace of Okinawa, destroyed by the Japanese, and tells me, proudly, that Professor Shō's husband is a direct descendent of the former king of the Ryukyus. When we drive by the front of her property, someone points out where the imperial palace once stood.

≈

After the formal dinner following my talk, Christine, an American professor at the University of the Ryukyus, offers to drive me back to my hotel. I had met her a few times in the United States and was awed by her adventurousness. She's traveled alone all over the world, including places in the Middle East where most Americans would never dream of going alone. She's a stunning woman, with a long-stemmed beauty-queen look that attracts attention in any culture, attention that I've watched her easily and graciously deflect.

"If you're willing to give up your fancy room in the Hilton"—Christine smiles as she drops me off at the door—"I could pick you up tomorrow morning and take you in a rickety boat through shark-infested waters to Kudakajima, a matriarchal island. We could stay with Mrs. Nishimae, a priestess in the Okinawan Religion."

We leave early the next morning. Kudakajima is less than an hour from the mainland. We don't see any sharks on the trip but the other people on the boat warn me, over and over, that they are everywhere here. I'm also warned about the jellyfish, the sea wasps, the cone shells, and the *habu,* a kind of snake. All are poisonous. One kills you in thirty minutes, another in sixty. The nearest hospital is on the main island, and the boat comes only once or twice a day.

When I arrive on Kudakajima, I understand the reason for these warnings. Sepulchers face the sea, as on the mainland, but on this tiny island death seems everywhere. Any place you look there's another of the tortoise-shaped tombs. This is a culture of remembrance, and it seems as if there is much here to remember, not just from the devastation of war but from everyday life, the poisonous creatures in this subtropical climate and also the typhoons that rip through the islands, the tricky tides that take their toll of fishermen each year.

"The mortality rate here is very high," Christine says. "Most of the men are net or spear fishermen; some of the women dive for pearls or shellfish. Every family has seen unexpected deaths."

It looks like paradise. One long road down the center of the island is lined with small date and banana trees, brighter than green against a sky brighter than blue.

Christine tells me how there is no distinction on the island between religious belief and social structure. The priestesses control the religion and they take care of the business of the island too.

"What do the priests do?" I ask.

She laughs. "There are no priests. That's *why* it's a matriarchal society. Women run everything."

One must be a widow to be a *nūru* (priestess), she explains, and a *nūru* cannot marry again. This seems a way of taking care of the disparity between the adult male and female populations, the men so frequently killed at sea. Every twelve years there is a ceremony, *izaihō,* in which the youngest widows are inducted as priestesses. And every year the priestesses meet and reapportion land according to which family has had a child, which has lost a son or husband at sea or suffered some other death or, more and more frequently, had a son or daughter depart for life on the mainland (Okinawa or Japan). Amazingly, everyone seems content with the division. The only fences are stones, the size of grapefruit, lined up in a row, demarcating one person's field from another's. Once a year, the *nūru* don their robes and headdresses and go out into the fields and move the stones.

Kudakajima, I am told, is the last communal, matriarchal

place on earth, a phrase that haunts me during my stay, like the tortoise-shaped tombs that face the sea.

We stop in front of a tiny ranch-style bungalow in which Mrs. Nishimae, the head priestess, lives. The house could have been transplanted from the Chicago suburbs of my youth. Even the color—Doris Day green—is one I know well but haven't seen in years. Through the screen door on the front of the house, I watch a tiny woman come toward us wearing a white cotton blouse and gray pants. Her hair is dyed black and permed. She looks like a normal, middle-aged woman—mother, friend, farmer, owner of a small business, and, I remind myself, a high priestess in the last communal, matriarchal religion. Only the gentle lines around her eyes fulfill my fantasies of what a *nūru* should look like.

Mrs. Nishimae welcomes us to her home. Christine understands only a little *Uchināguchi,* but that hardly seems to matter. People touch more freely in Okinawa than on mainland Japan, and Mrs. Nishimae cannot get enough of Christine. She strokes her arm, pats her shoulder, smiles up at her. Christine is the teacher of Mrs. Nishimae's son, a senior at the University of the Ryukyus. She has been helping him with his English and has also worked with him to collect books for the library and a community center he and his friends have set up on the island. They take turns coming back on weekends to run it. The priestess beams with pride as Christine tells her about her son's recent achievements at the university. It's clear she doesn't understand everything but she gets the point: her son's a star.

Mrs. Nishimae goes to a cupboard and brings forth an envelope for Christine. In it are photographs of herself, Christine, and a handsome young man, smiling happily together in this same kitchen on Kudakajima. She asks if I have children and I bring out a photograph of Ted, Charles, and me, dressed in *yukata,* taken during our night together in the temple on Mount Kōya.

Mrs. Nishimae says something in *Uchināguchi.* There is a sadness in her voice. Like so many of my conversations in Japan, this one is multilingual, but it requires even more translators than usual. Christine knows Japanese and a little Okinawan dialect. Two other people are staying in Mrs. Nishimae's house for the night. One is a spear fisherman who comes to Kudakajima a few months each year to catch eels, which he sells, smoked and cured, on the mainland. *Uchināguchi* is his first language but he knows some Japanese too. The other man is the *denki* (electric) man, here to fix the main generator on the island. He speaks both Japanese and *Uchināguchi* and even a smidgeon of G.I. English he learned during the War. He regularly exclaims, "Fuck!" as if this is a simple English expression of surprise or delight (like the Japanese *Hontō!*), and he is obviously pleased that he still has some serviceable English at hand.

When Mrs. Nishimae speaks, the spear fisherman and the *denki* man, after some discussion, translate for Christine, who tells me.

"They grow up" is what the *nūru* said of our sons.

I nod, sadly.

She then says something with a laugh, and the joke takes the same route from *Uchināguchi* to Japanese, each person laughing in turn, and, finally, to English: "And it's a good thing for mothers that they do!" is how Christine translates Mrs. Nishimae's punchline, and, finally, I get to join in the laughter.

I ask Christine if Mrs. Nishimae can tell us more about Okinawan Religion. A few years ago a film crew of women from Scandinavia made a movie about this island and the ritual induction of the new priestesses. Christine showed me a book based on their documentary and explained the captions under the photographs. I am especially fascinated by the *utaki*, the sacred grove where the new priestesses are inducted every twelve years. On mainland Japan, women are excluded from many religious rituals and can't enter the most sacred places. Until modern times, women weren't even allowed on top of Mount Kōya or Mount Fuji. But on Kudakajima, it's the men who are prohibited from entering the sacred grove and I'm curious why.

"Because they can go everywhere else," she says laughing,

though the *denki* man adds, editorially, that he's not sure he really approves of this answer.

I think about how Charles would have loved to see the *utaki* if he were here and ask if Mrs. Nishimae's son has ever been inside the sacred grove.

"Oh, I think he'd rather go to Shinjuku," she jokes, alluding to the famous entertainment district in Tokyo.

"Fuck! Fuck!" the *denki* man calls out and claps loudly after translating for Mrs. Nishimae.

The priestess is a cutup. She soon has us all in stitches, and I realize that, at the moment, she doesn't want to discuss Okinawan Religion. I know it is about ancestor worship and the ties that bind the living and the dead, ties against absence, the spirit's blending with the natural world, those tombs facing the sea which meet the land which meets the palm trees, the sky, the human soul simply part of the world's ebb and flow. Hardly a laughing matter. And tonight is a night for celebration: after all, the teacher of Mrs. Nishimae's smart son is visiting.

Things gets wilder as Mrs. Nishimae talks nonstop, only some of what she says making it through the rounds of translation, but nobody caring as she pours us more *awamori,* the remarkable local brew, the *denki* man shouting "Fuck!" with delight every few minutes.

Outside, there's music. We'd been told some neighbors would be coming by later to visit the teacher of Mrs. Nishimae's son.

"Everyone sings and dances on Kudakajima—and some of the local dances are pretty bawdy," Christine says, not knowing what to expect from the party making its way down the street.

An old man puts his head inside Mrs. Nishimae's kitchen doorway. He's holding a *sanshin* (the Okinawan three-stringed instrument, ancestor of the Japanese *samisen).* Other people have joined him from other houses and they are passing around more *awamori,* unself-conscious in the presence of two foreigners. It feels easier to be a *gaijin* here than on mainland Japan. The neighbors are roughly Mrs. Nishimae's age although some might be younger, perhaps still in their forties. Mrs. Nishimae sets out a plate of delicacies (dried cuttlefish, dried seaweed, and other dried things that I do not inspect too closely), and Christine asks if I'd like to learn the Kudakajima dance. Everyone watches, smiling, as she teaches me, twirling her wrists, moving back and forth, as in a Greek circle dance. The old guy motions us outside where we all dance together, hands clapping, feet moving back and forth in a way that, to Western ears, seems syncopated and arrhythmic. As in mainland Japan, the clapping here is on the off beat.

The music gets faster or slower, the words change with the tempo, but basically the step remains the same, with some simple variations. There's a lot of laughter during one song, and I assume it's one of the bawdy ones Christine told me about. There's a sea breeze here but still it's hot and humid, even this late at night, and soon we return exhausted to the house, more than ready for the requisite bath before retiring for the night.

Since Christine is the honored guest, she gets to take her bath first. Christine says to me in English that she'll be a while because she doesn't want to insult anyone by declining this honor but she knows the water will be too hot at first. She'll wait until it cools down just a bit, as if she's enjoying a good, long bath, something which will give Mrs. Nishimae great pleasure. She wishes me luck, opens the door to the bathroom, and disappears into a cloud of steam.

Mrs. Nishimae starts talking almost immediately. The spear fisherman translates a few words into Japanese, but I'm baffled, either by my own incompetence with the language or by his unaccustomed accent, I'm not sure which. It's something about dancing. I take a stab, get up, showing how I can do the Kudakajima shuffle, even by myself.

Mrs. Nishimae shakes her head. She gives up on language and points to me, toward my feet. I point to myself and make a little dancing motion with my feet and look quizzical. She nods. The spear fisherman explains, and this time, with the combination of language and pantomime, I get it: the *nūru* wants me to show her *my* native dance.

Fortified by several glasses of *awamori,* I decide to teach Mrs.

Nishimae the soft-shoe. I need a cane, but I don't know the word in Japanese so I draw a little picture. The spear fisherman nods, disappears outside the house, then returns with one of the dried eels that Mrs. Nishimae smokes for him in the little shed behind her house. The hard, black eel curves at the top, a perfect cane. Why not? I show the priestess and the spear fisherman the soft-shoe, singing "Tiptoe through the tulips, you'll come with me." I'm not sure I have the words right and I don't know any others and it doesn't matter. I begin again, joined by the priestess and the spear fisherman who hum along while doing something vaguely taplike with their feet. Tonight feels like a small miracle, laughing and dancing without language. I am filled with admiration for Mrs. Nishimae, a woman who has seen much tragedy and who yet retains her ability to experience joy. I find my eyes brimming with tears, grateful for her generosity and honored that tonight she has extended her welcome to me.

When Christine comes fresh from her bath, looking radiant in the *yukata* Mrs. Nishimae has lent her, I hug her and thank her for bringing me here. That night, we sleep on one side of Mrs. Nishimae's living room while the spear fisherman and the *denki* man sleep on the other. Mrs. Nishimae sleeps in a tiny room beside the kitchen. I close my eyes and listen: I can hear all of them breathing, can separate out the sleeping sounds and identify them, each to each, like the chorus of a wordless song. I can't stop thinking of the night Charles, Ted, and I spent together on Mount Kōya. Charles is now back in New York, just the right age to be harassed by neighborhood gangs, so far away. I miss him a lot. Mrs. Nishimae's son is in Naha, less than an hour by boat—but a whole universe separates him from the communal, matriarchal island of Kudakajima. He's a good boy, coming home regularly; some of the children return only for funerals, Mrs. Nishimae said. I wonder if Okinawan Religion helps with the whole process of raising a child, losing a child. They grow up, Mrs. Nishimae joked. What she does not say, but what is evident everywhere on the island, is that fewer and fewer young people are staying on Kudakajima. Despite the wealth of songs and the dancing, despite the sacred rituals, the culture is fragile. It's an anachronism, the last of its kind; and, unless more young people stay on the island or some of the others start moving back from the mainland, it is going to end.

"Someday, they'll come home," Mrs. Nishimae said resolutely, after I asked if all the young people were leaving Kudakajima.

I wonder where such perspective, such hope, comes from. Is it from religion or age or personal wisdom? Or just seeing children go away and realizing there's not much else to do but be philosophical. It's alarming to think of how many old people there are on this island. The tombs are everywhere—and some of the houses of the living stand empty.

Before we fall asleep, Christine says that she has asked Mrs. Nishimae if she will take me to the sacred *utaki*. Once again, I'm struck by Christine's intuitive generosity, arranging for a visit to the sacred grove with a shaman-priestess.

At dawn, there's a tap on my shoulder. Mrs. Nishimae points to my clothes and gestures toward herself, then points outside. I dress quickly and follow. Sunrise engulfs the tiny island, dawn all around us. I've never seen anything like this, the air itself brilliant orange and shimmering.

We walk. She talks. I am surprised at the tone in her voice, serious, urgent, significant. Even her posture has changed since the night before. In Japanese, I apologize several times that I cannot understand her, but she just looks past me and continues to speak. Is this a prayer? An incantation? An explanation?

Mrs. Nishimae stops and points at something. I look. At first I don't see anything at all; then she leans over, practically touching the ground, and I see a tiny mound of rocks, beach stones worn smooth by the sea, some thick shiny green leaves from a plant I don't recognize, a few sticks of matte black incense.

I know from Christine that this is one of the tiny altars that dot the island, part of its pantheistic religion. Somewhere on the island is a larger altar just like this, inside the *utaki,* the sacred grove that no man may enter.

We walk and walk under the gilt morning sun. This is my first experience of a tropical climate and everything overwhelms. Garish birds squawk and chatter, palm trees drip enormous strange fruits, lizards dart, gigantic insects make like lobsters, their pincers clawing the air. I know I'm walking with a priestess, but nothing about this island—lush, brilliant, noisy—conforms to my expectations for the sacred. Nothing ascetic or minimal or austere here, it doesn't feel at all like Mount Kōya.

Mrs. Nishimae is displeased. She has pointed out several of the tiny altars and I haven't been able to spot a single one myself. Now, impatient, she takes my hand, holds it, and physically points it toward another of the altars. This is a reprimand. We stand here a long time. She doesn't say a word, just looks at the altar. I look too. After two or three minutes, we start walking again. Slowly. I look over every inch of the jungle around us, then stop triumphantly when I sight one of the altars by myself. Mrs. Nishimae says something I can't understand, but I listen, then bow to her, solemnly. She smiles softly at me and pats me on the back. She claps her hands, making a little tap step. I bow deeply, then move my hands in the motion I learned last night at the Kudakajima circle dance.

We walk more quickly, cutting in toward the center of the island. Mrs. Nishimae stops, putting a finger over her lips, then disappears through a small opening in a tangle of undergrowth. I follow her in and find myself under an archway of tropical trees and plants so thick that I need to pause for a minute so my eyes can adjust to the darkness. I must hurry to catch up with Mrs. Nishimae again. She walks upright but I have to bend as we walk through this moist tunnel in the jungle. I have to fight against a feeling of claustrophobia here. I'm trying not to think of *habu,* the island's poisonous snakes, and must work to keep down my panic as damp palm leaves brush against my face. I don't like it here, how close it feels, the sweat clammy on my body in this dark, airless place. I'm tempted to turn back, to dash out into the open air again.

Suddenly we're in a clearing. I can stand, there is light. No snakes. The clearing is ablaze, with the sun beaming down on the gnarled tree, just like in the photograph in the book by the Scandinavian filmmakers, an altar of smooth stones and sticks of incense at the base of the tree: the Tree of Life in Okinawan Religion.

I make a deep bow and thank Mrs. Nishimae. I am in the sacred grove with a priestess in the last surviving matriarchal, communal culture on earth.

I think: I want to save this moment. I want to be able to flip back to it any time I need it—ten, twenty, fifty years from now. I want to remember exactly how it feels, the gasp of air again after the damp tunnel, the sun streaming down on the Tree of Life, Mrs. Nishimae with her laughter and her wisdom, the creases smiling in her weathered face. I know that in the Okinawan Religion the island is the center of the world. The sacred *utaki* is the center of the center.

For one moment, I am here.

8

ACCIDENT

Of course the moment didn't last. You can't dance with a priestess forever. Three months later, in late December, Ted's youngest brother, Ken, telephoned from Vancouver, Canada, to inform us of a family tragedy, a devastating car accident.

Jiko, accident, the unpreventable and unpredictable. In the Buddhist scheme of things, *jiko* is inevitable; it is the other side of the coin. But that coin doesn't just flip, it spins. As a commonplace expression has it, *"ura ni wa ura ga aru"*: the reverse side has a reverse side. For me, that simple phrase conjures up images of yin and yang, chaos and order, existence and nonexistence, the cycles of death and rebirth, a whole philosophical system. Yet I've lived in Japan long enough to know, painfully, that grief and loss are no different in one culture than another. Just because it's part of a philosophical system, doesn't make *jiko* any easier to accept.

When the call comes on Christmas Eve, Ted is grading a few last papers up in his office at Kansai Women's University. Since I've finished my grading, I'm down in the English Department office, where I sip green tea with some of our colleagues and the English Department staff. We're talking about how the term is going, plans for the holidays, typical departmental chitchat.

The mood is festive. It is the last day of class. For the foreign teachers, it is Christmas Eve. For the Japanese it is the end-of-year celebrations that precede *Oshōgatsu,* New Year, the most important holiday in Japan and one that brings the whole culture to a three-day halt. Miss Sumida, the head departmental secretary, explains that, although *Oshōgatsu* itself only lasts three days, the celebrations really fill a whole month. First there are *bōnen-kai* (weeks of parties to speed the passing of the old year), then *Oshōgatsu* (New Year, in which, for three days virtually all shops and buildings are closed), and finally *shinnen-kai* (another few weeks of parties to welcome in the New Year before normal activities begin again). The Year of the Monkey is about to yield to the Year of the Rooster, a lucky year.

When she's on the telephone, Miss Sumida uncharacteristically turns away from us as she speaks, first in Japanese, then in English, huddling her body over the phone, muffling her voice. Instead of calling me over, she puts the receiver down on the desk and comes to me. I cannot remember her exact words, but she conveys to me and to everyone else in the room that this will not be happy news from home. She takes my arm and solicitously leads me to the phone, as one might guide an invalid. It is an extraordinary gesture in a culture where people are respectful of one another's physical space, rarely touching one another as so often happens in casual Western conversation. Miss Sumida stands near, almost touching me, for most of the conversation. My colleagues—

another American and two or three Japanese—sit alert in their chairs, ready to help in any way they can, as I keep asking my brother-in-law to repeat himself, not wanting to believe.

The connection is terrible. My brain won't cancel out the static, attend to the blurred voice on the other end of the line. I can't seem to make meaning. Instead, my hand records what my mind resists. Somewhere, in the mass of clippings and flyers I brought back with me from Japan, I still have the small white piece of paper from Miss Sumida's desk on which I took dreadful dictation: *Christmas Eve. Driving home. Park and Sheena—dead. Bruce—multiple injuries. Ross and Karina—???*

We learn the details later. Ted's brother, Park, and his wife, Sheena, were driving home through the Canadian Rockies to spend Christmas Eve with Ted's parents and his sister. They were in a Volkswagen camper van, the three kids (Karina, a first-year college student; Bruce and Ross in high school and junior high) in the back of the van. A blizzard came up unexpectedly, ice first and then snow. The Mounties closed the mountain highway, but not soon enough to stop a pickup truck coming from the East and Park's van from the West. On a treacherous curve, both vehicles went out of control and met in a head-on collision. Park and Sheena were killed instantly. The kids were trapped in the car for several hours until the Mounties arrived.

I have said enough for my colleagues to know what has happened before I hang up the phone. Their eyes are large with concern and empathy, and everywhere there are enfolding arms. Later I realize that one of the American teachers at Kansai Women's University, an avuncular eccentric known as PK, must have come on the phone and taken my brother-in-law's phone number, because when Ted goes to call Ken, we find the number there, at the bottom of the sheet, in a handwriting we do not recognize. I remember saying over and over that I must find Ted and tell him. But my colleagues insist I sit for a few seconds and drink the rest of my tea. Someone—I do not remember who—says that it is unimportant now, of course, but at some point we will start worrying about our responsibilities at the University and he wants us to remember, then, that our colleagues will take over whatever needs to be done. We must not worry in any way about our responsibilities here. He says this in a commanding voice, more bracing than the tea. His practical comments bring me back an inch closer to the world of the ordinary.

A colleague walks me to the wing where Ted's office is and watches as I enter the room. How will Ted take this awful news? He and Park were born fourteen months apart, adorable together in baby pictures, blond-haired blue-eyed Ted in feet-pajamas holding his little brother, an urchin with masses of black curly hair and bright dark eyes. Ted's mother was a teacher in a small, four-room schoolhouse in Mountain View, Alberta, a ranching community in the foothills of the Canadian Rockies. She taught Park everything that Ted was learning so that Park could skip a grade and the boys could go through school together, eleven years in the same class.

"My brother Park and I only had one fight the whole time we were growing up," Ted sometimes would say. "It was over a pair of socks."

As adults, the two men were as different in personality as in appearance, yet they retained an eerie compatibility, almost like twins. And both had gone on from the four-room school in Mountain View to earn Ph.D.s, Ted in English literature, Park in psychology. We had been on the phone with Park only a few weeks before the accident, arranging for him to visit Japan to lecture at a nearby university where one of our Japanese friends taught psychology. Park was planning to come early in the New Year.

I still remember the details of that day. How Ted sits at his desk turned slightly away from me with his elbows resting on the traditional Japanese handmade paper in the desk blotter. The paper is of an intense, emeraldlike hue that we would call green but that the Japanese call *aoi,* blue, like the blue of traffic lights or grass. As I tell him what happened, he reaches over and takes the piece of notepaper on which I recorded disaster. He holds it in both hands and just looks at it, not reading, just looking. Ted's boyish face turns, for an instant, into something stony and mask-like. Color drains from his cheeks. His face is white; in any language, deathly white.

"We have to go home," he says quietly.

I am not sure if he means home to our apartment in Nigawa, Japan, a mile from the university, or home to Mountain View, Canada.

We walk down the hill to the train together, holding hands, ignoring the taboo against a man and woman's holding hands in public. At first, we are glad that we recognize no one. But soon I begin to realize that we are not just going unnoticed. We are being avoided. Normally, Japanese do not look at one another in public, do not make eye contact. But curiosity at seeing a foreigner up close often overrides the Japanese insistence on privacy and on maintaining a respectful distance from others in public spaces. As a *gaijin* in Japan, one grows used to stares. But today we must be communicating something different, tragic. Neither of us cries but we are obviously repressing deep emotions, and people, sensing this, avert their gaze.

I feel more alien, isolated, and alone than I have ever felt in my life. I am surprised by a sudden surge of something that feels like rage, as if our being here, away, has caused this terrible thing to happen. The emotion reformulates itself: terrible things happen when you go away.

Somewhere deep inside me is a strange, displaced emotion, guilt masked as anger, my hostility directed, inexplicably, at everyone who dares to ride that train with us and not feel what we are feeling. We violate public decorum again by sitting pressed against one another, holding both of each other's hands in both hands, the fingers as intertwined as we can make them. I am a *gaijin*—outsider, foreigner, nonperson—and I don't care what they think, these people who see green and call it blue.

We want to go home. Really home.

We begin the round of phone calls, complicated by the fact that in 1980 our area of Japan still does not have direct international dialing and we must go through a series of operators. Our Japanese escapes us so often and unpredictably that we finally write out the telephone numbers—our own, all of theirs—in *rō-maji,* phonetic Japanese, on a piece of paper that we keep taped by the phone.

We want to fly home at once, but Ted's family asks us not to. There will be no funeral. Neither Park nor Sheena wanted one. They say it would work much better for everyone if we finish up our school year as soon as possible and then fly to Vancouver to stay for a while, to help. The Japanese academic year ends in early March. If we could work things so that we could come home five or six weeks early—in late January, say—we could fly directly to Vancouver and be there when the kids get out of the hospital. We could then help to settle financial matters (there seems to be no will) and to set up new living arrangements. Ted's dad, a retired rancher in Alberta and recently divorced from his second wife, will live with the boys in Vancouver so that they won't have to leave their house, their school, and all their friends. He would like us to come to Vancouver to help him out for the first few months and before we have to be back at our regular teaching positions in the United States.

We agree. We know this makes the most sense for everyone. But we also feel severed, cut off from family, from rituals, left alone with our own sense of loss.

≈

The hardest call is to Charles.

Despite our glorious summer in Japan together, there was also a sadness lurking behind his visit. Originally, we'd made arrangements for him to live in Japan the whole year, but he found out his maternal grandmother was dying of cancer. He wanted to be there with her and his mother in New York, and we admired him for his choice. She was an extraordinary woman, whose kindness to me as her grandson's stepmother was one of the real gifts in my life; her death at an early age was a shock to all of us and devastating to Charles. Now we must call to tell him of more death. He had stayed with his Uncle Park and Aunt Sheena in

Vancouver for a few days on his return trip home from Japan. Now, they too are dead and his cousins, two of them roughly his age, are in critical condition.

Charles's voice sounds tiny on the phone, as if he is speaking from the bottom of a well.

It is impossible to tell if he's crying, he sounds so far away. We talk and talk, console, sympathize, express our love. Nothing.

The voice remains muffled and terse. Words aren't making this better.

We hang up, bereft.

≈≈≈

After the call to Charles, the Japanese apartment that we once found charming is suddenly a torture chamber. The walls have grown too close together. Soon we won't be able to breathe. My head is throbbing with pain; Ted feels dizzy. Yet we feel a need to go somewhere busy, distracting, loud, a place that can preoccupy.

We decide to spend the day in Osaka, a thirty-minute train ride from our apartment. It is Christmas Day.

Despite weeks and weeks of pre-Christmas hoopla, Christmas in Japan is a day like any other. The Japanese have taken up with gusto Christmas music, Santa Claus, and gaudy red-and-green decorations, but the month-long blaring of "Rudolph the Red-Nosed Reindeer" and "Silent Night" turns out to be an elaborate preparation for absolutely nothing. When December 25 finally rolls around, the Christmas trees and bows and bangles come down to be replaced by the ritual decorations for *Oshōgatsu*.

We spend the day wandering through department stores where shoppers busily prepare for *Oshōgatsu* amid the iconography of cute Baby Jesuses and adorable elves. The aisles are packed, and Bing Crosby croons "White Christmas" at ear-splitting decibels. We visit the gigantic food basement where salespeople in traditional cotton *happi* coats use electronic megaphones to announce specials on various seasonal items. They shout in highly stylized voices—like the piercing declamations in kabuki opera. The smells are strange too: seaweed, fermented soybeans, pink and yellow pickles, sweetly acrid like mildew and old fish. It's more than we can handle today.

We flee to the clothing floor, where there is, at least, less aural and olfactory chaos. Ted buys himself a tie. I purchase a tiny, collapsible umbrella. Both cost far more than we would normally spend, but it's Christmas, we say.

After a few hours, we realize how useless it all is and we return to our austere apartment, make a few more calls to Canada and to my family in the United States. Although some American expatriate friends had earlier invited us for Christmas dinner, we are in no mood for socializing. We remember still other invitations for Japanese end-of-year celebrations that must be canceled.

That is how we feel: canceled.

But our friends will not leave us alone. Normally no Japanese ever, ever comes to a home without being very specifically invited. It's unusual to entertain at home in Japan and frequently colleagues will work together ten or twenty years without ever seeing where one another lives or without ever meeting a coworker's spouse and children. Outside/inside, public/private. These are borders not easily crossed.

Yet Japanese friends keep showing up on our doorstep unannounced and uninvited. While we were away in Osaka someone managed to get into our apartment to fill the refrigerator with food. We are not alarmed at this because our apartment is owned by the university and people on the maintenance staff have a key. But we are astonished by this flagrant breach of one of the cardinal rules of Japanese sociability, something we learned soon after arriving in Japan.

"What does it mean," I asked Professor Sano, our department head, early on, "when someone says, 'Please come to my house'?

We keep getting invited, even by strangers we happen to meet in the supermarket. I don't get it."

" 'Please come to my house,' " Professor Sano said, smiling, "means 'Please *don't* come to my house.' No one ever goes to a person's house without an invitation that includes a definite, prearranged time—and a map."

The map is crucial. Since most streets are unnamed in Japan and houses are typically numbered in the order in which they are built, having just an address usually gets you nowhere. Business cards often have a small schematic map on the back, as do store ads in newspapers or other commercial announcements. Privacy— the home—is institutionalized by the very anonymity of the streets. The seeming public disorder is itself almost a system; it's a *choice* the Japanese have made. Tokyo has been destroyed twice in the twentieth century, once by earthquake, once by war. Each time the Japanese have chosen to rebuild the city as disordered as before. Maps to particular places allow one to penetrate the maze, by appointment as it were. Privacy is not just a privilege; it is a fundamental value and an escape valve for Japan's collective life. It is the still center amid the whirlwind.

Yet, mysteriously, our Japanese friends violate this rule. This isn't collusion, since people we know who do not know one another all show up at the apartment, uninvited. A colleague we barely know comes with a beautiful plant, an enormous yellow mum with russet edging on each petal. We've been told that chrysanthemums are commemorative flowers, used at funerals, but she explains that she has chosen these because yellow and orange are colors of life. The plant is for us because a lucky new year is coming, she says. She bows deeply before leaving, then, choking back tears, reaches out and grasps first my hands, then Ted's, as if intuiting that just now we crave touch.

Another colleague arrives with the papers we might need to leave the country for the funeral and then to reenter again. Mr. Higuchi is afraid we will be caught in the *Oshōgatsu* bureaucratic shutdown and will not be able to get the proper exit papers and entry visas. Somehow, without our aid or signatures, he has managed to secure every document we might require to make the trip home immediately and then return to Japan for the rest of the academic year. When we tell him that there will only be a very small ceremony at the graveside in Mountain View and that Ted's family has asked that we not come now but, instead, finish up our year as early as possible and then come to help with the kids in Vancouver, Mr. Higuchi doesn't bat an eye. This practical solution must seem incomprehensible to him: how unnatural to miss one's brother's funeral. But he shows no sign of surprise. Instead, he pulls a legal pad and a calendar from his briefcase and heads for the phone. After a few calls in which he makes arrangements in rapid Japanese, he returns to show us neatly and clearly how we can wrap everything up in less than a month and be gone. He gives us a choice of dates, then proceeds to call the airlines for us and changes our supposedly nonchangeable tickets. We can return home early without paying a penalty, he reports. He next calls the tax bureau so that we will have the necessary papers before we leave. We don't understand why he tells us that he has informed the tax office that Ted is the oldest son and that there has been a death in the immediate family. But when the tax assessment comes, we realize that Ted has received an official tax break because of each of those circumstances. Mr. Higuchi hasn't missed a thing.

Ted and I sit dazed. I heat and then reheat water for tea, a welcome distraction, as various visitors enter, tend to our lives, leave. At one point Ted and I discuss how strange this must be for the Japanese, our staying here in Japan instead of flying home for the funeral. Ted's family is not religious. A funeral is not what is important; it is putting together a life for our nephews and niece, helping to make things as comfortable as possible for Ted's father. Rationally, we know all this, but we still feel amputated.

We have heard that in Japan death stops the culture. A new set of rules and procedures comes into play when a loved one dies, but we don't know what the rules are. This is totally outside our experience—it's not in the guidebooks—and we have no way of knowing if the treatment we receive is typical or special because we are foreigners. We suspect that our friends are trying to compensate for our alone-ness. The closed quality of Japanese society, the collective nature of the culture, must make our situation— alone in our grief—seem unendurable. Our friends help us to endure. They intuit what it must be like feeling sorrow so far from home. Individually and collectively, they refuse to allow us to be foreigners through our worst pain.

Several people anticipate that, in the grief of the moment, we might forget to stock up on the food and supplies necessary for the three days of New Year, when the stores all close. People bring everything from milk to canned goods to toilet paper. Neighbors and students, some of whom we barely recognize, come only to the *genkan,* drop something off, and then leave. The *genkan* is where you remove your outdoor shoes and replace them with slippers. But like all features of Japanese domestic architecture, the *genkan* is also symbolic and serves an important cultural function. Physically inside the apartment or house, the *genkan* is symbolically outside, a mediation between the protective space of home and the outside world. The gap between inside and outside is so great in Japanese culture that you actually need this place to pause and prepare for the transition, from one kind of space (and self) to another. It is not just a space but a *concept.* We understand this function better when some acquaintances whom we barely know enter the *genkan* with gifts but refuse to remove their shoes and step up into the apartment itself. This, they insist, would be an invasion of our privacy.

Our Japanese friends do not leave us alone. We are moved by their attentions, including many reiterated invitations for the various events of *Oshōgatsu.* But we realize here, too, our Japanese acquaintances are violating a social taboo. Someone who has experienced a death in the family in the previous year does not normally join in *Oshōgatsu* celebrations beyond the immediate family. This is institutionalized in Japan through the ritual of the *nengajō,* the New Year's cards. The post office somehow collects and holds everybody's *nengajō* until New Year's morning, when they are all delivered to your home in a tidy bundle. It is exhilarating to run to the mailbox to find the cards and know that people all across the country are also reading dozens, even hundreds, of greetings from friends and loved ones. But if a relative has died in the previous year, you send a card edged in black, a wordless announcement and a way of excusing yourself from the festivities. *Oshōgatsu* is all about establishing good omens for the coming year. The bereaved stay home with their families and their sorrow, regrouping in privacy for the New Year. They skip the second and third days of *Oshōgatsu,* days reserved for visiting with business associates and friends. Privacy, again; but also a keen sense that one must be respectful of others' happiness. One does not inflict one's personal sadness on others at this happy time of the year. We know about this custom, and make a point of excusing ourselves from the traditional *Oshōgatsu* activities to which we have been invited by friends and colleagues.

≈≈≈

As New Year's Eve approaches, our close friends, Maryvonne and Ichirō Okamoto, insist that we spend *Oshōgatsu* with them.

"I'm French," Maryvonne argues on one of her food visits, this time bringing a wonderful bouillabaisse. "I don't give a shit" —she pronounces it "sheet"—"about Japanese customs or superstitions. It's New Year's Eve. You are spending the night with us."

"Maryvonne, we're just not up to it."

"Never mind!" she insists. "Ichirō and I and our friend Takashi will come to get you if you're not at our house by ten o'clock tonight. I mean it."

Maryvonne is five feet tall—but no one messes with Maryvonne. At ten o'clock, dreading having to spend the next three hours in celebration, we drag ourselves the block and a half to the Okamotos' house.

On television is the annual New Year's competition called the "Red and White." It's a rather inane exercise in nostalgia, where both past and current pop stars assemble to sing songs, the men against the women, the white team against the red, each song more lugubrious than the last. It's ostensibly a contest but no one cares who wins. What matters is how the songs evoke a torrent of *natsukashisa,* the bittersweet remembrance of things past, one of the most fundamental, powerful, and prized of all emotions for the Japanese.

When the last note of the "Red and White" dies out, when the points are tallied and the applause is over, it is midnight in Japan. The scene on the TV switches dramatically. A monk in yellow robes pulls a coarse hemp rope that is attached to a thick log that he swings back and forth with more and more force until it thunders against the striking seat of the huge cast-bronze temple bell. The sound is deep, melodious, impressive. At every temple in Japan, a bell booms forth the New Year 108 times, spelling, by one interpretation, the twelve months, twenty-four atmospheres, and seventy-two climates of the earth and, by another, casting out the 108 world worries of the year gone by.

Cameras are set up throughout the country so that, with each boom, the picture changes to show another temple, in another place. Urbanites in Tokyo or Osaka watch to see the bell of the local temple of their hometown, the place they left behind.

The Okamotos summon us outside to hear the ringing of the bell at Kabuto-yama Daishi. Often we have hiked up "Helmet Mountain" to visit the serenely beautiful temple there. Tonight the winter air is resonant with the somber sound of the bell at Kabuto-yama Daishi, 108 rings, repeated and distant like yearning.

It is a clear night with stars but too cold for gazing. We hurry back inside and huddle together under the *kotatsu,* the traditional heating device, the center of the Japanese home. Some people have argued that the divorce rate is rising in Japan because more efficient space heaters have replaced the *kotatsu,* a low square table containing a coiled heating element underneath and a long quilted skirt to keep in the warmth. Friends and families sit close together around the *kotatsu,* their legs extended beneath the thick quilt. The heat is so mellow and constant and close it seems to emanate from deep inside your body. Radiantly warm together

under the Okamotos' *kotatsu,* we now eat *toshi-koshi soba,* the delicious ritual New Year's "long life noodles," slurped from lacquer
bowls passed down for generations in Ichirō's family.

At one point, Ichirō excuses himself to bring *toshi-koshi soba*
to his mother. A *samisen* player and beloved teacher, she is ill in
her bed on the first floor of the house. Upstairs, we toast her with
the special New Year's sake, rice wine, and, on her behalf, slurp
the *soba* loud and long. Ichirō's father is impressed by how well
Ted and I have mastered this special slurping technique: it is
something we have practiced in the privacy of our own home.

It has been a pleasant evening. We have done our duty. We
have celebrated. But we are exhausted by this reentry into sociability. We want to go home.

"No!" Ichirō and Takashi say together. "It's time for the 'Red
and White,' American-style!"

Classical musicians by profession, Takashi was once Ichirō's
lute student. But both confess that they originally learned to play
guitar and did so from an adolescent adoration of Western pop
music. They realized earlier in the night that their favorite American songs are probably our favorites, too. Ted and Ichirō are the
same age. Takashi and I are each thirteen years younger ("And our
music is much better," Takashi jokes).

"Please sit for a few minutes," Ichirō leads us back to the
kotatsu. They tune up and I notice, not for the first time, the
beauty of Ichirō's delicate, seemingly boneless tapered fingers, and
remember reading once that most hand models in the United
States are Asian.

Like the New Year's Eve television show, Ichirō and Takashi
alternate songs. But these songs are all in English. Ichirō's English
is excellent. Takashi, who barely understands a word, *sings* English
perfectly. They both know not only every chorus, but every single
word to every verse of seemingly every American pop song of the
fifties and sixties. On and on they go, Ichirō playing every tacky
song from the early fifties of Ted's adolescence, Takashi countering
with the funniest songs from the sixties of mine.

"Snap! Snap!" Ichirō insists we snap our fingers as he plays

"Red Sails in the Sunset"; then Takashi urges us to help him with the motorcycle noises on "Leader of the Pack." Ichirō next launches into Jo Stafford's "Shrimp Boats Are a 'Comin'."

"Mashed Potato Time!" Takashi exclaims.

"They're playing your song," Ted teases, then repeats the story he's heard a hundred times of how I won a Mashed Potato contest in Chicago in 1962. Maryvonne insists that I teach her and Ichirō the dance while Takashi plays and sings. Pretty soon, we're all there, rotating our ankles back and forth like windshield wipers. Ichirō and Maryvonne ask me to help them coordinate their feet with the proper elbow action. Even Ted, who refuses to dance at home, is up and doing something that looks vaguely like the Mashed Potato.

By two A.M., Ichirō and Takashi still haven't exhausted the pop repertoire of our respective youths. Ichirō croons some silly song about a yellow-haired girl whose feet go "paddy whack," whatever that means. "One-eyed, One-horned, Flying Purple People Eater" is Takashi's rejoinder.

We all claim "Weemaway," both generations, even Maryvonne, whose birth year falls in between Ted's and mine, and who has only sung background vocals tonight. Maryvonne has the deep melancholy voice of a French cabaret singer. She has not sung a solo tonight, I know, because her Piaf style can coax tears from a stone—and this is not a time for tears. We've Tennessee Waltzed, Mashed Potatoed, and Twisted the night away. We are in a house in Nigawa, Japan, singing, dancing, and, miraculously, Ted and I are laughing.

In the morning, there is a knock on our front door. It is Mrs. Yanase, who refuses to enter past the *genkan* but who insists that we will come to her traditional New Year's dinner at one o'clock or her husband will send his whole football team to pull us out of our apartment and carry us to the Yanase house.

"But we know this is against Japanese tradition," we insist.

"It is also against tradition for me to be here now. Please be at my house by one."

A professor at a business college in Osaka, Mrs. Yanase is a superb cook who manages a household including two children, a father-in-law, and a seemingly endless array of international visitors. A nonconformist by disposition, she tools around Nigawa on her bicycle in her jeans, but her most disarming characteristic is the kindness that shines in her eyes. Mr. Yanase is a football coach, a psychologist, and a college president. He's also a character— hilariously funny in a wickedly self-deprecating fashion. His spare, wiry body twists and turns like a marionette's; his face is alive with expression. He is an athletic, graceful man, a powerhouse in the academic world, and such a cutup in any language that it is easy to forget how formidable an intellect he is. His lack of affectation is also very Japanese. The more prestige you have, the less you need to show it. Besides, since everyone knows who you are, your role is to play down your success.

At the Yanases, we enjoy the array of traditional foods of *Oshōgatsu* and one of the fellow guests kindly assumes the task of explaining to us the symbolism of everything we eat and drink. All the food is prepared in advance, we learn, so that even the cook has a three-day holiday from the usual domestic chores. Since Mrs. Yanase must run back and forth serving things during the whole of the meal, it hardly seems like a holiday for her, but she insists, laughing, that *symbolically* she's having a vacation.

The meal begins with water that was drawn at daybreak in order that we will have good health throughout the year, and then *ozōni*, a clear soup broth containing an assortment of unfamiliar vegetables, as well as *omochi*, a rice cake made from rice that has been pulverized with large wooden mallets to form a sticky paste. *Omochi* symbolizes long life. *Koi*, carp, is served both raw and pickled on *Oshōgatsu* because no fish is more able to surmount obstacles than the carp. The Japanese written character for chestnut is a pun on the word for *prowess* or *mastery*, so chestnuts, too, are part of the New Year's meal as are black peas (a pun on *robust),* and dried sea-weed *(happiness).* The root of the sacred lotus plant assures spirituality. No one explains what the *daikon* means, but the symbolism of this hard, white, foot-long radish is easy to guess.

All of these symbolic dishes are washed down with *otoso,* a form of sake flavored with Japanese pepper, yet another symbol of life, vitality, and energy: *genki,* as the Japanese say, the best thing a person can have.

Throughout the meal, food appears, plates are cleared, our tea and sake cups have been kept full. We haven't had to ask for or decide a thing today, as if our hosts realize that at a time like this mundane decisions become impossible. We can see the soft expression in their eyes, caring and solicitous, watchful. They are quick to change any conversation that might remind us of our sorrow and even quicker to respond to requests we don't even realize we're making. Once, my eyes start to fill with tears and I excuse myself and go to find the bathroom. Before I can get there, Mrs. Yanase is beside me, offering a tissue. Briefly, she holds my hand. Another time, when Ted looks sad and distracted, Mr. Yanase starts planning ahead to our next trip to Japan when, he suggests, he and Ted might think about team-teaching a course together. For a few minutes, Ted is removed from present pain and feels enthusiasm for the future. Silently, tacitly, they cushion us against loss and loneliness by showing us life again and friendship. They make us feel loved.

We are aware that our Japanese friends are handling this situation differently than would our American friends. Back home, our friends would have wanted to talk about it all; they would have coaxed us to express our feelings, urged us to cry. Such talk is not the usual way here when a friendship is as new as ours. Out of decorum or cultural differences or simply not-knowing-what-to-do, our Japanese friends have not really mentioned the deaths, although in some other unspoken sense the accident has been the point of every interaction. An overt reference to Ted's brother might cause us to weep and, in a formal situation, where some of the guests are strangers, this might embarrass us. These Japanese friends do not want to add to our pain in even the slightest way. We can feel this in their gestures, in the way they hover over us.

They are taking care of us today, and we feel grateful for their attention. For days, Ted and I have done nothing but think, talk, weep. Now, it is a relief to be able to put the pain aside for a few hours. In this situation, at this moment, we feel comforted by this generous form of Japanese empathy which does not require our self-revelation.

At the conclusion of the meal, Mr. Yanase has all of the guests toast Ted and me. Once again, there is no overt mention of the accident but that is what this has all been about. Mr. Yanase says he knows that this is simply the first of many *Oshōgatsu* celebrations that we will spend together. We all applaud and drink to reunion. And then all of the guests, new friends, wish us *genki* in this, the new year, the propitious Year of the Rooster. We thank them, and, in turn, toast them, too. All the omens look good.

As we walk home, we talk about how both groups of friends have adapted the Japanese New Year's rituals to our situation. It is a cliché, of course, that the Japanese are brilliant at adaptation, but this is amazing. They have taken traditional symbols and reassigned them to us, an American and a Canadian reeling from death and loss and separation. Adrift after the news of the accident, we have been buoyed by their kindness. In the midst of this terrible time, they have given us something precious.

We are beginning to understand that there's another level here, too, something beyond simple kindness. The Buddhist causality. *Because* of this terrible accident, we have been offered something precious. Nothing we do, nothing anyone else does, will ever change the fact of the accident. What can be changed is how we view its relationship to our life. Everyone experiences pain; everyone has a story to tell. How one understands the story is what's important. This is a matter of choice. We can see the accident as an indication that the universe is fundamentally unfair and we can wrap ourselves in this unfairness, armor ourselves against the world. Or we can see the way a community of people, all strangers less than a year ago, has come together in our time of pain. Community is essential; it is the one bulwark against inevitable grief and loss.

Jiko. Accident. The grief doesn't go away. But the reverse side has a reverse side, too. We will always be *gaijin,* foreigners, in Japan but we are aware that, because of a tragedy, we have been given entrance to a different aspect of Japanese life.

≈

In a small park near our house, we stop to watch a group of children flying a beautiful New Year's kite in the shape of a large bird, a hawk or perhaps an eagle. Other children are returning with their parents from Mondō-Yakujin, the Shinto shrine near our house. The first shrine visit of the year is a grand event, and girls wear brilliant silk kimonos embroidered in the exultant colors of youth: daffodil yellow, cherry red, pumpkin orange, sun gold. The young boys look dignified in little Western-style suits and, occasionally, in the handsome Japanese men's kimono and *haori,* the black silk overjacket decorated with a simple *mon,* the family crest. The pace is slow today, almost dreamy, not like any other time in Japan, and whole families promenade together, from toddlers to ancient grandmothers bent halfway to the ground. Something must have changed in our faces for, today, people not only gaze at us openly but they greet us, wishing us a happy New Year. In the park, one of the old ladies comes up behind me where I'm sitting on a bench and strokes my hair.

"Kitsune-iro," she says (Fox-colored).

We are reminded of the story our friend Sally tells about a trip that she and her husband, Toshi, took out in the countryside. There, an old grandmother pushed through a crowd in order to touch Sally's silky blond hair.

"What did she say?" Sally asked Toshi, smiling back at the beaming little woman.

"She says she wanted to touch the devil before she died," Toshi translated.

The incident reminds us that our friends in Japan are not necessarily "typical Japanese." But are they any less or more typical than the old woman in the park? More to the point, are *we* typical North Americans? Is *anyone?* If I can somehow "stand for" the American people when I am in Japan, why can't these Japanese acquaintances with their extraordinary kindness represent their country? It offends me, now, when I meet Americans who insist that our experience of Japan was somehow "exceptional." What, exactly, does that mean? We don't know anymore, if ever we did.

What we do know is that these Japanese, whom we have known less than a year, have repeatedly violated the rules of their own culture in order to make us as comfortable as possible during a tragic time in our lives. We wonder if, in reverse circumstances, we would be able to understand what it might take to help a Japanese visitor in America through a lonely and difficult time.

We spend the second day of the New Year, the day of reunion with friends, with Professor Sano, our department head, and his family. He too has insisted we come to his house. We tell him how grateful we are to our friends. We say that we are astonished that so many social customs and rules have been suspended on our behalf.

"Rules are very important to us," Professor Sano says, smiling. "But sometimes foreigners don't understand that we have rules for how to break the rules too."

This is a feature of Japanese culture we are beginning to understand, the flexibility behind seeming rigidity. In the past week, since the call came to the office in Kansai Women's University, the Japanese have been breaking rules right and left. They have leapt out of their own culture to try to understand ours—because we needed them, we needed their understanding in as fundamental a way as ever a person does.

I try to explain this to Professor Sano, working hard to keep back the tears. I tell him how grateful we are, how overcome with emotion for the kindness of all of our Japanese friends and acquaintances during this horrendous time.

Professor Sano proposes that we toast the New Year with sake, but Mrs. Sano whispers something to him in rapid Japanese, and he puts the sake pitcher away. Mrs. Sano has a quiet, moonlike beauty and a soft voice that makes you want to listen. She disappears for a moment, then returns with a lovely decanter. It's filled with *umeshu,* a sweet liquor that she made herself from *shōchū,* distilled spirits, and *ume,* summer plums.

The plums are so bitter by themselves, Mrs. Sano tells us in her gentle voice, that they are almost inedible. Only after the *ume* have aged a while in the alcohol do they become sweet.

"*Umeshu* comes like a breeze during the hottest days of summer," she murmurs.

It's the best *umeshu* we've ever tasted.

Together, we drink to the New Year.

9

GOING HOME

It's a land of blue-eyed giants. Men more than six feet tall stride by, arms swinging, voices booming. *Kowai*, I think (Frightening). *"Gaijin!"* I want to call out bravely, the way little children in the countryside used to exclaim when we passed by. A huge man leans against a column. I gaze at the diamonds of flesh flashing between the buttons of his shirt, the white curve of *hara* (belly) above his belt, luminous and round as bread dough. With his great *ashi-koshi* (legs and hips), he has the perfect body of a sumo wrestler. *Sugoi!* (Impressive!).

The airport in Vancouver, Canada, is filled with surprises. It is noisy with announcements, airplanes landing and taking off, people talking loudly in public about private things, as if no one else were near. *Hazukashii*, I think, hearing others and knowing they hear me. Ted's family is waiting just outside customs. Although his parents are divorced, both are here today, waiting for us, along with Ted's brother, Ken, and his sister, Karen. It is the missing brother we feel keenly as we come out to meet the rest of the family. We've had a month to adjust to the news of the accident, but now that we're in Canada the accident feels as if it happened yesterday. Ted's family is experiencing something of the same thing. How sad to have a reunion without Park and Sheena, someone is saying. It feels awkward to be voicing our most personal pain above the din of the airport.

Ted's dad thanks us again for arranging to finish up early in Japan. Ted nods some sort of reply, but I notice that he, too, has set his face like a mask.

"Are you okay?" his brother, Ken, asks.

"Probably jet lag," his sister, Karen, answers for him.

"We're so glad you're home," Ted's mother says, slipping between the two of us, an arm around my waist, Ted's.

≈

What became clear to us within moments after arriving in Canada was that we were experiencing the double shock of returning home after a family tragedy and of returning to our own culture again. The weeks were consumed by long talks as well as visits to lawyers, accountants, insurance adjusters, bankers, doctors. Both physically and psychologically, all three of the children were doing far better than anyone could have hoped. Our youngest nephew was recovered from his injuries, while our niece was actually working part-time, despite a jaw wired shut and elaborate bandages on one knee. Our oldest nephew was in the worst shape, with multiple arm and leg fractures that required microsurgery and for which the prognosis was still uncertain. We helped Bruce get settled into a room on the first floor of the house and then helped set up a room for Ted's father, who would be looking after the boys once our niece went back to college and we went home to Michigan. It was a busy time, filled with sadness, and we tried to be as useful as we could be while fumbling to learn our culture again.

I don't really remember when North America stopped seeming exotic to us. The process was gradual enough that we barely even noticed. At some point, it no longer seemed strange to sit in chairs, eat with silverware, sleep in beds, or shake hands instead of bowing (although we drew the line at wearing shoes inside the house). Our first full day in Vancouver, Ted and I decided to go for our daily shopping trip, on foot the way we always did, then discovered it was rough walking back nearly half a mile with groceries for the whole family. We were impressed by the cleverness of our niece, Karina, who came to help as we struggled up the walk with our bulging shopping bags and suggested that next time we might want to take the car. What an adventure! Driving on the right, down boulevards where cars stayed in their own lanes, the traffic signs all in English! The jaywalking pedestrians were a little scary (didn't they know it was *illegal* to cross anywhere but at a marked intersection or crosswalk?), but the parking lot at the supermarket was a source of wonder. It seemed to stretch for miles and was filled with all these funny, oversized American cars. In Japan in 1980, only *yakuza* (gangsters) drove big American cars. It took a second before we realized that, no, Vancouver was not overrun with Japanese mobsters.

In the supermarket, we felt grand wheeling around our shopping cart, overflowing with groceries enough for a whole week. We marveled at steaks one could actually afford to buy. We stared, appalled, at the dead chickens in the freezers—obviously dead and obviously chickens. In our Japanese market, the chicken breasts were decorously skinned and boned before they reached the consumer. (*"Kawaisō!"* KWU students exclaimed in sorrow and sympathy when the whole turkey came out of the oven at a Thanksgiving feast an American couple had painstakingly prepared.) And we were frankly baffled by the rows and rows of junk food arranged next to the rows and rows of diet products.

"This whole bag of oranges costs only three dollars!" Ted

noted, recalling the time he spent that much for a single orange in Japan. It seemed surreal, being able to buy fruits and vegetables at low prices out of season. But then a week or two went by, and we thought nothing of flipping a pineapple into our cart alongside the T-bone steak.

It took a little longer to get used to walking into a restaurant or store where the employees greeted us with silent indifference. In Japan, there was always a hearty greeting of welcome for every customer, Japanese or *gaijin.* We were frankly shocked—even outraged—the first time we discovered that half of the strawberries we'd bought were spoiled, and realized that during our entire year in Japan we had never once encountered either spoiled food or defective merchandise.

"It's kind of sad, isn't it?" Ted said one day at the grocery store as he watched me suspiciously turning over some tomatoes to make sure there weren't any bad spots. But, quickly, it stopped seeming sad at all. Soon enough we were back to believing that caveat emptor was the motto of every good shopper.

In time we even stopped marveling at the diversity of North America. Ken's wife is Filipina and their neighborhood in Vancouver is made up of people from Southeast Asia, India, Pakistan, Africa, the Caribbean, and various parts of the Mediterranean. The Japanese aren't as homogeneous as they claim to be, but there is nothing in Japan comparable to the multiethnicity of a big North American city. After a week or two, it was no longer even notable to be standing in a grocery line with a woman in a sari or a man in a Sikh's turban.

My body began to readjust to North American life. I no longer had to stoop to wash my hands in public restrooms. I didn't have a chronic backache any more from bending down to cut vegetables at the kitchen counter. I went a whole week without bruising a shin on a support under a restaurant table, located precisely where my long American legs needed to be. And never once did I find myself the center of collective stares, simply by virtue of being a *gaijin.*

≈≈

Back in Michigan in time to teach the spring quarter, I began to realize how much I had changed during my year in Japan and how much I was changing back again. Mark, my department head, had a party to welcome me home and to welcome the new exchange professor from Kansai Women's University. As I talked and laughed with some American friends and colleagues, I noticed the professor from Japan examining me, a puzzled expression on her face. Finally, I walked over to see what might be bothering her.

"I can't get over it," she said, turning to Mark. "This is the first time I've seen Cathy as an American."

She went on to explain that in America my posture, my gestures, even my personality were all different. She said she was trying to figure out just what the differences might be.

"Well, what is it, Cathy?" Mark asked, amused.

"Sumimasen, sensei. Eigo ga hanasemasen" (I'm sorry, professor, but I cannot speak English), I said in my most polite Japanese female manner, bowing deeply.

Mark burst out laughing. So did my other American friends, who were surprised to see me suddenly transformed into a stereotypical Japanese woman before their very eyes. We talked about how I could possibly have enjoyed myself in Japan, that silly bow, that modest little manner.

Even as I tried to explain that the surface wasn't reality but allowed a different reality, I felt a wrenching moment of self-awareness. My instant of self-parody was profoundly unsettling: imitating myself imitating a Japanese. What did it mean?

"Less is more!" I joked, repeating the modernist dicta learned, centuries ago, by the Japanese. "In Japan, I felt compact, self-contained."

A week later, at another party, Mark asked me to "act Japanese" again. He wanted others to see my party trick, my metamorphosis into a Japanese.

"Sumimasen, sensei. Eigo ga hanasemasen," I obliged, repeating the exact Japanese phrase, bowing low.

Again people laughed, but not like the first time. I knew why. Even as I spoke, I sounded American to myself. There was an edge in my voice that hadn't been there before. When I bowed, I felt as if I were taking up too much space, as if the respectful gesture had taken on a kind of aggressiveness. It wasn't convincing.

Unbowed, I became American again.

Here's what I thought about during the week between my first party bow and my second: I thought about how, from the moment we landed in Vancouver, I had been expanding, like Alice, into my bigger American self, my Italian-American gestures and personality returning. Yet I felt less free—dare I say less authentic?—than I felt in Japan. What was still more curious to me, it didn't really seem a contradiction that in Japan I had felt both freer *and* more constrained. Partly, of course, this was the freedom that comes from being a foreigner, knowing that you'll never know all the rules and that, as a foreigner, you don't have to conform to them all anyway.

Yet the paradox that expressed itself in my gestures, in the nonrational experience of body, was also a matter of having known what at least some of the boundaries were in Japan and having had a clearer sense of how individuals *must* act for a group—a community—to survive. Once you have the rules, almost anything is possible within those rules. Without them, everything can be suspect, difficult to judge. We saw it over and over again in Japan—and we missed it in America. Those uptight, workaholic, conforming Japanese (we all know the stereotype) were often willing to feel, even to express, emotions that, in the West, we routinely deny.

I think this is partly because, on some level, we all internalize the myths of our own culture. In America, that means that we like to think of ourselves as forthright (not like those inscrutable Japanese!), and we're often deceived about just how open we're being about our emotions. In some situations where a Japanese would remain silent, an American well might express emotions extravagantly. At the very same time, we might not even be aware of how hard we're working to deny other emotions that are both deeper and more personal. In some ways the silenced feelings are harder to decipher because we have no schooling in our own inscrutability. Think of any business meeting. Think of a PTA meeting. Think of the politician's rhetoric. "Let me be frank," someone says, a sure sign that speech is being shaped to ends other than open communication; the real urgencies (jealousy, fear, anger) operate somewhere below the surface. Because we think of ourselves as speaking freely, our speech is hard to decode. In Japan, everyone knows speech is a code, a convenience that helps the group to survive until it reaches consensus. Few Japanese would confuse the "frank" speech in a public situation with a statement of how one actually feels.

Every culture has its cherished myths. In the West (and especially in the United States), one of our fondest ideals is individualism. Our legal system, our social system, and our entire philosophical system are based on the notion of some stable, continuous self that must be protected against others—one's neighbors, one's enemies, even one's own state. In Japan, the individual/group duality operates differently and is more about how you *act* in private versus how you *act* in a group. The emphasis is on how individual behavior serves or hinders the society as a whole.

In America, we have evolved elaborate structures to protect individual rights, sometimes, as with the right to bear arms, at enormous social cost. Because John Lennon was shot the year we lived in Japan, people kept bringing up the matter of guns, not as a criticism but as a very real question. They simply could not understand how a country could allow private citizens to buy and carry handguns or automatic weapons, even bullets designed to penetrate bulletproof police vests. Where might it end? Could citizens have rights to bazookas, they wondered? to tanks? to atomic bombs?

American litigiousness also kept coming up. "Why do Americans sue so much, especially for things beyond human control?" they would ask. "Is it true that doctors don't want to deliver babies anymore, for fear of malpractice suits, and that most drug companies are refusing to make polio vaccines now?"

In America, the public is conceived of as individuals or as individual collectives or special interests—oil tycoons, truckers, auto workers, GM executives, teachers, bankers, CEOs, veterans, millionaires, the disabled, various ethnic or religious groups. In Japan, the group is idealized as homogeneous. The dark side of this myth of homogeneity is xenophobia and deeply ingrained racism, especially against other Asians. But for all the spurious emphasis on homogeneity, there are also moments when everyone becomes a *gaijin,* an outsider. This is partly because of the structure of Japanese discourse, the way that in certain situations little is made explicit. On occasion, everyone will feel adrift, unsure of exactly what's going on. What this means is that a lot of time is spent making sure there really is mutual agreement *(gōi),* even after consensus has ostensibly been achieved. It's important to make sure the group is operating well, that every member is in sync with every other member.

This is one reason for the endless discussions over tea or drinks before any real business can get done, not just in foreign trade negotiations but also among the Japanese themselves. In such a collectivity, it's not easy to move from outside to inside. We never seem to understand, in the West, just how long this takes, how human beings have more layers than any onion and sometimes you can peel and peel until there's nothing left and you still haven't found the center. Japanese spiritual and philosophical traditions emphasize illusiveness, and Japanese businessmen often build into their interactions the sense that to know another person is the second-hardest thing in the world—the hardest being to know oneself.

≈

Four or five months after I'd returned from Japan, I thought I was over all vestiges of culture shock, and never more so than the night I picked up my friends Esther and Jane in Detroit and drove with them cross-country to Esther's loft in New York City. We planned to stay in New York for a week before attending a conference together in Connecticut. It was a glorious night—driving fast, down one interstate after another, the windows rolled all the way down, the volume on the radio turned all the way up. We joked about the tofu and hot pepper sandwiches Jane had packed for us and kept our fingers crossed that my jalopy of a car would get us there safely. We laughed together at stories that Esther told about Israel, Jane about Poland, me about Japan. I felt glowingly free, ecstatically *American* again.

We pulled into New York well after midnight. It was a balmy night with a full moon and the city shone Picasso blue. I waited for the rush I always feel in this most American of cities, the nostalgic recollections of another time, when I was a teenager in the Village in the sixties, and New York was magic.

We drove past guys in gang colors, shouting obscenities, throwing bottles, hanging out. Esther made sure all four doors were locked and insisted we roll up the windows. Prostitutes, junkies, homeless people in every doorway. Instead of magic, I felt stomach-clenching fear. I've negotiated cities all my life, sometimes in pretty scary circumstances. Never before had I felt so threatened and vulnerable, like a rube up from the farm for the first time.

Japan again. It was still with me. A year there and I'd lost my skills for surviving in urban America. Japan has not abandoned its cities the way we have over the past twenty years. Strict laws against both drugs and guns make the Japanese urban landscape look and feel different than the American. In Osaka or Tokyo I'd gotten used to enjoying urban pleasures without worrying about crime, without feeling the constant presence of the hopelessly and desperately poor. None of this was conscious for me until I returned to America and realized that I no longer remembered how to keep track of everything happening around me. I'd lost that sixth sense that tells you (even before there are rational clues) it's time to cross to the other side of this street or to not go down that one. I hadn't used it for a year and it had atrophied. Before going to Japan, I had deplored what was happening to U.S. cities, but actually experiencing an alternative made the pressing poverty and the implicit violence of American urban life intolerable.

It would be wrong to imply that there is no poverty in Japan (even though some Japanese insist there isn't). Visit Kamagasaki in Osaka, inhabited by over twenty thousand day laborers and migrant workers, and you'll find homelessness, chronic unemployment, despair. Kamagasaki, or its smaller equivalents in other industrial cities, is as shameful to Japan's self-image as a middle-class state as homeless people and decayed inner cities are to the American ideals of equality and freedom of opportunity. But real poverty in Japan is less extensive than in America, about one-fifth of ours, if official statistics are reliable.

Recently, two young Japanese friends, both graduates of Tokyo University (the equivalent of Harvard, Yale, and Oxford all rolled into one), visited us on their way back to Japan after two years' residence in New York. They expressed amazement at the low cost of theatre, opera, and symphony tickets, relative to Japan. But they were also shocked to see how "ordinary" people live in a U.S. city. Japanese cities are typically unattractive, but they work. There are basic services, including good public transportation, sanitation, a sound infrastructure. America's inefficient, noisy, and dangerous public transportation was unfathomable to these Japanese visitors, as was the degree of urban poverty and filth. But worst of all was the violence.

"The United States is a great place to live," one of them observed, "so long as you are very, very rich."

By the winter of 1982, we were missing Japan unbearably. In the two years since we'd left, we had come to see it as more idyllic than we had when we lived there. We even began to consider the possibility of moving there permanently. At the time, Ted and I were teaching in two different states, Michigan and Illinois. Every Friday one of us would board the train to join the other, and then on Sunday there would be another seven-hour trip back again. If we moved to Japan, we could teach in the same area and live together in the same apartment.

We had a professional convention in San Francisco that December. I was starting a semester's sabbatical leave and Ted's teaching didn't begin again until February, so we decided to just keep going west, to head back to Japan for five weeks. We made arrangements to give several talks as a way of paying some of our expenses. Our old apartment, conveniently near the train station, was vacant, and Kansai Women's University very kindly let us rent it.

As we rode in the rainy night from Osaka International Airport to Maison Shōwa, our apartment building in Nigawa, we felt overwhelmed by *natsukashisa*. We were here, in Japan again. We eagerly opened the door to our apartment.

It was *small*. In memory, it had been perfect, compact and efficient. Now that there was a possibility that this living arrangement might be permanent, it felt like living in a RV.

Our friends were still wonderful. The country and the culture were still much the same, but our Japanese was even worse than when we left two years earlier, and the charm of struggling through dictionaries to complete the simplest transaction had worn off. And it was cold. Houses and apartments in Japan aren't centrally heated; our bathroom had no heat at all. After our overheated apartment buildings in America, there were days that winter in Japan when I was sure I would never be warm again. I bought thick long underwear and quilted, padded clothes and slippers. Swaddled, I still shivered.

Then the pipes froze and we had no water, hot or cold. A *gaijin* neighbor, a professor renting one of the other university apartments, said that this had happened each of the two winters he'd been there. Pipes are outside the buildings to minimize damage in case of an earthquake. Officially, they don't freeze, but in fact they regularly do. For three or four days there was no water other than from an outside tap on the ground floor. Every flush meant carrying a bucket of water up three flights of stairs. And once more my shins were bruised from supports under too-low tables at restaurants.

It wasn't that we didn't love being back in Japan. It was just that we were seeing it differently than we had on our first visit. This time we were watching carefully since Japan was not just a temporary diversion, but a possible future. We kept noticing things we found difficult or troubling, emblematic of what life might be were we to live there permanently.

One of our Japanese friends who taught at a large university nearby complained that half his department wasn't speaking to the other half. Since the university's business was conducted by consensus, this meant that they were having endless meetings, several times a week, until late into the evening, with nothing ever being resolved, as each side waited for the other to give in. So much for consensus and group consciousness! With the department divided into two silently warring camps, the meetings wore on and on.

"I was so angry and frustrated," he confided to us one afternoon, "that I nearly expressed my emotion!"

His statement, as much as anything, made us realize how much this country might start to feel like a fishbowl were we to live here permanently.

Another acquaintance, someone we'd not heard from since our last visit, apologized for not answering our annual letters. She said her life was very busy now that her in-laws were living with her. We were surprised to hear that her husband's parents had moved in. This was something she had earlier promised to resist to her last breath.

"I found out that my husband went on a sex tour," she said, by way of explanation. "He told me it was business but it was a sex trip to the Philippines. For two weeks. So I invited his parents to come live with us. They put their house up for sale and moved in by the time he got back."

"But, Sumi-san, I thought you didn't like his parents?"

"I hate them. But he hates them even more."

I could not take pleasure in Sumi-san's purported "triumph" over her unfaithful husband. I was reminded of the masochistic revenge ending in one of Fumiko Enchi's novels, where a long-suffering wife insists she doesn't want a proper burial. After the wife dies, her last wish becomes known and her husband faces public humiliation. Finally he is forced to recognize how badly he had treated his wife. There is a modicum of justice in his final public reckoning, but, in practical terms, what good did his eventual humiliation do her? It made me sad to think how much my friend Sumi-san's actions would cost her over the next years and even sadder to think of the self-effacing logic motivating her actions.

Mostly we saw, again and again, just how incompetent we were at things Japanese. Nowhere were we more incompetent than at what should have been a sad and solemn occasion, the funeral of Ichirō's mother.

On our way home from the train station after a two-day trip to Tokyo, where we each gave talks, we passed the Okamotos' house and saw the mourning banners draped over the entry along with the black-and-white lanterns that signal a death in the family. I immediately called Maryvonne and she confirmed that Ichirō's mother had just died. She said she couldn't talk now, the house was filled with relatives and there were still a million things to do, but she knew Ichirō would appreciate it if we attended the funeral the next day, held, as is traditional, at the house.

We wanted to be supportive and sensitive, just as Ichirō and Maryvonne had been after the death of Ted's brother, but we didn't have the slightest idea about proper comportment at a Buddhist funeral. I called Professor Sano, our former department head, and asked his advice. I told him there were problems—for example, we didn't have anything with us that even approximated the formal mourning clothes worn by the people we'd seen entering the Okamoto house.

"It is your spirit that counts," Professor Sano insisted. "Please don't worry about your clothes. Your friends will understand."

I also remembered that Japanese give money at a funeral but had no idea how much was appropriate or just how the gift should be handled.

"You're a foreigner," Professor Sano tried to reassure me. "No one expects you to know these customs. Besides, it will be easy. You'll be in a long line with the other mourners. Just follow along and do what everyone else does. It will only take a minute or two, but your friends will be grateful that you came to pay your respects."

We ransacked our suitcases for the most restrained clothes we had, a dark blazer for Ted, a dark skirt and white blouse for me. Every other man at the funeral was in a full black suit with a black tie. The women wore severe black dresses or full-length black kimono. The pervasive smell of mothballs made us aware that these were special clothes, tucked away in drawers except on occasions such as this. We had brought a number of ten-thousand-yen bills (approximately seventy dollars each), intending to give what we saw others giving, but it turned out that our money wasn't properly dressed either. All around us people held special white envelopes folded in a complicated *origami* style and tied with an elaborate black ribbon, their names on the envelopes in fancy calligraphy. They formally presented the gift, then wrote their name and address in a special book so that the family of the deceased could send them something later. We should have guessed as much. In Japan, every present gets a return present.

We backed out of the gift line and tried to disappear into the line of mourners waiting outside the house. Suddenly a middle-aged Japanese woman came rushing toward us and grabbed our arms. "This way! This way!" she urged in Japanese, dragging Ted and me inside.

The house had been transformed. A large altar was set up in what had been the father and mother's living room. There was an urn, holding the ashes, a memorial tablet, and presiding over all a black-and-white photograph of Mrs. Okamoto. There was a smile on her face and a sympathetic expression in her eyes, as if she regretted the sorrow she was causing her family and her friends.

"Here!" the woman said definitively in Japanese, pointing to where we should kneel in a small alcove near the back of the room.

"I thought Professor Sano said we'd just have to go through a line?" Ted whispered.

"Maybe this is a different Buddhist sect?" I suggested, trying not to panic. The space was so cramped that there was no alternative but to kneel in the formal *seiza* posture, our legs tucked under us, a position that Ted can't maintain for very long. Ted gently touched the paper doors that formed the walls of the alcove, and we both held our breath as they started to wobble. These were the *fusuma* that normally created rooms in the house, now leaned here, out of the way. One wrong move, we realized with horror, and the doors could come tumbling down.

There were maybe twenty or twenty-five people kneeling around the altar. Across the room, our friends Ichirō and Maryvonne knelt beside Ichirō's father. They looked pale and drawn as one person after another came before them, presumably paying their respects before the service began. An elderly woman came and knelt in front of Maryvonne and bowed so low that her forehead seemed to touch the tatami. When she righted herself, she said something that left Maryvonne visibly moved. I watched my irrepressible friend return the same deep bow, and then the two women, from such different generations and cultures, looked long at one another, sharing a silence intimate and deep. I felt like an intruder. We had met Ichirō's mother only once. Her quiet dignity and solicitousness, despite her illness, impressed us. It was easy to understand why people grieved over this woman's loss— relatives, friends, and the students whom she had taught to play *samisen*. I felt as if I had no right to be in this room with people who had loved her. My inappropriate clothes, my rumpled yen, even the wobbly *fusuma* all seemed to signal how out of place I was.

In impressive robes, the *jūshoku* (head priest) entered and took his place before the altar. We were kneeling directly behind him, so we couldn't see what he was doing, but the chanting and the incense and the photograph of Mrs. Okamoto were overpowering. By the end of the priest's prayers, everyone in the room was weeping openly, sobs sustained and heart-wrenching, *morai-naki,* mingled tears of sympathy, one of the few times in Japanese society where a public display of feeling is permissible.

After the priest stopped chanting, others in the room approached the altar one by one, knelt, bowed respects to the family, contemplated the memorial tablet, then did something with incense powder. From where I was kneeling, all I could see was a rippling of shoulders, a bowed head, movement of hands from one side to the other.

I knew that soon it would be our turn to go to the altar and asked Ted if he could tell what they were doing.

"No, not really," he whispered, sounding every bit as disconsolate as I was feeling.

I kept thinking: today is the antithesis of the wordless solemnity I found in those sacred places, Mount Kōya and Kudakajima. No transport, today, into a realm beyond mere words. Not at all. If the Buddhist goal is transcendence of the nightmare cycles of self-consciousness and self-absorption, then this, for me, must be what Buddhists call hell.

I was summoned first. I bowed before the altar, did something or other with the incense, hoping the contrite expression on my face would convey to Ichirō and Maryvonne that I didn't intend to be disrespectful, even sacrilegious. As I slunk back to the alcove, I noticed half-suppressed smiles on the tear-stained faces of several of the mourners. There were more smiles and knowing nods as Ted slowly and painfully unbent himself from his kneeling position, did something self-conscious and quick at the altar, and limped back to our alcove.

"*Gomen nasai!*" the middle-aged woman in the kimono was there again, now apologizing to us loudly in Japanese. "Your knees must be hurting," she was saying, in a full voice, not even a decorous whisper. *"Gaijin* can't kneel such a long time, *gomen nasai."*

Again she imperiously took us in hand and conducted us into a different room, this one filled with cigarette smoke and very old men in Western-style armchairs. They were visibly shocked to see us, and the woman explained something in rapid Japanese. I caught the word *shimai* (sister), but nothing else.

"Good afternoon. We happy to meet you at such sad time," one of the elderly men said in painstaking English. These men were all of Ichirō's father's generation, and I realized that, like him, they probably had learned some English as young men.

"Gomen nasai," I said, bowing deeply. *"Nihongo ga hanasemasen"* (I'm very sorry, but we do not speak any Japanese).

A look of relief came over their faces. They again bowed to us, smiling now, and immediately went back to telling one another in Japanese about recent deaths, new illnesses, what hurt and where and what this or that *kampō* (Chinese medicine) doctor recommended.

"Do you think we can just leave?" Ted asked.

"Let's," I agreed.

After bowing good-bye to the old men, we tried to quietly slip out of the sitting room and away from the funeral. Our friend Ichirō met us just as we were leaving. We bowed deeply, telling him how sorry we were about his mother. He thanked us, and then started to smile. He said he kept wondering why we were at the service for the immediate family, then ran into his bossy relative and learned that she had decided I looked exactly like Maryvonne and so must be her sister, here for the funeral (even though Maryvonne doesn't have a sister).

"Nothing went right—and we're really sorry, Ichirō," Ted said humbly. "We didn't mean to be disrespectful—we wanted to show our sympathy but—"

Ichirō shook Ted's hand again, in both of his. "My friends," he joked seriously, his eyes glistening, "anyone willing to embarrass themselves for a friend is a friend forever."

We spent the rest of our month doing what we could for Maryvonne and Ichirō. Out of friendship, of course, but also out of some vague need to make up for not having known how to comport ourselves at the funeral. We brought them meals as they had previously done for us. We had Ichirō's father to dinner a few times. We had a small surprise party for Maryvonne's birthday. But the image of our intrusion into that solemn funeral wouldn't go away. The offense in and of itself wasn't so bad, we realized, but it became emblematic of all the things that we didn't know about Japan.

Gradually, we acknowledged that we could not live there permanently. There was, first, the language barrier. With effort and time, we could get over that. But we'd never get over being *gaijin,* the sense of always being different. We also weren't sure about how we could lead our professional lives in Japan. Ted's field is Canadian literature, mine American studies. How would we pursue our research in Japan? I had loved the experience of teaching Oral English for Non-Majors for a year. Would it continue to fascinate for a lifetime? It also bothered me that living in Japan would have been too *easy,* the standards automatically lower because we weren't Japanese and couldn't know any better. As with the funeral, one could not be expected to get things right, and even the worst mistakes did not really matter. It was a "win-win" proposition that made me feel like a loser.

Even minor aspects of Japan that had seemed charming on the first visit—the little fastidious rituals like folding an umbrella or eating soup just right—began to feel oppressive when I thought about living the rest of my life like that. Nor did I want to be the kind of *gaijin* English teacher who endures Japan ten months of the year, then makes the break for freedom back home each summer. I didn't want to turn into a *gaijin-gaijin.*

These personal responses to Japan resonated with larger social and political discomforts that we had felt on our first visit—over the role of women, the sadness of the schoolchildren and the businessmen, the racism and xenophobia. On the plane back to America once more, I found myself moved to tears. We had returned to Japan for a month because we missed the country desperately. We had even contemplated living there permanently. Now we were leaving Japan behind and, with it, a passion. I no longer wanted to fit into this other culture, to master every rule, every detail. On the contrary, I was excited to be returning to the vigor, vitality, and nonconformity of American life.

When our plane landed at O'Hare Airport outside Chicago, I didn't experience anything like the culture shock that I had after the first time I came home, in 1981. But this second return to America, in January of 1983, brought its own form of culture shock. Japan was no longer an option for us, we had admitted that. Now I also had to admit that America didn't look as freewheeling and expansive as I had imagined it from the perspective of Japan.

First, I was shocked to notice how little nonconformity there really was in the United States. Walking around the small liberal arts college where Ted taught, I was alarmed that American college students looked every bit as alike, in their dress and hair and style, as did the Japanese. Commuting into Chicago to work at a research library on the book I was writing during my sabbatical, I was struck by how the American businessmen could have been *sarariiman,* there was so little variation, one man to the next.

And in Chicago there were even more bodies sleeping in the doorways. Politicians in 1983 kept saying America was more prosperous than ever before, but it didn't look or feel that way. A new term was invented to describe life in the Reagan eighties, "cocooning": wrapped up in your comfortable material life, just you and your family, you could forget the rest of the world ever existed.

During my lunch hours, I leave Newberry Library on the Near North Side of Chicago. I've worked out a small ritual for my post-Japanese American life. I stop at a local bakery, buy something, then wander through an area of the city filled with art galleries and bookshops. This simple pleasure, eating a croissant in the street, reminds me of one of the small things I cannot do in Japan.

On my noon walks, I like to visit a store that specializes in Oriental prints and books. For the last week, they've had a beautiful edition of Hokusai's *Thirty-Six Views of Mount Fuji* on display in the window. The book is open to my favorite print, the well-known "Great Wave off Kanagawa." In the foreground is an enormous wave that threatens to capsize three fishing boats. In the boats are little heads, each one as fragile as an egg. Each human face is paralyzed by fear, eyes riveted on the sea. No one in the boats has the luxury of seeing the big picture, of viewing Fuji majestic in the distance.

After I've been to this bookstore, I walk back to the library down a certain street where I know, every day, a man will be crouching on the corner, across from Treasure Island, a swank Chicago food store. The man's hair is long, uncombed. He's about my age, and sometimes I think I recognize him from long ago, maybe from when I was a teenager singing in Chicago, maybe not. He gives no sign of recognizing me. He never bothers anybody. He doesn't even panhandle. He just crouches on the corner at lunchtime and occasionally bays, like a wolf or coyote. People coming out of the store sometimes offer him food—an apple, a loaf of bread, a sandwich, a bottle of wine. He asks for nothing. Today, I bought a second croissant so I could leave it as I passed, placing the bag near him, avoiding eye contact, walking fast.

When I reach the library, I find myself so gripped by emotion that I have to stop and sit on one of the steps, draw a breath from down deep, restore calm. It takes a while before I can identify what I'm feeling. It's homesickness. But for which home? Japan? Or the "America" I had constructed from the other side of the Pacific?

Home. The word means something different than it used to.

10

SEA OF
JAPAN, OKI,
1987

The first thing you see when you come into my house is a green glass bowl filled with green and blue glass balls. These are floats, blown from bottle glass, and used to hold up fishing nets. I found them on Oki, a cluster of islands between Japan and Korea, where I spent a summer with my friends Maryvonne and Ichirō and their music group, the Danceries.

Each day around 10:00 A.M., the captain, a local fisherman, would pick us up at the dock and take us in his boat to a new beach, usually deserted, each one more spectacular than the last. We spent our mornings snorkeling, spearfishing, and diving. We stopped for a lunch of rice balls and whatever fish or squiggly raw things we had caught that morning. In the afternoons the rest of the group would dive and fish again, but I would set off alone, with my inflatable plastic life preserver, looking for new garbage beaches, *gomi hama,* we called them, places where the currents had washed up the sea's detritus—driftwood, bleach bottles, a zori or two, broken oars, fish skeletons, fishing nets. Japanese nets are held up by plastic floats now. But the Korean nets still use glass balls. My friends kidded me that I was in one of the most beautiful places on earth and I somehow managed to spend my afternoons pawing through garbage. But there was a payoff. Amidst all of that rubbish, suddenly there would be a glass ball, gleaming and pristine like the ocean itself.

I became obsessed. If a day went by without my finding a glass ball, it was a tragedy. Once I was almost killed because I was so determined to get to a new garbage beach that I overlooked all the signs of treacherous waters. I was trapped for a good half hour in a current that threatened to dash me against barnacle-covered rocks. On another day the captain almost bottomed out his boat trying to get into a cove that looked perfect for glass balls. He too was caught up in my quest. He'd never thought of them as anything special before—if you lived on Oki you saw the glass balls often enough to think of them as garbage—but suddenly he was inspired by it, the ritual.

My enthusiasm was contagious. Every evening a few kids would wait at the dock for our boat to come in. Each night another of them received a glass ball from the *gaijin* lady. They would wave to me on the street or join me in my morning walks or follow me to the post office where I often mailed small packages of the glass balls home to friends in America. The kids invented a nickname for me, *"Bin-Dama Onēsan,"* Glass Ball Elder Sister.

Oki was a good place to escape from death.

≋

I went to Oki during the summer of my third stay in Japan, in 1987. Ted had recently been hired at Michigan State University, which made him eligible for the faculty exchange program between MSU and Kansai Women's University. Charles had just graduated from college and was living in Japan for a year before going on to graduate school. His fiancée, Susan, had joined him, and they were renting a traditional Japanese house in the center of Kyoto, an hour and a half from our old apartment in Nigawa. It promised to be perfect.

I didn't want to go. In rapid succession, three of my friends had died, one suddenly in her sleep from a stroke, two after lingering illnesses, cancer and AIDS. A trip to Japan seemed sacrilegious. What right had I to be happy again after others had died? My father's mother, then in her nineties, was also ill. Always loving, generous, and kind, she was my "good grandmother," as I called her when I was a child (not like the violent other one), and remained the woman who meant the most to me. I couldn't face the fact that she might die during the coming year and I would not be there.

For the last few years, no one had applied for the exchange. If Ted didn't go this year, the program would probably be canceled. It might be our last chance. Reluctantly, I agreed to go. Ted made most of the arrangements, did the packing, and got us both to Japan, where, he insisted, I could grieve for my friends as well as anywhere. If it turned out that my grandmother really was dying, I could fly back to be with her.

That didn't console me. Neither did the cherry blossoms, which were in full bloom when we arrived. They were beautiful but, falling, they whispered death. We walked hours and hours along tree-lined streets and riverbanks. We saw old friends. We taught our classes. We spent weekends with Charles and Susan. I felt distant, remote, not really in Japan or America but in some other place, buried inside my grief. Ted was right. I could mourn in Japan as well as at home, and I was mourning.

As summer approached, Maryvonne and Ichirō invited us to join them on Oki. They would be there for six weeks, and we could stay as little or long as we wished. Oki would be a good diversion.

A few nights before we were to leave, Ted admitted that he wasn't looking forward to the trip at all. He can't swim and gets seasick, and Maryvonne had said several times that there was nothing to do on Oki but take a boat each day to some new beach and then snorkel or spearfish or go diving. He had visions of himself cooped up in an uncomfortable hotel room while the rest of us enjoyed the sea. He also suspected that we would all keep trying to come up with something fun for him to do, something he probably wouldn't find fun at all. He said he'd be much happier staying in our air-conditioned apartment in Nigawa working on the book that was due at the publisher's in September than resisting the blandishments of beaches and beachcombers.

"Besides," he said softly, "I think you need some time alone."

On the ferry that took us from the main island in the Okinoshima chain to the small one that would be our home for the next few weeks, Maryvonne mentioned the glass balls. She said the previous year the Danceries had come to Oki with a Swiss family. The wife spent her days diving with the rest of the Danceries. The husband and his daughter spent their days walking all over the island, peering down the cliffsides in search of new beaches, then climbing down the cliffs, searching the beaches for glass balls, then climbing all the way back up again.

"Last year they found 114 glass balls," she said.

"Glass fishing balls?" I could hardly believe my ears. "The green kind, made of bottle glass?"

I remembered seeing them first as a child. My father and one of his friends, both navy men, had brought some back from the Pacific at the end of World War II. The balls had disappeared years ago, but sometimes I came across others in antique stores or in seafood restaurants. I was fascinated by their shimmering beauty, the way you looked at them and felt as if you were looking into the ocean.

I found seven glass balls on our first full day in Oki. It was too hot to walk along the coast and then climb down to the beaches, so my method was to put on my snorkel and my flippers, get my plastic life preserver, and then swim by myself to a place that looked like it might have glass balls. For several hours each afternoon, it was just me out there with the ocean. Not a person, not a boat, not a sign of humanity. It gave me lots of time to be alone, to appreciate again what it meant to be a living body in nature. At the end of the afternoon, I couldn't remember having had a single thought. That summer I felt like a giant sensorium, letting the waves play against my body, marveling at the beauty of the coral reefs below, hearing the sound of the waves crashing against the shore, smelling the salt air.

About two weeks after we came to Oki, I swam alone past the coral reef, past the drop-off at the base of a cliff where the water turned abruptly from Singer Sargent turquoise to bruise blue. Looking down through my mask at the ocean floor, I saw an old motorcycle, probably from the fifties. It was covered in barnacles, silently grotesque, riderless beneath the waves, almost a thing of beauty.

One day the captain said that he wouldn't be able to take us in his boat until noon or one o'clock for the next week or so because he had contracted to do some cargo work in the mornings. We thought about ways to get out to the other islands and beaches by public transportation—ferries, the rickety bus on the main island—then decided we'd rather wait until early afternoon and go with the captain whenever he was ready.

"Let's go out for lunch today!" Ichirō joked.

"Out," on our island, meant one of two tiny snack bars. One we'd already tried—it specialized in curried rice and pizza toast. The other was named "Big Ben." On the outside it looked almost like an English pub, with a flower box filled with zinnias and bright marigolds, and a sign painted with a picture of the famous London clock.

We loved Big Ben immediately. The inside continued the English motifs, with flags and posters of famous British sites—

Balmoral, Buckingham Palace—and lots of clocks of every description. Like most Japanese snack bars, this one was run by a woman. She told us her name was Akiko Suzuki and, no, she'd never been to England, but hoped to go sometime. She did all of the cooking on a small grill and stove set behind the bar. She also did the waitressing, hostessing, and everything else for the small restaurant, which had maybe eight or ten bar stools and three tables set in a row against the wall. The other room at Ben was a six-mat tatami room off to the side. A small girl played quietly in the room with her dolls. Possibly Suzuki-san and her daughter slept there at night. Possibly they lived somewhere else.

Suzuki-san greeted everyone with a beaming, open face, her eyes soft and alive. She handled the full noon crowd like a ballet dancer, taking orders, making jokes, cooking the simple meals, pouring drinks, all with perfect composure and grace.

"This is *our* place," Maryvonne said definitively. We had added a new ritual to our easy Oki life, lunchtime at Ben.

"Look, Cathy-san!" Ichirō pointed. Suspended in a net above a tiny sink in the hallway that led to the bathrooms was an enormous, crystal-clear glass ball.

When Suzuki-san came over, I asked about the ball. She told me how she found it when she moved here. It was in an abandoned storehouse behind the restaurant. She said there had once been a glassworks on the island, maybe a hundred years ago, and this was one of the balls that had actually been made right here, on Oki. Isn't it beautiful? she asked us. Had we ever seen a clear one before? Did we notice how the light got caught inside and just glowed there?

"Oh, no! Another one!" Maryvonne joked in English, and then in Japanese she explained to Suzuki-san in high-comic terms that she had started calling me *Gomi Hama Obasan,* the Garbage Beach Matron, because I spent every afternoon scouring these disgusting places for glass balls.

"Good taste!" Suzuki-san joked in Japanese, then went off to retrieve a beer for someone at the bar.

Big Ben became our Oki haunt. We went almost every day.

I gave Suzuki-san's daughter one of the apple-size glass balls I found and told her it was a magic one. I had found it in a tree, so far off the ground that I had to climb up the tree to reach it. A glass ball that knew how to fly! I told her how other kids on the island would wait for our boat in the evening and I would show them the day's glass balls and tell stories about how I found them. I invited her to come sometime. Or maybe she would visit us at our *shukusha,* the austere government-run inn where we stayed, to see all the balls I had found. She smiled shyly. She never came.

During my first year in Japan, 1980, I met an American woman writing a dissertation on geisha. In 1983, on my second visit, I met another young American woman doing an oral history compiled from conversations with *mama-san,* the women who run the snack-bars and other small night spots of Japan. Both were fascinated by the role of women in the Japanese demimonde. So many Western men have written about the open, promiscuous, male pleasures of the Floating World without noting the life—the *sociology*—of the tough, capable women who run so many of the establishments in this world. What's in it for the women? these Western students of feminism needed to know. I wondered too.

The night I went with Professor Itō through the entertainment district in Osaka I had asked him about one of the *mama-san* I had just met, joking that her IQ must be up there somewhere with Einstein's. He laughed and told me she was the illegitimate daughter of a well-known corporate executive. Her mother had been the man's mistress for decades, and, when the daughter came of age, the executive set her up in business. Her snack bar was roughly equivalent to a trust fund. She had married once, in her twenties, decided she didn't like it, and now lived as an independent woman, taking lovers, he said with a strange smile, "when she chooses, but mostly she chooses not to." His comment didn't surprise me. The woman was lively, even bawdy, but there was something reserved, steely, behind her levity. Professor Itō added that this *mama-san* had recently made a killing on the Nikkei, the Japanese stock market, and her customers were always bugging her for tips.

I had also met Nomura-san, who had retired from the Takarazuka Revue and now operated a small restaurant near our apartment. Nomura-san was wry and aloof, even when acting friendly toward her customers. She was tough, like the *mama-san* I met in Osaka. Nothing at all like Suzuki-san, with her infectious, charming, high girl laugh.

The members of Danceries, like most musicians, are night people. If they awaken by ten in the morning, it's early. When the captain started coming after noon, they were not unhappy. Nor was I. I usually crept from my room, had breakfast in the dining room with Ichirō, the only other morning person in the bunch, then walked around the island by myself.

Sometimes on these early morning walks I find Suzuki-san preparing Big Ben for the day—sweeping and washing the front stoop, the sidewalk, the street in front of her snack bar. One morning she's on a step-ladder, cleaning the windows with a squeegee; another day she's on her knees scrubbing the floor, the door thrown open to sea breezes. These are morning rituals repeated by every merchant in Japan. Each time we meet, Suzuki-san interrupts her routine to talk to me. If she's at a stopping place, she invites me inside Ben for coffee.

Suzuki-san doesn't speak a word of English. Without a translator, our conversation is limited to my Japanese, which is even worse now than on my previous trips to Japan. I spend a lot of time thumbing through the pages of my pocket-size bilingual dictionary and racking my brain for synonyms that might be in the little book. We supplement our simple vocabulary with the generous language of pantomime, exaggerated facial expressions, theatrical gestures, philosophical shrugs or smiles.

Suzuki-san asks where I'm from. When I say Chicago, she goes, "Rat-a-tat-tat," a machine-gun noise and a gesture like a mobster, something I've seen a hundred times in Japan. Then she apologizes, aware that she has insulted my hometown.

I laugh and tell her not to worry, I'm not insulted at all. Everyone still thinks Chicago is run by Al Capone. I ask where she is from.

"Kyushu," she says, southwestern Japan. "I'm a *gaijin* here too," she smiles.

I've never been to Kyushu, I tell her, but would love to go. It looks so lovely in the travel books.

"It is," she says quietly. "And warm. Not like here."

It's hard to remember that Oki is formidable in wintertime. The calm summer seas turn stormy. Sometimes the sea is so rough that the islands are cut off from the mainland for weeks at a time. It's why two emperors were exiled here centuries ago. *Okinoshima:* the name means hidden islands, divided, isolated from society. The islands are remote enough that they still aren't on the tourist maps. They've remained relatively undeveloped. It's what we find so seductive about Oki but we also know the other story—the poverty, the way the young people must leave here to find work on the mainland. We have heard stories about how sometimes in the stormy season the boats that bring fuel to the island stop running. You can go a week or more without power, without communication with the outside world, without food or supplies coming in, and with no way to leave the island in case of a medical emergency. Paradise has its other side.

"What's your *toshi?*" Suzuki-san asks. A *toshi* is one's birth sign according to the twelve-year cycles in the East Asian zodiac. If you say your sign, you are essentially telling how old you are. One reason it's useful to know this is that the forms of address in Japanese differ depending on age. I tell Suzuki-san that I'm an ox, *ushi.* Suzuki-san is a horse, *uma.* Two stubborn women, she jokes. She is five years younger than I am, thirty-two. She is entering her *yakudoshi,* the "bad luck year," traditionally the worst year in a woman's life. Neither of us comments on this. Instead we each express surprise at how young the other looks. And then vocabulary fails. Or courtesy. I find myself caught up in the awkwardness of not knowing how much one is allowed to reveal or ask on a first meeting without seeming like a hopeless boor or a snoop.

"Come by sometime for breakfast?" Suzuki-san suggests.

I bow quickly and leave. She has work to do.

On another visit, I bring some photographs that I have with me, film left in the camera when I came to Okinoshima, pictures mostly of Ted and Charles and Susan. They were taken in lovely Arashiyama, a northern section of Kyoto, on our last trip together before Charles and Susan flew home to North America. I also have a few photos of me with my Japanese students and colleagues, and one or two of our apartment back in Nigawa. I hope that by showing my family and friends, my students, my husband and how we live in our Nigawa apartment, I can let her see the parameters of what my culture considers permissible and put her more at ease about whatever she does or does not want to tell me about herself.

I hand Suzuki-san a photograph of Charles and Susan smiling in front of the beautiful Katsura River, the low mountains of Arashiyama behind them. On the river is a long dark wooden boat, a cormorant fisherman. None of the birds can be seen in the photo nor do I know the word for *cormorant* in Japanese. I find myself pantomiming a bird with large wings, diving into the water, catching a fish in its beak. Its throat is tied so it cannot swallow the fish, which the fisherman then plucks from its beak and slips into a basket, a cruel way to catch a fish, but a hilarious pantomime.

Suzuki-san and I are laughing together and I am very happy. For reasons I don't fully understand, I like wordless communication. I love the feeling that comes when there is understanding—and even appreciation—without history, story. There's both anonymity and revelation, the opposite of what, in psychobabble, is known as self-disclosure. The Japanese have a term for this kind of language: *ishin denshin* (wordless heart-to-heart communication). It's considered a profound kind of communication. Perhaps I'm self-deceived, but it feels profound to me too, *real*. One of the first

things that attracted me to Japan and that I continue to find in-
finitely seductive is this cultural knack for being able to trust and
to be trusted without actually knowing much about one another.
Things we consider basic—meeting a friend's spouse or family, in-
quiring about someone's occupation—are as irrelevant (and impolite) in Japan as asking someone's salary would be in America.

But at Ben, today, it's time for show-and-tell, and I'm very
proud that I finally have the chance to show off what I learned in
Japanese 101: this is a photograph of my son, Charles. This is his
fiancée, Susan. This is their traditional Japanese house. It is in
Kyoto. This is my husband, Ted. He is sitting in the living room
in our tiny apartment in Nigawa. Declarative sentences that, in
this context, feel like small talk, American-style.

"Your *son?*" Suzuki-san asks.

She knows I'm thirty-seven. How could this man, who looks
at least twenty-five in the photograph, be my son?

"*Yōshi,*" I explain, a Japanese term for a child through legal
rather than biological connection, a term more common a few generations ago when poor parents would allow one of their children
to be adopted by and to take the family name of a richer, childless
relative. More commonly now, a grown man will become a *yōshi,*
taking his wife's name upon marriage, becoming the adopted child
and legal heir of his in-laws, with more rights than even their natural daughter. This is relatively common when wealthy families
have no son to carry on the family name. "*Yōshi*" is as close as I
can come in Japanese. *Stepson* in the Western sense has virtually no
Japanese equivalent. Once or twice I've heard the phrase "*otto no
tsureko*" (the child of my husband's former marriage), but it must
carry a connotation different from what I intend when I talk about
Charles. When I've used the phrase, I've drawn stares of wonder-
ment and embarrassment. *Stepson* is barely a concept in a country
where divorce is still rare and where one divorces a whole family,
not just a spouse.

I try to explain that Charles was only four when I came on
the scene. Now he's twenty-three. I try to explain how he's getting
married this summer and already I feel the loss. I know the word

for *empty nest syndrome* in Japanese, and I tell Suzuki-san that I'm feeling this. I am very happy for him, and Susan is wonderful, as nice a daughter-in-law as one could ever hope for. But that doesn't mean I don't feel *akinosushōkō,* an emptiness, a loss.

This conversation is misfiring, I can tell. No one ever told me either that a stepmother could suffer so badly from empty nest syndrome. There's virtually no category in our own culture, even in its present "blended family" stage. No wonder it's not translating into Japanese. Suzuki-san keeps looking from me to the photograph of Charles and Susan.

"You are a very kind person," she says, but I can feel her pulling back, embarrassed, as if she fears she has pried too closely or has missed something important. It was easier to act out the cormorant fishing.

Suzuki-san tells me to wait a moment and goes into the adjoining tatami room to bring out her own small album of photographs. Her home in Kyushu, two brothers, her parents, several photographs of her daughter in her parents' small tile-roofed house near Kagoshima Bay. In one photograph a tiny woman stands just inside the shadows of a house.

"Who is this?" I ask, pointing to the woman.

"*Obāsan,* my grandmother," she answers. "Eighty-eight years old, *beiju,*" a very lucky year. I do not ask Suzuki-san if she has gone home to Kyushu to celebrate this special birthday with her grandmother.

I rummage in my wallet, then pull out a small photograph of my own grandmother, Mae Notari, age ninety-three but a mere ninety when the photo was taken. Her head is tilted to one side. She is smiling, her enormous dark eyes both demure and canny, like a young girl up to mischief.

"Ninety? And still so pretty! She must have been very beautiful when she was young," Suzuki-san says. We exchange photos. For a moment we hold each other's grandmother.

"Your grandmother is beautiful too!"

"No, never beautiful," she smiles. "But very funny. *Very* funny." She laughs quietly to herself, as if she is remembering some family story, then looks sad. Suddenly I am awash with lone-liness, wishing I were with my grandmother. I struggle not to cry. In most contexts, it's impolite to reveal your emotions in Japan, not because emotion is bad but because emotions matter. It is not right to burden someone else with your feelings, especially with your sorrow. Wordlessly, we return our grandmothers to one an-other.

We finish our coffee, put our photos away, and bow good-bye for the morning.

Sometimes on Oki I swim for as many as six or eight hours a day. I am swimming away from my friends' deaths, from depression and an empty nest. Even my job has been going badly lately, but I've lacked the energy for a major career change. I am swimming away from all of these things, but mostly from my grandmother.

At ninety-three, she has outlived her life. She retains her hu-mor and kindness to the end but she is desperate to die, and I have let her down. I cannot help her. One day she fell. They found her on the floor with a cracked pelvis and a heart that had almost stopped. The paramedics came and revived her. Waking to find herself in yet another hospital, she looked at her doctor accusingly: "The Good Lord came for me today—and you wouldn't let him take me."

When I visit her for the last time in the nursing home before leaving for Japan, we have our usual, serious talk. I tell her of how three young friends have died recently—a stroke, breast cancer, AIDS—people who were close to me, now gone.

"Grandma, life is too short," I say, falling back on clichés, as one does speaking of death.

"Sometimes," she answers, gripping my hand, "it is too long."

"I wish I could help you, Grandma."

She closes her eyes. "You and Mari, you always help me. You're so good to your grandma, you two." I'm relieved that my cousin Mari will still be around after I leave but that doesn't absolve me of my own sense of guilt. I am returning to Japan, my special place, and my grandmother's dying here and I can't help her.

"Sweetie," a nurse whispers as she enters the room. "Sweetie, we need to change your bedding."

"Thank you, my dear," Grandma says. "Oh, you smell so good—new perfume?"

"Your grandmother always has something nice to say." The nurse smiles at me. "Most of these others—you can have them."

The nurse is black. All the nurses in this Chicago nursing home are black. The patients here are mostly old white women, immigrants—Irish, Polish, German, Swedish. My grandmother is one of the only Italians in this part of town.

"We'll take good care of your grandmother while you're gone," a nurse says to me, but I can tell she doesn't approve of my going off to Japan, not with a grandmother so sick. "You're very lucky to have a grandmother like that."

"You and Mari," my grandmother says, working to release me from guilt. "You and Mari are always good to me. You never forget me. Take lots of photographs of Japan to show me. You're my traveler. You see the world for me, dear." She pats my hand again and again.

When I pull on my coat, the tears are streaming down my face. My grandmother refuses to notice. "You look so nice in your pretty red coat," my grandmother says as I kiss her good-bye. "I'll always think about you in your pretty red coat."

≈

Mornings are leisurely on Oki. Two friends, Becky, an American, and Monique, a Swiss woman, arrive on the island. Soon all four of us—myself, Maryvonne, Becky, and Monique—are going almost every day to Big Ben. We go before the lunch crush and Suzuki-san sits with us, pulling up a chair to the long bench where we sit in a row. I take a photo one day and bring it in to Ben after it's developed. We look like revelers. Every day we go to Ben to laugh and talk and joke with Suzuki-san and Ami-chan, her daughter.

One day when we come in the atmosphere is changed. There are men at the bar whom we've never seen before. Suzuki-san's movements are abrupt and nervous. She greets us in a desultory way, nothing at all like her usual greeting. She serves us mechanically, mixing up orders, claiming some of the things that we order aren't available. In fact, if we want anything *cooked*, we'll have to come back another time. We order some cold sandwiches and cold drinks. We feel she wants us out of there as soon as possible so we bolt down our food. She clears our glasses away before we're finished and hands us our check.

The middle of the three men at the bar barks commands at her in a voice I've only heard on television—a macho Japanese *yakuza* (mobster) voice, monosyllabic and guttural. The whole scene is like something out of a B-movie, so much so that I look to see if he is missing any fingers, the traditional sign of contrition that a *yakuza* makes to his boss. But the man's back is turned and I can't see his hands. His hair is cut short, like a *yakuza*'s. Most frightening, on the back of his head someone has buzz cut the letters B-E-N, all the way down to his scalp. It was done crudely. Maybe with a dull razor. There are scabs and flecks of crusted blood in the bald letters. He looks at me a few times, back over his shoulder, but never turns to look at any of us straight on. He is an ugly man, with a weasly face, bad skin, brown teeth.

After we leave, we four foreign women talk with sadness about what we have seen. I've been told that some snack bars are controlled by *yakuza,* supplying booze, cigarettes, sometimes prostitutes. But somehow we thought here, on remote Oki, that Suzuki-san would be exempt. We don't like to think of her as part of a world that can be brutally violent, a violence that is pretty much allowed so long as it is contained within the group. The Japanese tolerate organized crime, as more than one commentator has observed, because they are sure that unorganized crime would be so much worse.

Later that afternoon I ask the captain about it as he drives us in his big fishing boat to yet another beach that looks like some tropical paradise right out of a travel brochure. The captain's aunt runs the other snack bar in town, and he does not want to talk about any of this, not snack bars, not Suzuki-san, and certainly not mobsters. He refuses even to say the word *yakuza.* He grunts, as if not hearing, until I mention the man with B-E-N carved on his head.

"*Goshujin,*" he uses the polite, honorific term. "Her husband."

I ask Maryvonne to ask again, in her excellent Japanese, because I'm sure I haven't asked the question correctly. *Goshujin.* The man with the scabby skull is Suzuki-san's husband.

"We must go back tomorrow," Maryvonne insists. "That poor woman will be very ashamed."

The next day is as if nothing has happened. We enter making our silly *gaijin*-on-holiday jokes and Suzuki-san rolls her eyes the way she always does, teasing back, enjoying the silliness of it all, laughing so hard we can hardly stand it, "crying with laughter," Maryvonne likes to say in her wonderful French-Japanese-accented English. Suzuki-san laughs along with us. Her daughter watches wide-eyed from the tatami room adjoining the coffeehouse.

I cannot remember how I learned that the daughter was not the child of the man with B-E-N carved on his head. I know no more details of Suzuki-san's story. Whether I see her alone on my morning walks or later with my other friends, I never dream of asking about that husband, her family life. Ours is a friendship based on an eccentric love of glass balls, an exchange of a few photographs. Two strangers here, we both have found inexpressible beauty in the glass balls blown from old bottles, tossed against the shores in winter storms, and overlooked by others as garbage. Whenever I find a particularly beautiful one, I bring it to Big Ben and show it to her.

~~~

I am excited about two strange ones I find next to one another at Mimiura Beach, a magnificent inlet with a rocky coast. This is where I finally hear the *shiosai,* the sound of the waves. When I read about it in a Mishima novel, I couldn't imagine the sound. But here it is. Not the sound of waves breaking. For the Japanese, the sound of the sea comes with the wave's aftermath, the crackling sound of water retreating through beach rocks. And there across an inlet, in a garbage beach, I found these two dripping glass balls, curved as if they belonged together, perfectly matched, one green, one blue.

I show them to Suzuki-san and tell her about the *shiosai.* I have finally heard the sound of the sea. She takes the two glass balls from my hands and holds them lovingly.

"Please take them," I say.

"No." She returns them to me. She is firm. "Give me some others. These are special. You must give them to someone you love."

Someone I love. It's as if she has plumbed my loneliness and my sorrow, too many deaths, my grandmother's long life. She understands this is a painful time for me. Where is my husband, after all? Why is there so much laughter? We don't talk about any of this, but I note how when she returns the glass balls, her hands linger in mine an instant longer than a Japanese would normally allow. We look at each other. The next day I bring her two other glass balls, very beautiful ones. One could be Venetian spun glass. She accepts them tenderly, making a deep bow.

"*Tomodachi,*" she almost whispers. Friend.

"*Tomodachi.*" I smile back. "*Bin-dama tomodachi,*" Glass Ball Friends.

On my last day on Oki, Suzuki-san and her daughter drive up to the *shukusha* in their car. I'm sitting on the stoop cleaning some sand off my snorkel and mask. I have never before seen them away from Big Ben. Suzuki-san gets out, then reaches into the back seat of the car. She brings forth an enormous brilliant green glass ball, green like the sea before a storm.

Suzuki-san presents the glass ball while her gentle daughter stands solemnly at her side. There is something ritualistic about the moment. None of us wants to break it with words. She passes me the ball. My arms encircle it completely. I am hugging it. I press my cheek against its cool surface. I feel warm tears running down my cheeks.

Suzuki-san and her daughter bow. I'd love to hug them but it's the wrong culture. Besides, my arms are full.

Suzuki-san explains that this ball was in the storehouse too, along with the clear one that hangs from the ceiling in Ben. It is over a hundred years old, made right here on the island. And now that she has given it to me, I will never forget her. *Giri*, reciprocal responsibility, every gift implies a return gift, every gift is also a burden, a responsibility, a tie that keeps bringing one back.

I know, without asking, that Suzuki-san will not join the other villagers for the farewell in the harbor. As the ship pulls away, streamers will be tossed from those on the deck to those waving good-bye on the dock below. The colorful ties are held until the ship pulls too far away, and then they break and flutter out upon the ocean, gay and sad.

I muster all my best Japanese to thank Suzuki-san. I wish I could stop the tears but it's not possible. She bows. I bow. She bows more deeply. I bow as deeply as I can with an enormous glass ball in my arms. She bows another time, then turns away. There are dark spots on the ground. At the car, she turns back. We look at one another a long time.

≈

"She's gone," Maryvonne says on the first day of my fourth visit to Japan in November of 1990, three years after I left Oki. We are sipping tea. I haven't unpacked my suitcase yet. "I didn't want to tell you over the phone," she says.

"Suzuki-san is *gone?* What do you mean?"

Maryvonne explains that the last time the Danceries went to Oki, they were shocked to walk into Big Ben and find that

Suzuki-san wasn't there anymore. The snack bar looked exactly the same—the posters of Balmoral and Buckingham Palace, the clock collection, including the clock I had sent her from England as a "return present," even the beautiful crystal ball hanging from the ceiling. A thin, humorless old woman was working behind the small bar. She claimed never to have heard of Suzuki-san. When Maryvonne asked her how long she'd been working there, the woman refused to answer. She wouldn't answer any more questions and made it clear that the Danceries were not welcome there.

"Where could Suzuki-san have gone?" I ask.

"No one knows—or no one will say. We asked everyone in the village about it. No one knew anything. One of our friends finally told us to stop asking."

After a pause, Maryvonne adds, in Japanese, *"Shikataganai,"* the ubiquitous phrase, resignation, acquiescence to the inexplicable, it can't be helped.

"What do you think happened to her?" I wonder aloud.

Maryvonne doesn't answer.

We let the silence last a long time.

Maryvonne picks up one of the small glass balls I gave her that summer together on Oki.

"You look at these," she says quietly, "and you know glass really is a liquid."

She holds it up, letting the light play inside.

"They always make me think of the ocean," is all I add.

We can almost taste the salt air.

11

TATAMI ROOM
IN
CEDAR GROVE

I never felt more nostalgic for Japan than when I first visited Paris. It was January of 1989, between our third and fourth trips to Japan, and we were exhausted from the process of looking for new jobs, trying to weigh the pros and cons of one kind of university over another, one area of the country over another.

"How about Paris?" Ted suggested one dreary winter afternoon.

He tossed me a tourist pamphlet featuring a photograph of Notre Dame bathed in rosy sunset light. "Look at these winter rates!" he added. "We couldn't fly to Chicago for that."

We made a pact. We'd go to Paris for a week and not mention jobs once. It would be a carefree week in the most romantic city in the world.

Although neither of us is fluent in the language, we assumed that communicating for a few days in French would be a snap after the years we spent scraping by in Japanese. I dug out some old French textbooks and thumbed through the pages. I felt confident reviewing a language with recognizable cognates, familiar rules of grammar, even an alphabet. At a local bookstore, Ted bought some maps and I picked up a dual-language French-English phrase book. He would be the guide; I the designated translator.

What I hadn't counted on was the extent to which living in Japan three times in the last ten years had changed me. When the French customs official asked me a question at Passport Control at Orly International Airport, the words that leapt from my lips were Japanese. He repeated his question in accented but perfectly comprehensible English. I tried again to answer him. *Still* Japanese.

"Hazukashii!" I muttered in embarrassment, turning to Ted for assistance.

"We have nothing to declare, sir," my husband answered the official in impeccable English.

The whole time we were in Paris, I didn't manage a single correct, coherent French phrase. In restaurants, taxis, Metro stations, my sentences might start French but they ended, every time, with the verbal equivalent of a bow. It was as if the compartment in my psyche labeled "Foreign" was now irrevocably changed to "Japanese."

Fortunately, world geopolitics being what they are, this had certain advantages. The first thing we encountered when we arrived at our hotel in the Sixteenth Arrondissement was the concierge trying to communicate with a group of impeccably dressed young Japanese women. He addressed them in loud, slow, exasperated English.

" 'Ave uuu ah rrrreservat-i-on?" Pain was palpable in every syllable.

"Vely solly. We do not speak Flench," one of the Japanese students answered politely. "Would you speak Engrish prease?"

The concierge looked ready to cry. I repressed a certain de-

light in the situation (I'd heard tales of monolingual Americans reduced to jello by haughty Parisians) and intervened.

"*Sumimasen. Yoyaku shite arimasuka?*"

In Berlitz-book Japanese, I inquired after the students' reser-
vations.

"*Merci! Merci!*" the concierge sighed with relief.

The Japanese women literally clapped their hands.

We soon settled all problems, the concierge asking questions
in Parisian English, me translating into Japanese or sometimes
merely into Japanese-accented English, then translating back again
for the concierge. Once the Japanese were duly registered and on
their way to their rooms, the concierge thanked me profusely and
insisted on upgrading our accommodation to a room with a better
view. A day or two later, when I helped him with another Japanese
transaction, he presented me with a small box of candy from La
Maison du Chocolat.

"Interesting," Ted observed after the second encounter. "The
Japanese are the Ugly Americans now. The French almost like us
these days."

For myself, I was happy. Just *happy*. It felt natural negotiating
between cultures. As the Americanized child and grandchild of
immigrants from various countries who had married, intermarried,
and remarried but who never liked one another very much (Italians
and Poles, Catholics and Jews), I had learned over the years to get
by on inklings of cultural differences, scraps of words, the inter-
stices between America and some other culture—some history—
far away but never forgotten.

In one of my fondest childhood memories, for example, when
I was six or maybe seven, I watched Grandma Notari lean forward
and gesture excitedly, with both hands, to her cousin, an older
woman named Ottovina. Ottovina had been in America almost as
long as my grandmother but she lived on the South Side, in the
Italian ghetto, and barely spoke any English at all. Ottovina
smiled at me a lot, patted my head, and said, "Nice-a, nice-a," and
then turned back to my grandmother. In their fifties and sixties,

the two women huddled together like schoolgirls with secrets to tell, happily engrossed in their conversation.

After her cousin left for her house in the Italian neighborhood, my grandmother looked lost and lonely. I said something to her but my English suddenly felt paltry. I wanted her to look the way she had a moment ago, bursting with energy as she laughed with Ottovina, the kind of name one never heard in our neighborhood of Swedes and Germans.

"Why is she named 'Ottovina'?" I asked, enjoying the sound of the word.

"It means she was born eighth in line," Grandma Notari explained. "Ottovina means eight."

"Like on the piano, an octave?"

My grandmother hugged me then and whispered something in Italian. I didn't understand the words but I knew that I'd gotten it right. Ottovina, octave, eight: translation was something like love.

I was hooked. From an uncle on my mother's side of the family, Pete Kotowski, I learned how to say *Jezus, Maria, Józefie święty*. I imitated the way Uncle Pete cursed like it was one long word, the consonants so tangled and guttural that the other kids shifted back when I said it. I could even swear in front of my teachers without getting into trouble. The words made me feel powerful and exempt. To this day, if I stub a toe or jam a finger, curses erupt from my mouth in Polish.

And in France, I realized that my language for cultural embarrassment, for not quite knowing just how I should act, is Japanese. If I were blindfolded and tossed into absolutely any foreign country—France, Hong Kong, Zaire—I'm positive that within two minutes I'd be bowing, apologizing, and exclaiming, *"Hazukashii!"*

Since this is our first visit to Paris, we decide we'd better take in at least some of the standard tourist sights. We visit the Eiffel

Tower but decide not to wait in the long line of tourists (mostly Japanese) who will be ascending to the top. We stop at Notre Dame but discover that, even in this off-season, there are so many visitors that they've had to adopt crowd-control measures to preserve the building. Dozens of Japanese wait outside the door for their number to be called, at which time they'll be shuttled through on twenty-minute guided tours.

We wait, surrounded by Japanese. They are talking freely because they assume the *gajin* don't understand what they are saying. Shopkeepers here aren't nearly as friendly or helpful as they are in Japan, they say. The guidebooks insist that everyone in Paris knows English, especially if you speak very slowly, but most of the time the French won't answer even their simplest questions. One young woman says people have been so rude to her that it is making her nervous, she's afraid she will develop a complex, something (I know) that the Japanese worry about a lot. I've been told that in Japan they've set up an emergency counseling service—even a telephone hotline—for Japanese suffering culture shock due to a visit to Paris. This young woman seems a prime candidate.

We decide we'll skip Notre Dame, the line is just too long, but before we go I lean forward and tell the young woman that I hope things go better on the rest of her trip. Her mouth drops open. She stares for a moment, bursts into a big smile, then accosts me with a volley of Japanese. I apologize hastily, saying I know only a little Japanese, *sukoshi,* and she slows down and asks me some formula questions. Where am I from? Have I been to Japan? What part of Japan did I live in? How long? Did I like it there? All of my answers please her. She is from near Himeji, a famous castle city, and she attends a junior college in the suburbs of Osaka, not far from Kansai Women's University. I know and name a few of her train stops and she cries out with delight. We bow and bid one another good-bye. A quarter block away, I glance back. She and her friends are still waving.

It's a strange way to see Paris, but Ted and I are having a great time. The presence of Japanese everywhere infuses our excitement at being in France with a bittersweet aura of *natsukashisa*. We yearn for Japan.

We push on to another standard tourist site, the almost grotesquely ornate Opéra. Most of the building is closed off, under repair, with ropes cordoning off huge sections.

I stop to use the women's restroom. There is a small rap on the old wooden stall door.

"Chotto matte kudasai" (Excuse me a moment, please), I blurt out in Japanese, automatically, even involuntarily, and then feel very silly, realizing that I'm still stuck in my "foreigner" mode.

When I leave the stall, I discover that the woman who knocked is Japanese. Her mouth drops open in astonishment when she sees a tall "Frenchwoman" exit the stall. I wash my hands quickly and flee from the restroom. It's too complicated to try to explain to a stranger why I, an American, have excused myself in colloquial Japanese in a restroom in Paris. The Japanese woman doesn't even try to cover her embarrassment. *"Hazukashii!"* she mutters quietly, and enters the stall. I am certain that she spends the rest of her trip trying to ascertain what, precisely, about her way of knocking had tipped off a Frenchwoman that a Japanese was on the other side of the door.

I tell Ted about the incident in the restroom as soon as we hit the street, and he predicts, archly, that there will soon be a spate of Japanese newspaper or magazine articles about proper comportment in international public restrooms.

His prediction is not that farfetched. Westerners tend to think of the Japanese as an insular people, not much concerned with the rest of the world. We know that their textbooks evade responsibility by ignoring past military aggressions such as Pearl Harbor or atrocities like the rape of Nanjing. It's easy to assume from this that typical Japanese go about their business with little regard for how others might view them. Wrong. The Japanese have to be the most pathologically self-reflective and self-conscious people in the world. They are *obsessed* with how they are viewed by non-Japanese, which may well be one reason that they prefer to travel in the relative anonymity of a tour group.

Many Japanese bookstores feature a whole section devoted to Japanese translations of books about Japan originally written by Westerners for a Western audience. For over a hundred years now the Japanese have been buying up even the most racist and derogatory Japan-bashing books that Westerners have written. They read these accounts greedily (if resentfully), seeking to know exactly what we say about them when we talk among ourselves. The only American equivalent I can think of is the recent success of *Made in Japan,* co-authored by Akio Morita, founder of Sony. Highly critical of American workers, Morita's book was intended for a Japanese audience. Translated into English, it became a bestseller for a short time as outraged Americans rushed to read what those presumptuous Japanese were saying about us now. Japanese newspapers and magazines are filled with interviews with *gaijin* who report on foreign attitudes toward the Japanese. "Returned Traveler" columns are also popular in Japan, especially accounts of how Japanese tourists managed to survive humiliation abroad.

The bathroom incident at the Opéra perfectly fits this format, for it plays into one of the deepest fears of the Japanese—the fear of being identified as the Other, outside the group. Metaphorically, being a *gaijin* is about exclusion and isolation, precisely what Japanese society, from infancy on, is geared to prevent. No wonder anxieties run high when the Japanese venture into foreign territory and the metaphor becomes reality.

Ted and I are walking together down the Rue St. Sébastien Froissart. It is cold and drizzly today and the sidewalk is jammed with Japanese tourists. We must duck continually to avoid the onslaught of umbrellas, the spokes jutting out at exactly eye level.

"This *really* feels like Japan," I say to Ted, recalling the inconvenience of being a head too tall in a rainstorm.

We stop at a postcard-perfect French café, hoping something hot and warm will revive us.

The waiter gives us a conspiratorial wink. It takes us a moment to figure out why. We peer around the restaurant. Except for us, every patron in the place is Japanese. Their umbrellas are neatly folded shut and placed in the stand at the entrance, the handles all facing the same direction. There are too many coats for the rack, so some are folded into neatly squared bundles and stacked on a chair near their table. Two rows of bulging designer shopping bags are lined up like soldiers against the wall. Although the café is full, these Japanese are so quiet one would barely know they are there. They talk and laugh in whispers, their gestures efficient and contained. They are a mixed group, men and women, all about the same age and seemingly from the same social class. It's probably a company tour group.

"You will see," the waiter confides to us in English. "They will all order the same thing, exactly."

When, one by one, they each order a café au lait, then a croissant, the waiter can barely control his mirth.

"Is he right?" Ted asks. "Over here, do they all start to seem alike?"

The question floats there in the air. They? Us? Here? There? It's been building since we got here, this sense that Japanese tourists are everywhere, buying everything and anything at top dollar, driving up prices that are already too high for cheap American dollars. We've heard other Westerners insist that the Japanese all look alike to them—camera-toting tourists all in a group—a preposterous and racist stereotype. But for the first time since we began our association with Japan, we find ourselves seeing the Japanese as many Westerners seem to view them: predictable, inexplicable, uniform.

Ted and I talk about this, keeping our voices low. What does it matter if they each want café au lait and a croissant? Nothing, except that it fulfills a stereotype. And that is what is bothering us. We are seeing them as "them," foreign. *Gaijin*.

The waiter comes to take our order.

"Café au lait and a croissant," Ted says, an edge in his voice.

"I'll have the same."

The waiter doesn't even notice.

When I lived in Japan, the Western stereotype of Oriental uni-formity seemed incomprehensible. In my classroom at Kansai Women's University, I'd look out at row upon row of students, all the same age, all from upper-middle-class families, sometimes a hundred in a room, and be aware of the endless variety in the faces and personalities. Seeming similarities—such as hair and eye color—turned out not to be similar at all. Once, during an exam, the sun streamed in the high windows onto the glossy hair of my students, heads bowed over their test papers, a hundred different hues of black gleaming like rainbows down the rows.

One day our friend Toshi asked us if it was really true that Westerners thought Japanese all looked alike. I said, yes, some Westerners did think so.

"Good, I'm glad," he said thoughtfully.

"Why?"

"Because I had the same feeling when I visited California to meet Sally's family. All the Americans looked alike to me."

He explained that he found America utterly confusing. There were so *many* possibilities, such an extreme range of sizes, skin tones, hair and eye colors that at first when he tried to classify people, he kept making mistakes. He told us how twice, even as they were waiting for their luggage, he started up conversations with a tall blond woman he thought was his wife's sister—and both times he was embarrassed to discover he was chatting with some tall blond stranger who just happened to be standing close by.

After we leave the café, we spend a wonderful afternoon in the Musée d'Orsay. As we admire art, rain beats heavy against the glass skylights of the lovely nineteenth-century train station now converted into a museum. It's almost rush hour when we button ourselves into our trench coats again, pull up our collars, and open our umbrellas against the weather.

As we make our way down the street to the Metro stop, I notice a young woman walking maybe thirty feet ahead of us. She's dressed in a style I call "High Japanese." Her stunning shoulder-length hair fans out against a pure white wool suit under a fantastic raincoat, transparent except for crisp, black piping around the hem, collar, and cuffs. She wears white spiky heels and has a tiny white beret balanced asymmetrically on the side of her head. With gloved hands, she grips the handle of an umbrella that threatens to blow away in this rainstorm, a black umbrella with gold spokes. She looks like a painting against the gray Paris day.

"Come on," Ted says, "the light's green."

We dash into the street, looking down to avoid the biggest puddles, and run up against the people immediately in front of us who have suddenly stopped. Then I see the Japanese woman in the white dress, sprawled there in the intersection, splattered with mud. Obviously she has fallen and I'm afraid she might be injured. She looks dazed and helpless, utterly defenseless, the careful façade spoiled and nothing left between her and a world of honking cars, the extended hands of strangers, admonitions shouted loudly and in French.

"*Sumimasen*" (Excuse me), I address her, surprised by the quiver in my voice. "*Daijōbu?*" (Are you okay?).

The woman stirs to the familiar words. She pushes herself up from the pavement.

Ted and a solicitous Frenchman in the crowd help her to her feet and safely to the curb. I walk behind them, holding her purse, watching how she limps for the first few steps, then begins to pull herself upright again.

I recognize the fragility and the swagger, the sense that the world can be controlled with a series of perfect gestures, like a tea ceremony, and the helplessness when those gestures fall away. I have felt it myself, more than once, on a morning before a big meeting or just before I've had to give a lecture, looking in the mirror, carefully coloring my lips, encircling each determined eye with a ring of smoke gray like a fortification.

"*Daijōbu*," she says to me softly once we're safely out of the traffic. She makes her voice steady. She is answering my earlier question: I'm okay. "*Hazukashii*," she then adds quickly, looking down.

She bows deeply, apologizing to us, which is to say, in Japanese, she thanks us for our help. Looking over the wreck of herself, she seems on the verge of tears again. Then she looks at me. In this pouring rain on a busy street corner in Paris, I watch her face go soft with recognition. I'm a breath away from crying too.

"*Gambatte kudasai!*" (Good luck!), I urge. You can do it! Go for it!

She giggles, covering her mouth with her hand, her culture's acknowledgment of embarrassment, but also a sign that she's okay.

"*Gambatte kudasai!*" she repeats to me.

I hand her back her purse. She snaps into action. With a brisk motion, she brushes at the stains on her white wool dress. She smooths down her hair, tipping the beret back to its original angle. She secures her purse in the crook of her arm and grasps her umbrella, women's gestures I've seen a thousand times, it doesn't matter the country. Simultaneously, we bow and bid one another good-bye.

≈

"Where are we going?" I keep asking as Ted leads us down one of the busiest and most expensive shopping streets in Paris, the boutiques crammed with Japanese tourists.

"Come on!" he says, avoiding my question.

We turn off the main boulevard, walk a few more blocks, then stop in front of a small shop down a winding, cobblestoned side street.

"*Sakura?*" I say, recognizing the *kanji* for "cherry blossom" on the door.

Ted had found this place on one of his walks. It's the Paris branch of a favorite Kyoto tea shop.

I know how it will smell even before we enter.

I breathe in the distinctive aroma of *matcha,* the thick, dark green tea of *chanoyu* (tea ceremony). The tension leaves my shoulders for the first time since I've been in Paris.

I'm beginning to understand the English matron insisting on her silver tea service in the jungle. She's not just an imperialistic Brit comically adrift without the amenities of her class. She's a traveler, any traveler, succumbing to the seduction of the familiar when she's feeling far away. I can't help smiling to myself over the fact that it is Sakura—not McDonald's—that relieves my homesickness. There is something entirely comforting about leaving behind the gilt and glitz of the rue du Faubourg St. Honoré for the peace—the *predictability*—of the ancient wood and stone minimalism of this Japanese tearoom.

Except for a French waitress, except for us, the occupants of Sakura are all Japanese, Japanese as calm as a Kyoto Zen garden. The scurrying tourists with their Nikons and their designer shopping bags are transformed the instant they enter this muted space. Home territory. Postures change, pace slows, bustle becomes murmur. The sounds in the tearoom are hushed, minimal: the whispered hiss of Japanese (a more euphonious and sibilant language than World War II caricatures allow) and the slightly louder sipping of the foamy green tea from ceramic bowls cupped securely and tenderly in both hands, the tips of fingers gently touching.

"Itadakimasu," Ted and I say as we bow to one another, the ritual salutation before partaking of food or drink. Like the other customers at Sakura, we lift and turn our tea bowls, taking in the beauty and form of the pottery with the sensuality of a Frenchman sniffing the bouquet of a fine cognac. We rotate our bowls clockwise with the right hand, then sip with the most beautiful side away from us as we drink. With a tiny twig, exquisitely stripped of bark on one side, we pierce the delicate *nama-gashi,* the traditional *azuki* bean sweet. Mine is white and shaped like a flower,

perhaps a camellia. Ted uses his twig fork to take a small slice from an elegant maple leaf.

"I wouldn't mind living *here*," I whisper to Ted, the first time either of us has broken our pact not to mention the decisions that await us back home.

"Perhaps we will," he responds.

Neither of us speaks for a long time. We sip the green tea. We are liking France better and better.

≋

People laugh when we say that we moved to rural North Carolina because we decided we couldn't live permanently in Japan, but that's pretty much how it happened. Sitting in a Japanese tearoom off the rue du Faubourg St. Honoré, we found ourselves thinking about the various jobs we'd been offered and suddenly knew that we wanted to take the positions at Duke University, situated in the lush, overly green Carolina countryside that reminded us of rural Japan. Since we had never owned a house during the twenty-odd years we'd been married, we would be starting from scratch, but land prices were inexpensive enough there that we could build a little house, and it could be Japanese. If Sakura could survive in downtown Paris, why not a tea house in the rural South?

We talked about it tentatively at first, as we walked, arms linked, over rainy cobblestone streets. We talked about it on the plane ride home to America. Two weeks later, we were back in North Carolina, trying to see if this were possible. We contacted a realtor, Anne Sanford, and told her we wanted to live on a lake. She said she knew of five acres of hardwood forest on a lake way out in the country. We visited the office of Dail Dixon, a brilliant local architect whose work we had admired. Dail had never been to Japan but he understood about simplicity, about siting a house in harmony with nature. He showed us photographs of an exquisite Japanese house he had designed for a retired army couple who had been stationed in East Asia. He'd also designed a striking house for Arabic scholars longing for Morocco. Dail drove out with us to the lot. We turned down first one small road, then another, then down a dirt road and stopped in front of a plot of land so dense with trees and brush that, even in winter, we could hardly see the lake only a few hundred feet away.

Dail charged ahead through the brush. "Look! A ravine!" he exclaimed. We followed the sound of his voice and found him standing in a ravine that ran diagonally through the property. It was lush with Christmas ferns. The light came in slant and glowing here, illuminating a druidic-looking tree stump, probably a hundred years old, from which maple saplings grew tall and limber. It reminded me of the Tree of Life on Kudakajima.

"Here's where I'd site the house," Dail gestured with his arm, as if he could already see it standing there, running along the edge of the ravine, facing toward the lake.

The four of us followed the ravine down the sharply sloping hillside, under a canopy of beech and hickory trees, pushing branches out of our way until we came again to daylight, the shoreline. It was a quiet cove, lined with willows, with the lake winding diagonally out of sight. A gnarled red bud tree slanted out over the water.

"This could be a scene in a woodblock print," Ted exclaimed.

On our way back to town, I expanded on my idea of a Japanese house. I said I wanted the front of the house to be pretty private, but with small windows marching down the stairway, something I'd seen in a traditional Japanese house out in the countryside near Shiga, one of our favorite pottery villages. I described the way each small window in the Shiga house framed some aspect of nature—a patch of tree bark or the tips of a dogwood—so that as you walked down the stairs you came to appreciate nature not as a huge and impersonal force but as something intimate, human, artful, framed. And we knew we wanted a tatami room.

"Wait! Wait!" Dail laughed. "You're way ahead of me. What I'd like you to do is send me photographs of all your Japanese things, your art, your furniture. And since you're both writers, send me letters about your sense of what a Japanese house looks like."

"Actually, I don't really want it to *look* like a Japanese house," I said. "I want it to *feel* like one."

"That's much harder," he said, smiling.

We knew we had our man.

That same morning, before flying home, we bought the land, commissioned Dail to design the house, and stopped by the Dean's office to sign contracts for the jobs we'd been offered.

"May I ask you a personal question?" our realtor asked as she drove us to the airport. "How long did you two know one another before you got married?"

When we told her we'd known each other ten days, she smiled. "I thought so."

From the beginning, we knew that building a "Japanese" house really meant creating, in America, a fantasy of Japanese life. It meant putting into solid, visible form our *interpretation* of Japanese-ness. Tricky business. At the time, we had little definite experience of a Japanese house to go on, and certainly no personal experience. Our 2DK in a poured concrete apartment building in Nigawa was hardly a traditional Japanese house. In fact, what we learned from living in Japan is that the uncluttered aesthetic found in Japanese architecture books is, like so many of our romantic notions of Japan, more an ideal than a reality of daily life. The Japanese apartments we visited were typically crammed with a combination of Japanese and Western furniture as well as all the other paraphernalia of families living in little space.

Yet the clutter of everyday life doesn't necessarily mean that the Japanese have lost their vaunted appreciation of the minimal. Japanese culture is metonymic by design—an association stands for the real thing, a part for the whole. A well-placed rock in a tiny garden becomes a mountain, a crooked little *bonsai* tree can be an ancient forest, and the tatami room represents calm, unhurried space. With the futon folded away, there remains a bare expanse of golden mats, a fresh straw country smell redolent of another, rural time before a *tsubo* of land (the equivalent of two tatami mats in size) sold for millions and millions of yen.

I'm sure awful things happen in tatami rooms as elsewhere—arguments, betrayals, acts of small cruelty. But I prefer to maintain a blind faith in the salubrity of straw. Within tatami rooms, time slows. People lower their voices. Even drunks at parties manage to crawl off the mats to be ill. Can a tatami room be transplanted to Cedar Grove, North Carolina? We aren't sure. But it is what Ted and I talk about with one another and with Dail. With a view of the ravine to the east, and the lake to the west, perfectly situated to catch the reflections of the setting sun, a tearoom would make a splendid place to unwind. For houseguests, it would be an intriguing guest room, and for us, occasionally, when we felt homesick for Japan, a bedroom. We also like the inside joke: Japanese temples, villas, spas, and retreats are, ideally, set in cedar groves. Ours just happens to be in Dixie.

As soon as we decide to build the house, old dreams return like forgotten friends. Moss gardens, straw-mat rooms, wooden bridges arching in the moonlight, paper lanterns with the fire glowing inside. Yet there is also a realization that building this Japanese house is solid, material proof of our decision not to live permanently in Japan. The tatami room in Cedar Grove is part appreciation, but also part rejection. Like most forms of nostalgia, it pays homage to a place we never really knew.

12

FESTIVAL
OF THE
DEAD

During the hottest, most humid part of summer, in mid-August, time stops for three days while Japan celebrates *Obon,* the Buddhist Festival of the Dead. The rituals vary from place to place, but everywhere there is a reunion of the living with those who have died. Since the dead return loyally to the village of their birth, the living must return there too. The entire country is in motion before *Obon.* Trains and planes are filled to capacity. Gaudy colored lanterns flash and whirl, guiding the departed spirits home.

And then there is calm. Families sit around together, the dead occupying the place of honor. They chat peaceably, the living among the dead. A friend tells of her surprise at hearing her mother confide loneliness and longing to the spirit of her late husband. The mother would never have spoken so freely were her husband still alive, and certainly not within earshot of the children. Another friend jokes about how her father-in-law keeps his deceased wife informed of the state of his false teeth—fitting or ill-fitting, lost or found. A student tells me that at *Obon* her family likes to consult with the ancestors about her behavior. The ancestors have objected to her riding with her boyfriend on his motorcycle. She has promised them not to do it anymore.

"It's much harder to disobey your ancestors than your parents," she observes glumly.

Obon is for closing off unfinished business, for restoring bonds, for healing and remembering. It is part and parcel of an annual commemoration of the dead bound by traditions ancient and arcane. Throughout *Obon,* prayers are said and repeated; graves are cleaned and adorned with new flowers. Ritual foods are served, each with a symbolic function. On the final day of *Obon,* a bull, symbolized by eggplant, and a white melon horse carry the dead back to *meido,* the Celestial World of Darkness.

Obon is particularly meaningful in a place as remote as Oki. During *Obon,* all those who have gone off to make a living in the cities on the mainland return to Oki to be with their families and their ancestors. Extra ferries are needed to bring them back home. And everyone together celebrates *sharabune,* one of the most beautiful *Obon* festivals anywhere in Japan. "*Sharabune*" is Oki dialect for "spirit boat." Each village in the Okinoshima chain spends the summer building a straw boat large enough to transport boxes of food and other gifts that will comfort those who have no grave except the sea.

For weeks before *Obon,* each community builds its own large model of a sailing schooner. The boats are made mostly of rice straw, woven and bound together. Tied to the wooden masts and riggings of twine are hundreds of colorful streamers, each one inscribed with a prayer, a wish, a message for someone in the spirit world. On the final day of *Obon,* the ships are brought to one central harbor for launching. The oldest members of the community come at dawn to chant on the shore. They kneel on straw mats in their dark clothing and chant in unison with a Buddhist priest.

The morning air grows thick with incense and the droning of ancient sutras, as lulling and profound as waves.

After the boats are loaded with the boxes of food for the netherworld, those boys and girls who have just reached puberty solemnly climb into the boats. They are dressed in shades of vermillion, the color typical of *torii* gates at the entrance to a Shinto shrine, the color of joy and welcome, the rising sun. Fishing trawlers tug the straw ships far out to sea until they are no longer visible from the shoreline, and then the fishermen snatch the children to safety and release the ceremonial boats. When the straw soaks up water, the boats slowly sink into the ocean. The spirits return to *meido* and the children have been initiated into a world of mystery and death, into adulthood.

Yet as serious as this initiation ritual is, it is also fun. What from the harbor looks solemn takes on a carnivalesque air when seen from a closer vantage point. Fishermen in their trawlers draw close to the straw vessels and throw candy, fruit, and other treats to the children. Teenagers in powerboats veer past, grinning and taunting, drenching the kids in the straw boats with sea spray and still more laughter, but also throwing them ice cold cans of soda. Everyone works to make the day festive for the children. With some sadness, they leave the boats bound for *meido* and return to ordinary Japanese life.

That night everyone rejoices at the *bon odori,* the final ceremonial dance. The spirits have been liberated from Buddhist hell; the young have survived a rite of passage; the villagers dance and drink and laugh with friends and relatives who live most of the year in other places, far away.

In 1990, three years after leaving Japan and during my first year teaching at Duke University in North Carolina, I was invited to attend a conference in Tokyo. The conference was scheduled for summer, my least favorite season in Japan. The heat and humidity, especially in the cities, are stifling. But not on Oki. I called

Maryvonne to see if the Danceries would be going again to Oki and if I might be able to join them there after delivering my paper. They were leaving in mid-July and planned to stay until after *Obon*. This was before any of us knew that Suzuki-san was gone, so Maryvonne and I immediately began to plan a "Glass Ball Reunion" to be held under the glowing crystal ball suspended from the ceiling of Big Ben. She called the friends who ran the *shukusha* on Oki to make sure they had a room available for me.

"Of course!" the manager said. "And we have a surprise for Cathy-san. Please tell her we found another of the big glass balls. We're keeping it here for her until she returns."

What Maryvonne and my friends on Oki did not know was that I too was planning a surprise. My past visits had been conducted mostly by pantomime, phrase book, and occasionally through my scattered knowledge of offbeat, colorful, but not very useful Japanese expressions. This time I'd be fluent. It was a promise I made myself. I would not return to Japan a fourth time without knowing the language.

I enrolled in a nine-week intensive language course at Duke that boasted one teacher and two teacher's aides for only three students. We met across the hall from the advanced class, and the teacher and her aides took turns rotating between the classrooms. We had class from nine A.M. until two P.M., five days a week. At lunch, we all ate together, the students in the introductory class conversing as best we could with the advanced students. After the class sessions ended, there were tapes to be listened to in the language lab as well as computer programs to teach the two Japanese phonetic alphabets (*hiragana* and *katakana)* along with the hundreds of *kanji* characters. Japanese films were shown on Wednesday nights. Saturdays were for cultural demonstrations and field trips—a tea ceremony, an incense ceremony, flower arrangement, a visit to the local Matsushita corporate headquarters. On every second Sunday, we went in pairs to spend the afternoon at the home of a resident Japanese family, our "host family," who fed us Japanese food and taught us Japanese games that we played with their children. I studied six or eight hours every night, more on test nights. It was a full and total commitment.

And it was a disaster, too. I have an idiosyncratic relationship to language learning. As a child, I liked to lace my English with Italian, Polish, and Yiddish words and phrases. Traveling in Spain, even in Hong Kong, I quickly picked up enough of the language to understand simple transactions. But whatever aptitude I might have for languages deserts me in the classroom.

I'm not entirely sure why this is, but it undoubtedly relates to my dyslexia. When I was in school, the word hadn't been invented yet. Then, I was just written off as a "problem student" because I could handle some subjects with ease and others not at all. It's painful for me to recall my days as a student and hard to explain why some subjects were so difficult. The patterns don't seem to make sense. As an undergraduate, for example, I concentrated on the philosophy of mathematics and loved reading topology books. Yet even now, when I try to do simple arithmetic such as balancing a checkbook, I'm as likely to write "27" as "72." My brain also misfires when I take standardized multiple-choice tests, something I remember keenly whenever I have to take a written driver's exam. I can't do recitation or rote memorization either. Conventional language learning depends on all the skills at which I'm worst.

But I resolved that, despite these obstacles, I *would* learn Japanese that summer. I decided to be very Japanese about the whole business: I would "wear my *hachimaki*" (set my mind to it). All of June and July could be devoted to the task, with only the occasional break to oversee the completion of our house in Cedar Grove. In August I would join my friends on Oki for *Obon* and I would speak Japanese. If the ancestors wished to chat with a *gaijin,* this time I'd be able to answer them back.

It's a miserable summer. I study ten hours straight for my first major exam. I barely sleep the night before, *hiragana* characters running through my brain along with conjugations of the *-te* form. Although the adjectives are difficult for me, the verb conjugations I somehow know without bothering to study, residual knowledge from my time spent in Japan.

When we arrive in class, one of the students asks *sensei* if she'll answer some questions about the tricky verb conjugations. The teacher kindly explains, with rules and exceptions marked off in neat rows and columns on the blackboard. She keeps looking at me to see if I'm getting this. I avoid eye contact. I want to scream, *"Stop!"* I want to cover my ears. I *know* this material but the diagrams are confusing me. Politely, I sit there, pretending to pay attention, but my heart sinks. I feel the verbs running away from me with each new rule, each new schematic diagram on the blackboard.

By the time *sensei* passes out the exam, I remember nothing. I glance at the test. A few adjectives, lots of verbs. My hands are shaking and, if I let myself, I would cry. It's like a bad dream. I make a 20 percent on the exam.

I imagine sitting with the ancestors for *Obon* on Oki.

"What will we do with her?" someone asks. It's a tribunal, everyone pointing at me, my *F* in Intensive Japanese emblazoned on my T-shirt like Hester Prynne's *A*.

The ancestors answer, thoughtfully, profoundly. In Japanese. I can't understand a word they say.

Over the years I've run into several *gaijin* who have lived in Japan a decade or two and still haven't learned the language. I find this incomprehensible, repugnant. I am judgmental.

After three trips to Japan, I still do not know Japanese and it's harder for me to criticize.

"You must speak Japanese very well," people inevitably say.

"Hazukashii!" I think instantly, burning with shame.

At the same time, I reluctantly admit to myself, I feel the seduction of subliteral peace. I am not good at language learning, but I'm confident in my abilities to read situations where there are no words. One part of me *likes* not knowing Japanese. There is a freedom in not-knowing, a selectivity in foreignness. I wonder, sometimes, if its silence is part of what makes Japan precious to me.

"I understand exactly what you mean," says a friend, a volunteer at a local hospital, when I try to explain how not knowing Japanese sometimes makes me more intuitive, more observant and feeling. "It's like when I play my guitar for the Alzheimer's patients. There's a level of communication beyond mere words."

As our son, Charles, once remarked, in Japan every conversation seemed meaningful. Being without language forced a kind of meditativeness, an inwardness, a dependence on one's innermost resources. If one took the time to unravel and translate, even the most mundane conversation became an accomplishment, a reward in itself no matter what its content. But most times, one simply tuned it out. The constant chatter on subway platforms and restaurants—distracting back in America—was in Japan a sublingual hum. Ads were aimed only at others. Humanity seemed smiling, benign, quiet. Or simply irrelevant. When communication did happen, it was a small miracle—precious, pristine.

I cherish nonverbal communication, but there's a big difference between not needing to say anything in certain special situations—and not being *able* to say it. I want to be able to speak on Oki. I want to see Suzuki-san again and ask her about her life there, its isolation, about how she is able to keep her buoyancy and poise.

Japan makes me want to communicate. The first year I was there, I worked at it, traveling with a dictionary, a phrase book, my flashcards and notebook, wherever I went. By the end of the year, I could understand most of what people said to me. Frustratingly, I could say almost nothing back except an all-purpose, barely grammatical *"Wakarimasu."* The expression is apt. It means "comprehension," in the sense of "I understand." But it's also often used simply as a way of forestalling further conversation ("I hear you talking; that's not saying I understand; in fact, I don't really understand; let's move on, *Wakarimasu! Wakarimasu!"*). When people spoke to me in Japanese, I answered with a bow, *"Wakarimasu,"* aware of the ambiguities.

Since I am a teacher by profession, it is impossible for me to view my companions in the intensive Japanese course simply as fellow students. I also imagine what it must be like to teach us and imagine *sensei* must be just about ready to commit *seppuku* (ritual suicide).

What a bunch! All three of us in the introductory course are auditors, an inauspicious start. One has already taken first-year Japanese several years before and is taking the intensive summer course as a review before signing up for the notoriously difficult second-year class in the fall. He makes it clear early on that he has no intention of participating in the many extracurricular events planned for the summer. The second student already knows Chinese but, since he has a Japanese girlfriend, wants to pick up Japanese too. He's a graduate student, very smart, who assumes Japanese is going to be a breeze. His frustration level mounts each day as it becomes clear that Japanese is far harder than he anticipated and there's virtually no transfer from Chinese.

The third student is me. Having lived in Japan three times, I know hundreds, perhaps thousands, of interesting, offbeat, and archaic words (I'm especially good at Buddhist sutras—the equivalent of ecclesiastical Latin). I know no grammar and can barely utter a complete sentence, although I do know the words for emotional states and how to use them throughout a conversation to situate the discourse the way the Japanese do: *hazukashii, natsukashii, okashii, sabishii, ureshii*—I'm embarrassed, nostalgic, funny, sad, happy. I also know dozens of quaint expressions such as *Mochi wa mochiya* (If you want rice cakes, go to the rice cake maker). The teacher doesn't have a clue what to do with me.

To make matters worse, I'm older than she is and a full professor at the university where she is an instructor. Although she's an Americanized Japanese, this upsetting of the usual hierarchy is unsettling to her. She can't believe that I'm failing her class. Badly. She offers apologetic comments about how it's harder to learn a language as you get older. This doesn't make me any happier.

I leave each day drained, from the not-learning as well as from the tense interactions among my classmates. There are too many distractions, too many conflicts. At first it feels like high school, then junior high, and finally grade school. Driving to class each morning, my stomach knots the way it did when I was a kid waiting for the school bus to come. After a week in this intensive Japanese course, I'm so demoralized that I actually make a stack of all the books I've written and put it on my desk, just beyond my Japanese homework assignments, as a tangible and consoling reminder that I am not that schoolgirl anymore but a professor at a prestigious university.

"How would you like to go out to the house with me today?" I ask a friend, when a meeting we're supposed to attend is canceled unexpectedly. "I love it there. The windows aren't in yet and it feels like the treehouse I used to hide out in when I was little."

My friend is a French teacher. We sit on the subfloor of my future study, and she listens attentively as I tell her about Japanese class and how much it is undermining my self-esteem. This course brings back all the horrors of having been a problem student. I wasn't just being unruly or defiant back then; I didn't learn the way most people do, and I probably never will. Now I'm not learning Japanese and I hate the sense of failing.

"There are other ways to learn languages," she says, soothingly, "more natural, less structured ways. You should be taking a totally different kind of class."

But right now there is no other kind. I'm going to Oki. I need to learn Japanese and I need to learn it *now.*

Sometimes, after the carpenters leave for the day, I go to the house to study Japanese. I sit in what will be the tatami room, taking in the view of the path that winds down the hillside between the beech trees, to the lake that looks cool even on a hot, humid June day in North Carolina. I breathe deeply and rhythmically, seeking Buddhist calm. I open my Japanese workbook and start to fill in the blanks. Helplessly, I start to cry.

Suddenly, there is a major problem that makes the humiliations of my Japanese summer seem insignificant. Ted's mother is seriously ill. She had been diagnosed the previous summer with congestive heart failure, but for a year a new medicine worked well. Now she is very sick again. We talk daily to Karen, Ted's sister in Alberta, Canada. It's not dire yet, she says. No, she doesn't want me to drop my Japanese course and come to Canada.

"Mom's been a teacher all her life," Karen says. "She of all people would want you to finish that class. *I'm* not dropping the course I'm taking," she says.

She assures me that we have more time. "I promise I'll let you know if there's any change at all in Mom's condition."

When she talks to Ted, she says something she doesn't say to me. She says that, although Mom is not in any immediate danger, the doctors are sure she won't live much longer.

"I'm sorry, honey, but I won't be able to go to Oki with you this summer," Ted says quietly, when he finishes talking to his sister. "I'm afraid this might be my last chance to spend time with my mother."

When I went to Oki the first time, I needed to be alone, to sort out the pains in my life. Now I want Ted with me, to become part of this fantasy world of mine. I want him to meet my friends there, to feel the ocean breezes. I know he won't be able to snorkel to the garbage beaches with me, but the coral reefs are so close to shore that I'm sure with a life preserver and a diving mask he could go out just a little way and see that whole rainbow world beneath the waves.

"If Mom doesn't get better," I tell him, unable to face the fact that she is dying, "I'll cancel the trip to Oki for *Obon*. If she doesn't improve soon, I'll finish up the Japanese class and then join you in Canada. I can always go to Oki in the fall."

Inez Marie McCarthy Davidson. Ted's mother. Mom, I call her, and she's been a mother to me for the last twenty years of my life. If she doesn't get better, I'll miss Oki at *Obon,* the Festival of the Dead. Right now, death is closer to home.

≈≈≈

Here's what gets me through Japanese class. When the photograph cards have been flashed for the tenth or fifteenth time, so many times that the other students are ready to shriek with boredom, and when I am able to come up with adjectives that describe the photos but still cannot remember the precise word—the lesson word—that matches the cards, I pretend I'm on Oki. I re-create a scene from my last visit, only this time, in my fantasy, I am chatting fluently, effortlessly.

I pass Suzuki-san one morning in front of Big Ben. She's tossing a bucket of water over her stoop, cleansing it. Instead of our usual laconic conversations, this time I say in perfect Japanese, "I noticed that you weren't at the Bon Odori dance last night. I missed you. I hope you weren't ill." (Negative hope, hard to express in any language. I pull this off flawlessly.) In fact, my Japanese is so good in this fantasy that I can strip it down, the way the Japanese do, leaving things vague, without pronouns, allowing the conversation to proceed by context, nuance, emotion, intuition. Only the most boorish Japanese would deign to express the *subject* of a sentence. *"Bon Odori.* Healthy? Missed." I realize with a smile that this is exactly how I communicated before I started this insufferable course.

How is it possible to study so hard and learn so little? I tell friends I'm spending the summer un-learning Japanese. *"Wakarimasu, wakarimasu,"* I say and smile at the students we have lunch with from the advanced class, I hear you talking, I don't know what in hell you're saying.

The only thing I seem to be doing right is writing. Each day we are to keep a diary. On Fridays, we hand these in. I ask *sensei* if, instead of a diary, I might write letters to Japanese friends. She consents immediately. She's delighted that there's something I can do, something I enjoy.

I write my first letter to Professor Sano, my longtime guide to Japanese life, my former department head, my friend. I hope I have the form correct. I begin, *"Haikei,"* the standard formal greeting, then change to *"Zenryaku,"* the less formal one that translates, literally, as an apology for not using the more formal one. How's your health? I ask, the requisite opening. Please take care of yourself. *Sate,* well, now: the first third of the letter is a warm-up, an attempt to do in writing what one would normally do in conversation.

I then tell Professor Sano of my plans to visit Japan this summer, of the way I love Japan and how frustrating it has been to love a place without being able to communicate. Which is why I am studying very hard, taking an intensive course with other students younger than my son, Charles. Despite the best efforts of my excellent *sensei,* I write, I am a poor student, the worst in the class. I try to make this funny but we don't get to humor in the first year. I do not tell him that the one-page letter consumes most of an afternoon and requires much consultation with my grammar books and dictionary. The letter ends with the date, my name in small letters at the bottom, his name in large ones at the top. I hope I have this right.

Professor Sano writes back by return mail. He is honored that I sent him the first letter I've ever written in Japanese. He will cherish it for the rest of his life. He answers, kindly, by using *hiragana* rather than the difficult Chinese characters. I can tell he is writing to me simply, so that I might understand. *Gambatte kudasai!* he ends his letter. Good luck, but also, literally, work hard. The Japanese don't leave much to chance.

My second letter goes to Naomo-kun, the son of Ichirō and Maryvonne. When we were on Oki together, Naomo-kun was my *sensei,* teaching me Japanese words and phrases, constantly frustrated at my ineptitude.

"She could at least make an effort," I heard him say to his

mother one night in Japanese. He still doesn't comprehend how I can understand more than I know.

"Dear *sensei,*" I begin my letter to Naomo-kun. I tell him I am studying hard, about how even this simple letter will go to my teacher first as an assignment and will, I know, come back to me covered in red, with corrections everywhere. I tell him how I know from his mother that he has just begun to study English, at *chūgakkō* (junior high), and I tell him I hope he has his parents' wonderful abilities with language.

"*Gambatte kudasai!*" I end my letter.

"Useless!" Maryvonne says when she calls a week later. "Naomo got your letter. He was very moved. He's been trying to answer in English but he's useless—no ear at all. He's even worse than you! Don't hold your breath for a reply," she warns me.

"Thank goodness!" I exclaim. "Maybe he'll be more sympathetic to me next time I'm in Japan."

My third letter is to Suzuki-san at Big Ben. I tell her how excited I am to return to Oki for *Obon.* I tell her that I am learning some Japanese so perhaps this time I will be able to communicate better. I tell her that I hope her grandmother is still *genki,* healthy. I wish I could write about how my own grandmother was still alive when I got home, how I had to fight with the doctors and demand that they let her have painkillers; and how, two months later, finally, after a struggle, she died one day in her sleep—but not before she had seen and admired the photographs of Oki. When she died, one of the small glass balls from Oki was on the bed table beside her.

This is not anything I'd write in a letter to Suzuki-san, even if I knew how. It would be presumptuous to write such a thing given our brief acquaintance; in Japan, death would come more formally, by a card with a black border sent at New Year's, nothing stated. Just that black border and then calls would be made, discreetly, to find out who died, when, where, how. Instead, I tell Suzuki-san how the huge glass ball she gave me occupies the place of honor in my living room in North Carolina just as it did before in New Jersey, during the year I taught at Princeton, and, before that, in Haslett, Michigan. I tell her when I look at it I think of Oki. I tell her I am happy I will see her again at *Obon.* I want to write that maybe this time she will join my friends and me for the *sharabune,* the launching of the straw boats, and perhaps she will dance with us at the *bon odori,* she will join the moving circle, two steps forward, one back, the sad-happy final event of *Obon,* when we laugh and sing and dance together before friends and relatives depart for distant cities and the spirits return to *meido,* the world of darkness. Instead, I write that I hope to see her soon.

Suzuki-san doesn't answer my letter.

~~~

Mom isn't getting any better. I decide to call off my trip to Japan for the summer.

"Will you give my best to Suzuki-san?" I ask Maryvonne, after explaining my change in plans. "Will you tell her that I'll come in November, when the seas are rough, and we can talk then, in Japanese?"

"I will tell our friends on Oki," Maryvonne says, "that you will send your spirit to Oki for *Obon* and we will all dance together at the *bon odori.*"

"That will be fun," I say, wistfully.

~~~

In her next call, my sister-in-law tells us that Ted's mother is much worse. Although we have all promised her that she can die at home with dignity, Karen has relented and taken Mom to a hospital because the doctor assures her that there Mom can either recover or die comfortably, out of pain.

"I don't know if I did the right thing," Karen says sadly.

"We'll be there immediately," Ted says. "We can fly out tomorrow afternoon and be in Calgary tomorrow night."

Out of a sense of duty, I drag myself to class. I fail another big exam, not quite as badly as the first one, but I'm still not passing the course.

After class, I call *sensei* aside. I tell her what is happening, that I'm leaving immediately and probably won't be back to finish the class. It feels like a reprieve. But I don't say that. I apologize again—yet again—for having been such a terrible student.

"Give me a break, Cathy," she says in her delightfully idiomatic English. "How many foreigners have you met who speak perfect Japanese and don't get a thing? Would you trade their language ability for your Japanese friends?"

"That's a nice thing for you to say," I answer halfheartedly, "but I notice that you said it to me in English."

"Don't be a *baka*" (fool), she teases. "What's your favorite saying, '*Ura ni wa ura ga aru*'?"

I laugh. The reverse side has a reverse side.

"*Wakarimasu*," I bow humbly, parodically.

She puts her hand on my forearm. "I'm very sorry about your mother-in-law. *Gambatte kudasai!*"

When we arrive in Calgary, everyone looks pale, exhausted. It is late and we go immediately to Mom's hospital room. She lies on her back, her body propped up with pillows, fluids dripping through tubes into her veins. She opens her eyes for a second, recognizes us, then closes them again. Ted goes to her, kisses her, and takes her hand in his. He talks to her, even though she cannot talk back. Mom's whole body seems suddenly at ease: I hear you talking, son. There is a glimmer of a smile. Her breathing relaxes. *Wakarimasu.*

"We've been telling her all day that you were coming," Karen says. "She waited."

We stay for several hours, speaking to this unspeaking body, and then Karen says we should probably all get some sleep, Mom too. They've been here all day and the hospital will call us if there is any change.

That night we make a call to Vancouver where the rest of Ted's family is staying with our nephew, Bruce, who is undergoing complicated microsurgery on the leg that was crushed in the car accident several years ago. No one refers back to that accident tonight but we're all thinking about it. Once again we feel death's imminence and the distance between us.

Next day, we assemble again at Mom's bedside: Ted and me, with Charles and Susan; Karen with her teenage daughter, Jo, and Jo's boyfriend, and Karen's husband, Sykes. Ted and Karen each take one of Mom's hands. They talk to her. She cannot speak but we know she understands. Ted and Karen whisper memories from when they were growing up and then tell stories from Mom's childhood, stories made familiar over the years by her telling. Ted says how proud they all were that she was their mother and talks about her teaching, over fifty years in the classroom, such a legendary teacher that someone's written a master's thesis about the way she inspired her students to get out of Mountain View and to win scholarships to the University of Chicago or Oxford. I think how Ted, Charles, and I always tried to go back every August. Like *Obon,* returning to the ancestral village. Others returned too, including the students who had gone on to careers elsewhere. No one passed through Mountain View without stopping to visit Mrs. Davidson.

When it's my turn to talk, I find myself gripping Mom's strong hand tightly, telling her about my Japanese class. I tell her that I've worked hard but I'm just not good at languages. I tell her that many times I've wished she were my teacher. I have a feeling that she would be able to figure out why I'm not making the right connections and she would know what I need to learn to speak Japanese.

Even the least academically gifted kids in Mountain View swear Mrs. Davison could teach them anything. I remember the story of Rodney, Ted's best friend growing up, who just couldn't do math. One day, Mom noticed him counting on his fingers under the desk. She watched him, and realized he had figured out a system for getting through some pretty complicated math by calculating with his fingers. She gave him an abacus, explained the basic principles, and showed him how to make his trick work even better. For the rest of his life, he could sell cattle at auction or do any other kind of arithmetic by inconspicuously touching his fingertips.

"You're so good, you could even teach me Japanese, Mom, I know it!" I whisper, and everyone in the room laughs. She squeezes my hand.

She is dying and I still look to her as a guide. I tell her about the new house in Cedar Grove.

"Ted says the local store looks just like the one in Mountain View forty years ago, when he was growing up. You'd like Cedar Grove, Mom."

I tell her we're near the Smokies, the oldest mountains in North America, and maybe someday we'll bring back a pine tree from there for our yard, something she loved to do after a drive through the Canadian Rockies. I tell her how we found a dwarf Alberta spruce at a local nursery and we planted it on a small knoll at the entrance to our property. It makes us think of her whenever we come home.

I invite her to come visit us sometime in North Carolina. Sometime I think she will.

≈

A kind nurse supplies morphine when Mom needs it. A doctor comes in to explain that the heart machine has been running without interruption for three days, which means her own heart has stopped functioning. It is the same with the kidney machine. Mom knew when she began taking pills a year ago, for congestive heart failure, that they would restore her health but might shorten her life. At eighty-three, she's had a full, rich life, and, judged by her own terms, the medicine proved to be a good bet. She's had a great year, cheering at each of her granddaughter's basketball games, at her grandson's football games, going once a week with her son-in-law, Sykes, to the Calgary Stampede Grounds to watch the thoroughbreds run, never placing more than a two-dollar bet but betting on every race and cheering and coaxing on the horses like a high roller, poring over the daily racing forms at the breakfast table.

"I like to watch the horses run, whether I win or lose," she'd say. "But I like it lots better when I win."

Now this woman of endless stories, a teacher, lies without words, waiting to die.

The doctor comes in to talk to us again. He is a Sikh, a religious man, very calm, kind. He explains in medical terms that our mother's vital functions have all stopped. She could be kept alive on the machines, but she will never be able to leave the hospital again. All the evidence indicates total kidney and heart failure. She'll never speak again. But she can remain indefinitely in this semicomatose state on the machines.

"We promised our mother we would never allow her to die like this," Ted insists. "If we have to, we'll check her out of the hospital and let her die naturally, at home."

Ted and I have talked about this a lot. He knows the medical battles my family endured when my grandmother was dying two years ago. We know from a friend whose father is dying in the States that without a Living Will death can be prolonged, barbarously. But this is Canada. The family's wishes count here. And the patient's.

"She wouldn't want to stay here like this," Karen agrees.

Somehow, out of the silence of her dying, Ted's mother hears this conversation with the doctor. She summons extraordinary strength and responds, nodding her head vigorously, agreeing. We are all startled by this sudden movement. We have no doubts about what this iron-willed woman wants. Even deprived of words, she makes her wishes clear.

"We can keep your mother comfortable until she dies," the doctor says calmly. "And, of course, if it is the wish of the family, we can remove the artificial support system."

"Yes!" we all say, the children and grandchildren in the room together. Again Mom nods her head. Yes.

"I'll ask you to leave the room while I unplug the machines," the doctor says. "After that, her body will be on its own. She will live out her natural life. It could be just a few minutes or maybe hours or even days."

Tears are streaming down our faces. Mom grips Ted's hand, Karen's. A firm grip. A woman who has lived her life on the farm. She is saying good-bye.

We all decide that we want to be in the room when she is dying. We want to be there, no matter how hard it is. We're doing this for Grandma. We have celebrated this woman's life together, and we will do what we can to ease her into death. Our culture has no *Obon* ready-made, but we are filling in as best we can.

Death starts at sunset. Her favorite time. How often have we driven her to the mountains or to a nearby lake to watch the sun set? From her hospital window, we look across the coulee, the deep gash in the parched prairie landscape, the last gasp of flatlands before the Rockies. It is a wide landscape, the sky streaked red and orange.

"I knew she'd wait until sunset to die." Jo, our niece, a young poet, reaches for symbolism. "She loved sunsets better than anything. This is hers."

Jo's boyfriend, a Catholic from a Portuguese immigrant family, whispers a prayer, bowed head, and makes the sign of the cross. With my Catholic and Jewish family and my Protestant education, the only prayer I can remember at the moment is a chant I heard repeated over and over by pilgrims who—like Ted, Charles, and me—were visiting Mount Kōya to pay respects at the burial place of Japan's great holy man, Kōbō Daishi. *Namu Daishi Henjō Kongō, Namu Daishi Henjō Kongō:* "We two, pilgrims together, the Daishi and I."

We stand here—children, grandchildren, in-laws, cousins, friends—holding hands in a circle around our mother's bed. Together we represent nine different ethnic groups and five different religious backgrounds, all in one room, a "mosaic," as they say in Canada. We grapple with the moment, trying to make sense from polyglot tradition. We have no eggplant bull, no white melon horse to ease Mom's journey to the other world.

Karen's husband, Sykes, has been watching out the window. He finds what he is after on the mauve horizon, an eagle soaring quietly there. Sykes is Metis, a descendant of Cree Indians who married early French settlers of Canada. Sykes's parents are from the far north. His mother was sixteen before she saw a white person. Although she's a devout Catholic, she's never found Catholicism a hindrance to her Native beliefs. I have heard her tell stories of shaking tepees, of wolfmen disappearing in the moonlight, their footsteps visible and transcendent in the snow.

"Grandma, the eagle is here," Sykes whispers, leaning over his mother-in-law. He brushes a strand of hair from her forehead, giving her permission.

She doesn't answer. In a moment her body is still.

The sky settles into a deep violet, the eagle is gone. We hold on to one another, an unsteady circle, and leave the room together. I think of the *bon odori,* the shifting circle on the last night of *Obon,* the Festival of the Dead. We hold one another, then we return, one by one, each person saying a private good-bye. We've never been taught the words for this farewell. We find words all our own.

13

PHOTO ALBUM: THE FOURTH JOURNEY

Is it the silence of the photograph—the untold story lurking behind the formal pose—that the Japanese find so compelling? Or perhaps photography appeals because it memorializes, freezing an image in time. The captured instant often takes on meanings far more portentous than the actual event. Especially after tragedy—a death, the end of a relationship, or just the inevitable passage of time—a photograph can become as poignant as a haiku. The classic Japanese snapshot, *kinen shashin* (a significant or exotic scene validated by the posed presence of a familiar figure in the foreground), seems designed to simplify what Buddhism renders problematic, the very nature of existence, the self. "I was here," the photograph brazenly asserts. "I exist."

I finally returned to Japan in the fall of 1990. A major photographic exhibition was being held in Kyoto as part of the commemoration of the 150th anniversary of the invention of photography, and a number of Japanese universities had invited me to give talks on the beginnings of photography in the West, the subject of my current research. I thought it would be a perfect opportunity to learn about the beginnings of Japanese photography and to talk with philosophers and artists about the Japanese obsession with the camera. Why, I wondered, are the Japanese such ardent picture takers?

Returning in November also meant that I'd be in Japan for the investiture of the new emperor and in Kyoto for late autumn, my favorite time of the year—a season of fiery maples, golden gingkos, the light incandescent on the mountains. And I could go claim the big glass ball waiting for me on Oki when the islands would be at their most storm-tossed and dramatic. Then, in December, after his classes were finished, Ted would join me for another month and together we'd celebrate our fourth *Oshōgatsu* in ten years.

The only problems with the trip were logistical. Ted and I could spend December in a furnished house at Kansai Women's University. But for November, I wasn't sure where I would be staying or for how long. Except for the week on Oki, the rest of my time would be broken up, three nights here, two nights there, sometimes a guest of the universities where I'd be speaking, sometimes on my own. I had invitations to reside with various friends in their tiny Japanese spaces. They kept assuring me that they *wanted* me to stay with them, but I wasn't positive that I was reading the invitations right and was intensely aware that I was invading their privacy, an uncomfortable situation anywhere and especially so in Japan with its fierce separation of private and public. I was also nervous because this was the first time I would be in Japan on my own, without an institutional affiliation. I felt like a *rōnin*, literally a masterless samurai.

I'm not good at dealing with this kind of practical uncertainty and I fretted long-distance to Maryvonne. "Besides all these other problems, I'm feeling superstitious," I told her. "It's my *fourth* trip."

In Japanese, four is the unluckiest number because the character for *four* is pronounced *shi,* the same as the character for *death.* The Japanese avoid the number the way some Americans avoid thirteen.

"Now you're *really* being ridiculous!" Maryvonne scolded me. "How can you come back a fifth time, a sixth, without making the fourth journey?"

"My god, Maryvonne, you sound like Bashō!"

"It happens after you live here twenty years," she said wryly. "You get cryptic and profound."

I told her that I planned to pack my Buddhist charms for safe passage.

"And I'll have father-in-law burn incense for you in front of the *butsudan"* (home altar), she mocked. "Seriously," her voice changed again, "I need to talk to you. I am very happy you are coming now. Besides," she said cheerily, "think of what fun we'll have on Oki."

I should have known the trip would be a disaster.

The first setback came when Maryvonne revealed that Suzuki-san had left Oki, without a trace. The second came immediately after.

"And we'll have to delay our own trip to Oki for a couple of weeks," Maryvonne said. "The Danceries are having a busy year. I can't get away just now."

Besides being an artist, Maryvonne is the manager, costume designer, and lighting and set director for Danceries. *"Nandemoya-san,"* everyone in the group calls her jokingly, Ms. Jack-of-All-Trades. She suggested that I could still go to Oki by myself, but, when pressed, confessed that she would love to come with me, to experience those famous rough winter seas. It would be good for her painting.

"I'll wait 'til you're free," I insisted. "But why didn't you tell me before I came? You know how much I hate crashing with friends. I was counting on the week on Oki—now I have to figure out something else. I could just as easily have come a little later . . ."

"That's why I didn't tell you," she said, cutting me off. "That's what I've been trying to tell you all fall—I *need* you here. Now."

Only then did I acknowledge that she had said something like this in several of our phone conversations. Preoccupied with worries over where to stay—how long, with whom—I had not been listening to what my friend was trying to tell me. Sitting in her house in Nigawa, I recognized the droop in her shoulders, the eerie monotone of her voice. I felt as if I were looking into a mirror and seeing myself three years earlier, on my previous trip to Japan. At a time when I felt dead, Maryvonne helped me as much as any friend could. For the past weeks, when she was trying to tell me how much she needed my friendship, I was fretting about accommodations.

"I'm listening now," I told her quietly, touching her hand. "Is it your art? Is it something personal?"

"That's just it. I don't know. I can't say. I don't understand it but everything's wrong."

"Is it your friend's death?" I asked more directly. She started to cry.

As a girl back in France, Maryvonne went through convent school with two friends. They were inseparable. One of them died a few years ago of cancer. This fall, the second friend died in a car accident in ambiguous circumstances. After the death, Maryvonne was given some of the woman's personal effects, including a diary that revealed how seriously depressed the friend had been.

Maryvonne told me about her nightmares, every single night, violent images of rape, murder, dismemberment. She showed me her recent paintings. Instead of her usually serene landscapes, her new paintings were filled with hideous evil eyes glaring red from under rocks, behind trees, in sunsets.

When Ichirō came in, we embraced French-style, a hug and a kiss on each cheek. I produced some warm socks with leather bottoms for him and a bottle of North Carolina corn whiskey, *omiyage* (souvenir presents) from North Carolina. We laughed and joked, Ichirō trying the whiskey, me sipping a little sake. Maryvonne grew quiet.

After he went to sleep, she and I talked in whispers. Ichirō is one of the most wonderful people I know—witty, smart, decent. Their marriage has been the kind you read about in romance novels. They met as art and music students on an idyllic island in Greece and have lived in Japan happily ever after.

"I'm worried that he's killing himself," Maryvonne whispered. She said that he'd been so stressed out and so exhausted that he hadn't been able to fall asleep at night and sometimes he needed a bottle of sake before he collapsed into bed. "He's like a *sarariiman* these days," she said, sounding worried.

For three days Maryvonne and I talked and talked, nothing but talk, whenever Ichirō left the house.

"What does he say about your friend's death?" I asked her.

"I don't talk to him about that. How can I? This is Japan. Death isn't something you keep talking about. Besides, he's so exhausted these days. *Shikataganai*" (It can't be helped).

"But the tension is terrible, Maryvonne. Maybe if you talked to him about your nightmares, your fears, it would be better. I'm worried about you, I'm worried about him. I'm worried about both of you, and your marriage. You have to do something. A great marriage doesn't just—"

"*Shikataganai,*" Maryvonne repeated.

The fourth journey. No one said it was going to be a picnic. Yet part of me felt almost relieved. On my previous trip, the third one, I was the one who was fragile. Japan got me through it, especially Maryvonne and Ichirō. It was my turn now. *Giri,* reciprocal responsibility, the glue of this society. Without it, nothing works.

The fourth journey. I was no longer a tourist.

≈≈

Every night is a talkathon. Maryvonne says it's a relief to have a Westerner around with whom she can talk, really *talk* about her problems, something that rarely happens in this land of nuance and indirection, strategic silences and politely changed subjects. Even the other foreigners here—the permanent residents—seem drawn to this place partly because they like its reticence. Or maybe, inperceptibly, one grows quieter after living in Japan for a while. I know that after my first year I, too, had become more circumspect and suspicious of words. Maryvonne has waited for my presence, for a friend who can bathe her in words.

I understand more about this silence that Maryvonne is finding so oppressive when I stay for a few nights with my friend Chizuko Ozawa. Chizuko lives in the countryside outside of Kyoto, and she invites me to stay with her while her husband is out of town. She says she'd enjoy my company. We meet at a local train station and then drive slowly, in a downpour, over the narrow back roads to her house.

We stay up late and reminisce about past times together, during the years in which she was a student in the United States and then later, when we met again after I came to Japan. I cannot help but notice that she looks unusually tired and pale, and I keep waiting for her to say something that will leave me an opening to ask if anything is wrong. She wards off my attempts to get too personal.

The same thing happens the next day. It is as if she both wants and fears talking about what is happening in her life. Once, when I ask how her son is doing, she practically runs from the room. Our visit isn't going well at all. The atmosphere in her house is thick with tension. On Saturday, my last day with her, I ask if she'd like to go browsing around secondhand bookstores in Kyoto. I know she loves to do this, and it would be a good chance for me to look for material on early Japanese photography. She seems enthusiastic as we set off but then decides we should split up, with me going to bookstores while she runs some errands. We can meet in the afternoon for tea, she insists, before I take the train back to Maryvonne and Ichirō's house.

When I walk into the tea shop, I see Chizuko staring off into space, a look on her face so desolate that I hug her and insist that she tell me what's wrong. Perhaps she feels safer here, in public, away from her house, because finally she answers my question. She tells me that her son flunked his college entrance exam to a national university for a second time and now plans to spend yet another year as a *rōnin,* adrift and without a clear direction. He will study independently at home (not in a *juku*) for the next entrance exam. I know what this means. The whole family will devote another year—an entire year—to his endeavor. They will walk cautiously around him. They will shape their lives to his schedule of studying twelve or eighteen hours a day without relief, all to get into one of the nation's prestigious universities. If he succeeds, he'll be set for life. Another year on eggshells.

I appreciate Chizuko's candor, but it's clear that still more is going on than she is telling. When I try to push, she abruptly changes the subject. I realize that her years in the West have changed her boundaries for self-expression, but have not removed them entirely. It occurs to me that if I were better at expressing my own feelings, I'd probably be able to coax Chizuko into self-disclosure. Not for the first time, I realize that it may be my own skepticism over my generation's cant about "getting in touch with feelings" that attracted me to Japan in the first place.

Chizuko and I make small talk about the miserable fall weather we're having, both aware that this is not our real concern. Then, suddenly, she reaches into her purse and pulls out a newspaper clipping. She translates. It's about a mother who committed suicide when her son failed the entrance exam to a national university.

"For godsakes, Chizuko, it's not worth *this!*"

"I know, I know," she assures me. "But it's like on shipboard where someone goes around the deck checking on the people who are really seasick. There's always some passenger who'd rather jump than be sick one more time. The discomfort is so unbearable they forget the journey will soon be over."

My friend Hiroko-san doesn't talk at all. Usually a cheerful person with a delightfully wicked sense of humor, Hiroko-san is uncharacteristically somber when I call. I try to talk to her about our favorite subjects—sumo wrestling, the various pottery villages we've visited together—but she is distracted and tense. She says she is enjoying her new life in Tokyo, but the tone of her voice is utterly unconvincing. When I ask if anything is wrong, she ignores my question. She suggests that we meet at Sakura, the Tokyo branch of our favorite tea shop, when I come to do research at a photography museum.

On the three-hour *shinkansen* trip from Osaka to Tokyo I think about the tension I heard in Hiroko-san's voice and her denial when I asked if anything was the matter. For most of the ride, rain streams down the train windows and I think again about this strange time in Japan, all this moving around, all this talk with friends whose lives are in turmoil. Overwork, stress, career setbacks, familial discord, children having problems in school, midlife crises Japanese-style. Even the weather has been terrible this trip, and the weather is never bad in the legendary Japanese autumn.

The second I see Hiroko-san I can tell something is drastically wrong. It's been six years since we last saw each other, when she visited me during a business trip to the States, but even allowing for the intervening years, the change is frightening. Instead of my ebullient friend, I see a woman with hunched posture, a tentative walk. Her shoulder blades are visible through her light sweater.

We bow to one another, then hug, something for each of us. "It's so good to see you," we say, looking one another over. She avoids my eyes. I fear she sees that I'm alarmed by how she looks. We go inside.

She stares blankly into space, then smiles at me vacuously, apologizing. I keep having to remind her of the thread of our conversation. I ask her several times how she is doing and she assures me that everything is fine, absolutely fine. I refill her teacup once, twice. She forgets for so long to refill my cup that I try, discreetly, to refill it myself after pouring more tea for her, a violation of Japanese etiquette, filling one's own cup. When she realizes this has happened, she goes through an orgy of apology.

"It's okay, Hiroko-san," I soothe, speaking of more than unpoured tea. "Please tell me. I know something's bothering you."

She stands up abruptly, looking at her watch, saying she has to get back.

Back *where?* I want to ask, but I hesitate. My friend is obviously on the edge, and I don't know where the edge is. I do not know if asking more will help—or push her over.

Although I'll be in Tokyo a few more days, I suspect I will not see her again this trip. She will make excuses, and if we meet a few years from now, she will act as if nothing has happened.

Blame it on the weather. When friends call, they begin with the ritual lament about the rain, the clouds, the leaves turning strangely, some say late, some say early. Hiroko-san told me that in her neighborhood the leaves are withering on the branches and falling without ever turning at all.

≈

There are times when I love Japan's silences. Away from the din of urban Japan, deep in a bamboo grove, the ground thick with leaves, I swear you can *hear* the stillness. Then a breeze stirs, and it's like the whole world breathing, the swaying of the bamboo, synchronized, inhaling and exhaling, like a sigh.

I've had moments exactly like that with some of my Japanese friends. *Ishin denshin,* wordless heart-to-heart communication: there's nothing like it.

At other times Japanese silence is a prison. You know there's someone inside, desperate to break out, but language, culture, and tradition are powerful jailers. The most you will see is a scrawny arm waving desperately from between the bars.

Even with Japanese friends less troubled than Hiroko-san, there are often awkward silences as they try to describe what they are feeling. Some linguists insist that it's easier in English than in

Japanese. Our language is unusually precise in the fine distinctions it makes among different levels and degrees of certainty, intuition, feeling, and insight. Even psychoanalysis, ostensibly a way of delving into the irrational and unconscious, is firmly rooted in the rationalist assumption that articulation can uncover the cause of particular emotions or behaviors. The "talking cure," as it's sometimes called, is very much part of our Western *cogito* tradition, our concern for ego, rationalism, and intellectual articulation (i.e., "I think, therefore I am").

Contemporary Japanese psychology, on the other hand, derives from very different philosophical traditions, including meditative ones in which ego, rationalism, and articulation are devalued (and sometimes condemned). Such popular Japanese psychotherapies as Naikan and Morita emphasize meditation, gratitude, and humility. In Morita therapy, feelings are considered less significant than will. Indeed, one can will a change in behavior regardless of one's feelings. Both Naikan and Morita are based on the Buddhist principle that selflessness is the goal one should strive for.

For many Japanese, the analysis and expression of personal feelings do not come easily. From early childhood they are schooled not to inflict themselves on others. To tell your problems is to demand attention. Several of my conversations in Japan are filled with pains that I learn about only indirectly or intuitively. Freud in haiku: the withered leaves on the trees near Hiroko-san's house, falling without ever turning beautiful. That's as close as she'll come to self-revelation.

What does one say in a culture that hesitates to speak its mind? Psychologists in Japan are just about as rare as lawyers and possibly for similar reasons since both professions rely on clients who are willing to spend time and effort expressing themselves and voicing their demands. What happens when even the concept of a "self" is a matter for philosophical debate? My former department head, Professor Sano, likes to remind me that Japan never had an Age of Reason. The very concept of "humanism" is regarded as both arrogant and naive. Although Japanese life can be intensely contemplative and introspective, this is not a psychoanalytic culture. Complaint is a ritual in Japan as it is everywhere, but problems here are often addressed situationally or materially, not as part of some Freudian pattern of personality beginning in infancy.

Later, when I'm staying at Maryvonne's again after a stint at another university and an overnight visit with a friend teaching there, I mention how hard I'm finding my new role. I'm being called on to talk, to confide, but the solutions that seem most obvious to me ("You two need to talk about this. You have to let him know you're angry. You both should be seeing a counselor . . .") are irrelevant or simply impossible here.

Maryvonne tells me an anecdote that confirms what I'm thinking. Several years ago she was beside herself when her son refused to go to school, insisting each morning that he had a stomachache. After arguing with him endlessly, after alternating between solicitous concern and "tough love," after trying all the Western motivational techniques she could think of, she decided to follow her mother-in-law's advice and take Naomo to a traditional Chinese medicine doctor.

"He examined Naomo all over and pronounced there was a serious imbalance," Maryvonne laughs. "His *ki,* his spirit, was all out of kilter. The doctor assured us he had exactly the right *kampō* medicines to cure the problem and if Naomo took them faithfully, absolutely every day for a year, he would be fine again. I thought it was crazy! But sure enough, Naomo took the *kampō,* a white powder in the morning and a black one at night. It made him feel very important and adult. He and his grandpa took their medicine together, at the same time. Pretty soon he was going to school every day, no stomachaches!"

Common solutions to everyday catastrophe. Keep busy, work hard, go to the *kampō* doctor. Of course there are deep and abiding friendships in Japan, friendships where (as in the United States) confidences are exchanged and where solace is sought and proffered. But I've seen very little of our Western habit of dissecting hidden motives and neuroses or of trying to locate the cause of present-day problems in childhood disappointments or deprivations. Pharmacists do a brisker business in Japan than psychotherapists.

When psychology fails, fall back on fate. Good luck, bad luck, an elaborate system of beliefs, superstitions, symbols. Omens occupy the same dark, half-acknowledged space in Japanese life that the id does in our own. We believe, puritanically, that if we control the id everything will be all right. No promiscuity, no adultery; no smoking or drinking; no red meat, egg yolks, or high-cholesterol food. Jog three miles a day. Work on that heart rate and all will be well. Such are our (current) curative rituals. For the Japanese it's fortune tellers, charms, palmistry, Chinese astrology, numerology, rituals (never sleep with your head to the north) that cushion existence and make for happiness.

≈≈≈

After I deliver a talk on early photography, I am the guest of honor at the usual formal dinner. The party breaks up early, and the two professors who arranged the lecture, Professors Ueno and Matsushima, colleagues and friends, invite me to go somewhere pleasant for a drink before I go back to the tiny room in a "business hotel" where I'm staying for the next two nights. I think they must feel sorry for me, here alone. They probably would not have asked a Japanese woman out for this drink. Once again I am aware of how talk has a gender and a country.

It's a curious night. I know, from mutual friends, that each of these men is going through a difficult time but neither will admit that this is the case. Because there are two of them, I have no way of knowing if they are reserved because they wouldn't want to tell their problems to a woman (even a *gaijin* woman) or because they don't want to speak of anything personal in front of one another.

Professor Ueno is very ill, probably cancer, I have been told, although no one knows for sure, including Professor Ueno himself. It is standard medical practice here not to tell the patient about potentially fatal illnesses, especially cancer. Not even the emperor was told that he was dying. Several times today, mutual acquaintances have told me that they are extremely worried about Professor Ueno's health, but no one mentions the subject in his presence. At dinner, when I ask after his health, he first answers, simply, "Fine," then, probably seeing some doubt in my facial expression, he adds, heartily, "I can't complain. For someone my age, I'm very *genki*" (vigorous, energetic). Topic dismissed.

Professor Matsushima's problem is professional. He resigned from a high administrative position at his university last year out of a sense of principle when he discovered that dubious business deals were being negotiated by other officials at the university. Now that he is out of power, he is being blamed for the improprieties. His enemies imply that his resignation is a tacit admission of guilt. There's nothing he can say to clear himself. If colleagues have so little respect for his honor, mere words aren't going to be able to save him. Or so the Japanese logic goes. Old associates suddenly hesitate to be seen with him. I've heard all about this, from both sympathetic friends and gleeful enemies.

He too laughs heartily, his face growing red with sake. Only a few terse, even bitter remarks, passed off as jokes, hint at his anger over the loss of face, the unearned sense of shame. He tells us how he has taken a part-time job at a prestigious university outside of Tokyo.

"How can you do it?" I ask incredulously. "You're teaching full-time in Kyoto, part-time in Osaka—and now in Tokyo too?" It will take him almost five hours each way to commute to the other university. He also has a demanding scholarly career. "You'll kill yourself with so much work."

"*Shikataganai,*" he shrugs with resignation. "My *sensei* asked as a personal favor."

He is recouping his reputation at high cost. He drinks more sake.

An awkward silence falls over our table, and Professor Ueno clears his throat, filling in the gap. "Your paper today was very interesting. I was curious when you mentioned you were doing some research on early Japanese photography. What aspect," he asks me, "particularly interests you?"

"Yes," Professor Matsushima adds with new animation, "what have you found out so far?"

I tell them I've learned that the camera came to Japan in 1853 when Commodore Matthew Perry forcibly "opened" the country to trade with the West. A daguerreotypist aboard one of the ships recorded the historic event but also took dozens of photographs of ordinary Japanese life, of commoners weaving tatami mats, bathing communally, walking down the muddy streets in *geta* (raised wooden sandals), a hairdresser combing a man's hair into a glossy topknot, a maid painting white makeup on a geisha's shoulders, children flying fish-shaped kites, old women planting rice in the paddies.

The Japanese thought the Western photographs were very funny. Why in the world would anyone commemorate such prosaic scenes? The daguerreotypist left one of his cameras behind. By the time ships started coming regularly from the West, the Japanese had set up shops in the harbor villages where they sold photographs of Japan created exclusively for the foreign trade.

What were the subjects of these first Japanese photographs? Commoners weaving tatami mats, bathing communally, walking down the muddy streets in *geta,* a hairdresser combing a man's hair into a glossy topknot, a maid painting white makeup on a geisha's shoulders, children flying fish-shaped kites, old women planting rice in the paddies—everyday life in Japan.

"Very interesting," Professor Ueno says.

"Very Japanese," Professor Matsushima laughs.

"In what way?" I ask.

"The Americans came into Edo Bay with their ships and their guns. We'd been living off by ourselves for two hundred years, but now suddenly we have to be trading partners—*have* to be. They want us to change, be like Westerners, but they also want to take our picture, so they can understand the culture they're trying to destroy. Of course we sold them postcards of ourselves." He laughs again. "Can you think of a better way to hide?"

Professor Ueno nods agreement. "Give people what they want to know and they leave you alone."

"People." Does he mean me? Is he talking about our evening together? Have I broken a rule, tried to be too personal? These are precisely the kinds of questions I cannot ask for the answer will not reflect some "truth" but only what will ease the social situation. "No, of course not, Cathy-san, you would never be rude," is the only possible answer. Thus there's no point even trying to ask the question.

It's still pouring when we leave the restaurant. Professor Matsushima insists on helping me find a taxi, no easy task on a rainy night. He keeps his large, black umbrella over me, getting wet himself, and regularly runs out into the street, trying to hail a cab. By the time one finally stops, he is soaked. While we wait for the other fare to get out of the cab, he bows deeply and thanks me for coming out for drinks with him and Professor Ueno. He hopes they haven't kept me too late.

"Not at all," I say, first shaking his hand good-night then bowing, my usual merging of East and West. He looks sad and bedraggled, tired. I am fond of him, he has been unfailingly kind to me. I cannot help adding, "You are one of the kindest and most honorable people I've ever known. Please take care of your health."

He makes a very slow, deep, formal Japanese bow. In the rain, with the bright lights of the entertainment district blurry behind him, he looks like a snapshot of pain.

I walk through the photography exhibit at the Kyoto Museum thinking again about what a photograph really means. Perhaps because of how this trip is going, I keep wondering about the relationship between the photo and the ever-elusive self, about how the person taking a picture is the one who is not pictured. "Hidden agency" is the phrase one of the philosophers uses. The concept feels somehow Japanese.

Last night, I had another long conversation with Maryvonne. Another postponement of our trip to Oki. Three times now plans have been made, then changed. The trip is obviously not working out. I suggested that it might be easier just to drop the whole idea and not worry about it anymore.

"We'll go after Christmas," Maryvonne persisted, "after the concert season is over," she promised, yet again. "We'll go before *Oshōgatsu*. If we're lucky the sea will be rough. I'll take lots of photos. I need something, some new rhythms, for my paintings."

Maryvonne's new series is hauntingly beautiful. No more eyes, the reds are now muted greens and brown. Nature is the setting but abstract nature; feeling, not representation. She says this series is about repetition, the way life comes in relentless succession, bare trees in a winter forest, wave after wave after wave against the shore.

I'm thinking about this when I come to the photographs of Hiroshi Sugimoto. I've never heard of him, never seen his work before. It's magnificent. First there are three photographs of classic American movie theatres. The theatres are empty, the screens glow white and ghostly. Every detail of past and silent splendor is captured perfectly in the beautiful silver-gray tones of these exquisitely sad photographs. The perfection is a mask for desolation, apocalypse, the glowing screen with no story to tell, no sign of life, a theatre with neither movie nor audience.

But it is the next three pictures that take my breath away. There are three black-and-white photographs of the ocean. Each one is simply that, sky and ocean, the horizon line the only "content" of the painting, the difference between the grayer water and the whiter sky, a different sea in each photograph. These are minimalist works, technically speaking. There is also something infinite here. Beyond words. No familiar figure validates human life in these photographs. Existence—the self—is as irrelevant as meaning. Like his desolate sad movie houses, Sugimoto's ocean is perfect, precise, and fathomless.

I find myself lost in these photographs, noticing the clarity of the light in his photo of the Caribbean, the crisp articulation of each ripple, the firm demarcation of horizon and sky captured in black and white. I can almost feel the blazing sun, the blinding white beaches, although they are not in the picture.

His Mediterranean is softer, with a velvety horizon, as if sea and sky gently mingle here, in love with one another.

I recognize the mossy light of the third seascape even before I read the caption: "Sea of Japan, Oki, 1987."

≈≈≈

I'm back at Maryvonne and Ichirō's for the holiday celebrating the investiture of the new emperor. It's a day heavy with symbolism. Today the emperor sleeps with the Sun Goddess.

Well, we don't know if they actually fornicate (no one knows the ritual except the emperor himself), but we know there's a royal bed in the inner sanctum and, in the old days, before the end of World War II, some kind of physical union took place between the newly crowned emperor and his ancient ancestress (a temple priestess? a nun? a vestal virgin?). It was a form of symbolic incest from which the emperor emerged neither male nor female, no longer human but a god.

Maryvonne whispers that finally Ichirō's work load has eased up. He's been getting to bed early lately, and this morning he actually slept in until nine. His whole mood has changed; he's hardly drinking at all. He seems like the old Ichirō. We laugh and tell stories. I even confide in him. I tell him how everyone I've met this time in Japan seems to be falling apart. I'm not sure if it's the unseasonable weather or if I've brought bad luck with me, the fourth journey.

Ichirō teases that he doesn't think I'm causing *all* these problems, but maybe there's a reason why now, this time, I am hearing about them.

"I think sometimes when we're feeling happy and optimistic we only see what's good. Maybe it's *because* it's your fourth visit that you are able to hear such things."

I say that I've felt less like a tourist this time than any other in Japan. Maybe it is because I have no real agenda here that I am taking more time with my friends and noticing the pain.

Ichirō jokes that this conversation is getting too deep for

him. Maybe, he says, the weather might be a more plausible explanation after all.

"Everyone says so," Maryvonne adds. "Even on the weather report, they say so."

I'm not surprised. The Japanese expect connections between external conditions and internal ones. If the rainy season, for example, comes too late or lasts too long, everyone starts acting strange; it becomes almost a national obsession. The national meteorological service feels compelled to apologize publicly for the disruption and then makes impressive pronouncements about the new, revised dates for the official beginning or end of the season. In the West, our usual impulse is to deny that anything as significant as the ego could be influenced by mere nature.

"Actually, I have my own theory," Ichirō insists in the same whimsical manner. "Perhaps everybody is so upset these days because of the new emperor."

"The emperor?"

"Sure. You know we Japanese hate change. We had one emperor for almost sixty-four years. He was dying for a long time, then there was a year of mourning, now we have a new emperor. Of course people find it difficult!"

He explains that the whole calendar changes with a new emperor. It is now *Heisei gannen,* the first year in the new *Heisei* imperial reign. "It makes us feel like infants again. Our first year. You know we're a very simple people."

Ichirō always jokes—incisively—about Japanese life. When he says that a new era makes people feel insecure, I listen. Change. It's not necessarily a positive concept. I tell him that psychologists in America are gearing up for similar problems when the century turns.

"No change is good change," Ichirō jokes again.

On television, the emperor is wearing medieval robes, edged in gilt. They seem to be suspended from hoops, they stick out so far.

"Or maybe wires, like a marionette," Maryvonne says. "Some people insist he's sort of a puppet now anyway."

It's true. In a controversial speech—much applauded by some but despised by conservative Japanese—the emperor has said he will serve and abide by the Constitution. I admire the way he has virtually renounced ancestral claims to deification. He even refers to himself with the normal personal pronouns instead of the special ones customarily reserved exclusively for the emperor. For some Japanese old enough to have remembered the old system, this all must be confusing. The new emperor has even admitted, implicitly, that his late father should bear some of the responsibility for World War II, something that has outraged conservatives all over Japan. All of this is political but also, I think, intensely personal. The new emperor seems a shy, quiet man, an intellectual. One has the impression he'd rather be just about anything but an emperor. He's also quoted in a newspaper article as saying that he didn't really have sex with the Sun Goddess. He doesn't say what he did do in that secret room with the big imperial bed, but he certainly doesn't look as though he had much fun. He looks like he has a headache.

"I guess this is what happens," Maryvonne suggests, "when you're no longer a god."

At a large dinner I am seated next to a Japanese woman whom I know only casually but whom I've always admired and liked. She tells me insistently and repeatedly that she wants her son to go to college abroad, not just for a year but for four years, even though he speaks virtually no English. She asks if I'll help them fill out the admission forms. We meet a few days later at a quiet coffee shop, and I proofread a whole stack of them for her, then help her with some of the trickier parts. Only later, through a mutual friend, do I learn that this woman's only brother, a middle-level executive, has just died of a massive stroke, at age forty-one. The unofficial verdict is *karōshi,* death from overwork. She's convinced the only way she can save her son from the same fate is by getting him Westernized early on. I think back to the meticulous way she filled out his applications, ferociously dotting every *i,* as if his life depended on it.

I find myself internalizing all of this grief. I keep wondering what I'm doing wrong. Even when my friends have confided in me, I have had the sense that the real story remains untold. I get scraps of autobiography, the leavings of tragedy. What do you *mean?* I ask. How do you *feel* about this? I ask. These are *American* questions and sometimes my friends look at me like I'm a Martian.

"Hazukashii!" my friend Chizuko Ozawa apologized when a tear ran down her cheek. She was still holding the newspaper clipping about the woman who committed suicide when her son failed his college entrance exam.

I reached out and touched Chizuko's hand and she started to sob, something she probably would not have done in public around another Japanese. She was ashamed, but I felt enormous relief. For me, the tears were much better than the stony reserve I'd seen in her eyes. That expression reminded me of the close-up common in Japanese movies, the heroine's impassive face right before she plunges the knife into her gut. When I tried to get Chizuko to talk some more, she merely wiped her eyes and apologized for causing a scene. She asked me if I wanted more tea, then began asking if it was true, what she'd heard, that I'd built a Japanese house, with a tatami room, in North Carolina.

I find myself hungry for American words.

My phone bills for calls home are enormous, hundreds and hundreds of dollars. I tell Ted that everyone we know seems to be falling apart. I tell him every detail, every nuance of every conversation, realizing as I tell the stories that there are enormous gaps that require filling in, crucial information never conveyed and that I cannot begin to guess for myself. Ted and I talk and talk, analyzing, trying to understand. This is exactly the way I cannot talk with my Japanese friends.

When I hang up, I feel as alone as I've ever felt. Tonight I'm staying as a guest in a beautiful villa owned by a local university. It was built by a millionaire before the price of land soared astronomically in Japan. It's the most exquisite private residence I've ever been in, an acre of land, a tea garden, even a waterfall running into a beautiful pond filled with *koi*. The groundskeeper showed me a box filled with carp food and told me, if I want, I can lean down close to the water and the *koi* will actually eat from my hand.

I wish Ted were here. I am in Japan, yearning for my Canadian husband, for my tranquil new house—Ted says it still smells like new lumber—our Japanese fantasy in Cedar Grove, North Carolina. I understand what people mean when they use the word *homesick*. I actually do feel nausea. I am sick with longing to be home. It's silly but I can't resist: ten minutes later I call Ted again.

"What did you do today? What did you have to eat? What are you wearing? Tell me where you're standing. Exactly. Are there shadows from the low winter sun? Is the Japanese camellia bush in bloom? Do the tatami still smell fresh, like a rice field at harvest time?"

≋

I never did make it to Oki. In the lull between Christmas and *Oshōgatsu*, Maryvonne and I took the train as far as the coast, only to learn when we got there that the ferry wasn't running. The sea was too rough. At the ferryboat office, the ticket vendor warned us that the storm could easily last another week.

Unwilling to simply turn around and go home, we went to the local Japan Travel Bureau to find out if there was anything of interest that we could do nearby. We were told of an *onsen*, a hot springs resort, on the sea in the nearby town of Kaike. To Kaike we went, loaded down with our small hand luggage and large shopping bags filled with presents we were bringing to our friends on Oki.

We stayed in Kaike three nights, phoning Oki each night, telling jokes, always wishing our friends *oyasuminasai*, good night.

"Ask if Suzuki-san came back?" I told Maryvonne. She shook her head no when they responded that she was still gone.

One night, Maryvonne and I composed a comical letter to our

friends on Oki, a parody of sentimental Japanese love songs about people separated from one another by a stormy sea. I transcribed it into *hiragana* with a few *kanji* characters thrown in for good measure and felt triumphant that I'd remembered at least something from my torturous summer language class.

"Next time," we added in a postscript, "we will make it back to Oki even if we have to swim."

We enclosed the letter in a box with some of our presents and arranged for the owner of the inn to send the package to Oki as soon as the ferry was running again. The others we decided to eat and drink ourselves. Gluttonous, making up for our loss, we devoured cookies, chocolates, *marrons glacés,* and a big bottle of sake. The *onsen* we stayed at in Kaike was known for its crab so for three days and nights we ate crab legs, crab claws, crab soup, crab salad, crab soufflé, crab roe. We sat cross-legged on the tatami, looking out at the gray sea, the gray sky, the waves crashing against the breakers, picking the meat out of the crab shells, eating sweets, getting drunker and drunker on the sake, two middle-aged friends who don't drink very much, exchanging life stories, telling jokes that seemed funnier at the time than we knew they were, laughing until we cried.

"Oh no! I'm going to be sick!" Maryvonne jumped up from the tatami. "Thank god it's a Western-style toilet." She made it just in time.

I stood behind her, rubbing her back, trying to make her feel better. After several minutes, she came back and collapsed onto the tatami.

"How do salary men do this every night?" she asked, looking a little green.

"Beats me!" I said, feeling queasier and queasier.

We took turns being sick all night, each one tending the other, trying to laugh about it.

"We're probably the only two women who have ever gotten seasick on the way to Oki—*without* taking the ferry!" Maryvonne joked, when she called our friends on Oki our final night at the inn. "I never want to see a crab again as long as I live," she added.

When she handed me the phone, Shimura-san told me that the glass ball he'd found was there waiting for me, that he and his family would take special care of it until I came to claim it.

"We are all happy that you still have a reason to come again," he said, waxing Japanese.

"Our trip is now a family joke," Maryvonne said to me recently, in a phone conversation. "Whenever something doesn't work out as planned, we just say, 'I think I'll go to Kaike.' No matter how disappointed we are, that always makes us smile."

I return to the Kyoto Museum to see the rest of the photography exhibit. Last time, I was so moved that I had to leave the museum after I came to the photograph of Oki, sea and sky without human interruption. 1987. The year I was there. Sometimes coincidence has the feel of fate.

Now I start with Sugimoto's photograph. On this visit to Japan, his photograph is as close as I will get to Oki. I have to face the possibility that I may never return there. I stand back, too far back to see the caption on the little white card. I have never seen a more beautiful photograph. If I could afford it, I would buy this photograph. I would hang it over my desk and never leave Oki again.

The museum is even more crowded than usual. There seems to be a tour of some kind and everyone is moving together, in a huge clump, photograph to photograph. I let myself be carried along by the crowd. There is much I have not seen, and I'm fascinated by the jumble of new and old, Japanese and Western photographers, images I have never seen before.

I come to the photographs of Brazilian photographer Sebastião Salgado. I've seen these reproduced in magazines but I've never seen the original prints. I am astonished by the absolute clarity of the pain in these portraits of poverty and unimaginable hardship, bodies toiling in the gold mines of Brazil. They look like Brueghel allegories of human suffering. One photograph is a misty long shot of endless bodies, hundreds of men snaking up fragile ladders, a body or two on each thin rung, hundreds more waiting down there, at the bottom, for the chance to climb out of the mine. Another is a close-up of a mud-encrusted hand reaching back toward a worker at the top of a precarious twig ladder. The worker on the ladder looks as if he is ready to keel over from exhaustion. Behind him is the abyss, the gaping cavern of the gold mine, down and down into the earth.

Everyone who sees these photographs gasps. Some people then stop and study them; others hurry by, as if needing not to see. An elderly woman in a kimono stands blankly in front of the second photograph. She was there when I came in and remains the whole time I stay, maybe fifteen minutes.

I go on to see the rest of the exhibit and then return to look at the photograph of Oki one last time. As I am leaving, I again pass the Salgado. The old woman in the kimono is still there. I notice how her lips move, as if she's saying something, perhaps talking to the suffering figure in the foreground. His head is bent forward, his mouth open, as if he is panting from his long climb. Her mouth is open too. No words come out. Just moving lips in front of human suffering. Soundless, and the picture doesn't change.

I have to work hard not to weep. I have a sudden urge to touch her, to hold her, to tell her I know how she feels. But this is Japan. One does not talk this way to friends. What could I possibly say to a stranger? I brush the sleeve of her kimono as I edge past. She doesn't notice. She is still there, talking silently to the photograph, when I leave.

14

THE
PRACTICE
HOUSE

"Good evening. Please come see our house," a young woman beckoned even as she opened the door of the Practice House.

In 1987, during our third visit to Japan, Ted and I were invited to dinner at this quasi-Victorian residence furnished in Western style. We were the guests of an American home economics teacher and six students from Kansai Women's University. Like other students from the university, these six had stayed in the Practice House for two weeks, mastering the basic domestic skills required of a Western homemaker. At the end of their stint, they had invited us, two *gaijin,* for an evening of food and entertainment. There were nonalcoholic before-dinner drinks served with little appetizers arranged elegantly on trays. There was an American-style dinner of pot roast, mashed potatoes, green beans with slivered almonds, jello salad, and a dessert of marble cake with chocolate icing. We were there to certify that they had done it all just right. One day any of these young women might marry a diplomat or an executive stationed abroad with some multinational firm. For two weeks, the students of KWU practiced for America.

It was intriguing (if a little frightening) to see our culture through Japanese eyes. The opening invitation to see the house was especially surprising since traditionally in Japan one does not show a visitor one's home. That would be presumptuous and prideful, as well as an invasion of one's privacy. The American teacher at the Practice House confided to us that she had asked the students not to greet visitors at the door with the request that they take a compulsory house tour, but the students ignored her request. They were fascinated by our custom of showing visitors our homes, and they insisted on acting out this exotic American ritual. Our coats still on, we toured the Practice House. They showed us everything: the insides of closets, the American-style bathtub behind the shower curtain, even the kitchen sink. There was no selectivity because everything in America, these students believed, is public. Ours is a country of disclosure.

Disclosure. Enclosure. The relationship between those two words is provocative in Japan. After visiting three or four small Japanese homes, Ted observed that the quest for a house in Japan isn't a quest only for more space but also for privacy. Often houses are little bigger than our 2DK apartment. Often the garden is nothing more than a four- or five-foot strip along part of the back of the house. But what is markedly different is the enclosure. A Japanese house typically has a wall around it, separating it from its neighbors, defining the boundary between us and them, mine and yours. In an apartment building, doorways are obscenely exposed. A neighbor shares a wall. Territory overlaps. People get a little crazy then and dream of houses.

As soon as we found out that we would be able to return to Japan for a fourth time, in 1990, we wrote to Professor Sano asking if we might be able to rent our old apartment near the train station in Nigawa. Professor Sano answered that it was already rented but the Practice House would be free in December and, if we wished, we could stay there. The school's offer was generous and kind. It would also be ironic, Professor Sano noted, if we lived in an imitation Western house in Japan after spending a year building an imitation Japanese house in North Carolina.

Professor Sano explained why the Practice House would be available that December. Kansai Women's University had decided to phase out its residency program. Some faculty members had argued that it was silly to train students to live in an imitation Western house when most of them lived in Western-style houses or apartments already. Fewer and fewer young Japanese sleep on futon anymore, so they hardly needed the Practice House to teach them the basics of a Western bed. And many KWU students had lived abroad, some for several years. Besides, one young professor observed indignantly at a faculty meeting, the whole idea was degrading. What better example of American colonialism, the imposition of Western values in Japan, than the Practice House?

Designed for Japanese students who might someday live abroad, in 1990 the Practice House was being turned into a residence for visiting foreigners. I would be the first visitor. Ted would join me a week later, but until then I would have the huge house on the hill all to myself.

I move into the Practice House during a typhoon. The students have all been sent home and Kansai Women's University is dark and deserted as a friend drives me to the English Department office, the lone spot of light on the campus. Miss Kitagawa, the head department secretary, and Professor Sano are waiting for me there.

"My goodness," Professor Sano laughs. "You have more boxes

this time than when you came for a whole year. You must be planning to get lots of work done!"

I'd mailed ahead several boxes of books and files, everything I might need to write a book on photography. I tell him I'm planning to work very hard in the Practice House.

"Well, I'm sure you'll find yourself a desk there," he laughs, aware that there are two desks in every bedroom.

We're all soaked by the time we've moved my things into the house. I suggest to my three Japanese friends that they should go home before the main part of the typhoon arrives, but they refuse to leave until they've given me a tour of the house. It's different than the tour I had back in 1987, given by the KWU students eager to display their Western social graces. This is more practical: how to turn on the heat, the stove, the shower. They make sure I know how everything works. The knobs invariably rotate in ways that do not come naturally to me, apt in a culture that reads from right to left, and I take careful notes as we go through, tacking up instructions throughout the house. At least the guts of this dwelling, I think, are Japanese.

They ask if they can help me put away my suitcases and boxes, but now I insist they should get home before the real storm hits. My friend offers to drive Professor Sano and Miss Kitagawa to the train station. The rain is getting heavier and heavier. The worst part of the typhoon is expected sometime during the next few hours.

"You'll be okay?" they ask.

"Of course."

When they leave, I sit in the living room. I've turned on the heat but the house hasn't warmed up yet. I'm shivering. I may be catching a cold. Rain rattles the windows. My boxes line the entryway. There are far too many—lots more work than anyone could get done in a month. I'm usually a light packer. This is ridiculous. I have no intention of spending every minute of this trip to Japan doing research, writing. Why all these boxes?

With a pang, I remember that when Charles was little he would make the shift from one parent's house to the other's by bringing all his important possessions. Suitcases and boxes of books, toys, hobbies. We kidded him when we went cross-continental camping that the tent, the camping gear, and Ted's and my belongings took up only about one quarter of the space in the car. All the rest was for his things. He'd sit in the backseat, surrounded by comics and books, reading *his* books, playing with *his* toys as we drove through North Dakota and Montana, Manitoba and Saskatchewan, to southern Alberta. He insisted on moving all those things into *his* room in the family house in Mountain View, Alberta, all by himself.

I look around the Practice House, and I look at *my* boxes. They are my reminder of who I am, *now*. They are my defense, my fortification. Against what? Ghosts, perhaps. The Practice House is filled with ghosts.

I find, more and more, that I hate this house. It is forbidding and cheerless, with an aura of high Protestant austerity. It could be a stage set for *Jane Eyre*—tall ceilings, long dimly lit corridors, waxy dark wood floors, walls once off-white but dimmed over the years to a kind of mottled grayish beige. There's a heavy, old, fifties-style black telephone in a little nook at the bottom of the curved mahogany stairway. I count twenty-six stairs as I dash from my study on the second floor to answer the phone and miss the call. People rarely let the phone ring more than three or four times here, perfect for a 2DK apartment but impossible in the Practice House.

"Well, *that's* certainly British," Maryvonne jokes when I phone her, hoping she was the one who just called. "I remember when I spent my junior year abroad in Sussex, we were always just missing phone calls."

"There's even a small locked door upstairs," I tell her. "I think it leads to the attic where the madwoman is kept."

The furnishings have been collected over the years, by different home economics teachers determined to make a Western house from what was available in Japan. Some of the living room furniture is of the somber overstuffed variety that a friend calls "Brooklyn Baroque"; it still fills the Western-style front parlors of elderly

Japanese businessmen with memories of the Meiji era, the first period of large-scale Westernization in Japan. Mixed in with the velvet are some blackish rattan pieces with beige cushions and severe Scandinavian lines, circa 1960. One rattan table holds a stereo system stocked with Christmas albums going back forty years—Frank Sinatra's Christmas, Mel Torme's Christmas, Patty Page's Christmas, Perry Como, Andy Williams, Mahalia Jackson, Montovani, 101 Strings. There's an LP of different renditions of "Rudolf the Red-Nosed Reindeer" as sung by a whole string of crooners with vaguely familiar names.

I know almost nothing of the history of the Practice House but find myself trying to "read" it the way an archaeologist reads the fragments layering an ancient dwelling site.

It's clear that something catastrophic happened here, sometime around 1965. The cultural clock has stopped somewhere after Beatlemania but before the Kent State massacre. That's when the record collection ends, the *Family Circle* magazines. Even most of the home ec books on the shelf were published before 1970, except for a few ugly things in plastic-covered three-ring binders with "units" on home management and human ecology, color-coded tabs separating one unit from the next, scientific and utterly unconvincing.

The decor is emphatically pre-postmodern. Nothing sleek, high tech, or matte black here. I can't help but think of the conspiracy of the home ec teacher and students who pretended for two decades that the Practice House was somehow like America now. Just about the only furnishings purchased in the last decade are electronic. A color television with a bilingual adaptor, a VCR, a stereo—all Japanese-made.

I think back to 1968—the Vietnam War (with Japan a fueling and supply station for American forces as well as the preferred place for officers seeking R&R), student dissent, Martin Luther King's assassination, Bobby Kennedy's assassination. Is that when the Japanese lost faith in the Practice House?

Or was it the women's movement? The model of Western womanhood in this house predates the feminism of the late sixties and early seventies. Housedresses. Aprons. June Allison and Doris Day would be right at home. The Practice House is an icon to another era, when the American ideal was a mother tending her three or four children in her suburban home, dinner at the ready for the husband commuting from his office in the city. The Ring-Around-the-Collar Mom. My American friends who stay home and take care of their children full-time don't act like that anymore. The American home ec teacher who presided over the Practice House until 1990 must have known it was a charade. In home ec classes back in the States, she'd probably be talking about safe sex rather than table settings.

Or perhaps the demise of the Practice House is connected to the trade deficit and the changing global economy. In *Conversations in Japan,* a memoir co-authored by sociologist David Riesman and his wife, Evelyn Thompson Riesman, about their trip to Japan in 1961, one of the central topics is the burdensome trade imbalance with Japan. The two Western authors worry about the billions of dollars owed——*by* the Japanese, not *to* them. Japan was the world's third largest borrower from the World Bank and had "less developed country" status. Ironically, the whole argument was the mirror image of today's, right down to Americans haranguing the Japanese about the need for greater "quality control" and a more dedicated, educated work force. The Japanese then bitterly decried the American protectionism that kept them out of the auto industry and electronics market where they thought they just might have an opportunity to compete with American products.

The Practice House is haunted by a ghost of America past. As Christmas nears, I wonder just what spirits of other times might come calling.

"Hello, this is the Practice House. _____ here. Who would you like to speak to?"

These words are printed in faded block letters on a yellowing index card thumbtacked to the wall above the telephone. Someone has crossed out and corrected the last sentence, "To whom would you like to speak?"

Every time I answer the phone at the Practice House, I see this card and feel a pang of something halfway between anger and pain.

"Hello, this is the Notari residence. To whom do you wish to speak?"

That's how I had to answer the phone as a child. If I answered it any other way, I was punished. We had moved to an upwardly mobile suburb of Chicago. Our neighbors were middle-class and their names did not end in vowels. Our house was immaculate. And we children answered the phone politely and grammatically. On holidays there were mother-daughter dresses for my mother, my sister, and me. And perms, our straight hair tortured into frizz for the Christmas or Easter gathering and the requisite smiling photograph. The Practice House is a tribute to the American suburbia of my childhood. I don't like it any better this time around.

As Christmas approaches, I am reminded of a color photo dated 1956 that I found in my grandmother Notari's dresser drawer after she died. It is Christmas in the snapshot and we are all sitting at the table, my family, my two grandmothers, my aunt and uncle, my cousin Mari, curly-haired and adorable in the front of the photograph, staring into the camera from her high chair.

The room could be the Practice House. On the dining room table is a white cloth, real candles, piles of homemade food. It's dessert time and there are pies of several varieties. My mother was a flawless if reluctant cook, and she loved to one-up my aunt by serving elaborate dinners at family gatherings. At each place there is both a water- and a wineglass, even in front of my plate and my brother's. We are seven and four respectively. Three generations and we are still foreigners, masquerading as participants in the American dream. The chianti for the children is a dead giveaway that this is not a WASP gathering in the suburbs. Grandma Notari is the only person standing in the picture. She looks as though she's been rushing back and forth between the dining room and the kitchen but has paused for this snapshot, a hand resting gently on my shoulder. My other grandmother is also in the photograph. Although everyone else looks warm, with sleeves pushed back from a house where the oven has been on all day, my Polish grandmother sits in a dark wool coat ("my cloth coat," she always called it), looking as if she's waiting for Cossacks to burst through the door at any moment.

The photograph has faded, as fifties color photos do, to a kind of sepia. My brother, sister, and I are each separated by an adult, no doubt to prevent fighting. That's what I remember about holidays, not the elaborate table settings but the fighting. In the photograph I am smiling hopefully at the camera. My brother wears his characteristic Ricky Ricardo grin. My sister, also characteristically, stares away from the camera, a silent, unsmiling, beautiful two-year-old wishing she were somewhere else. We're all a faded off-red color except for my mother. She's still in technicolor, in a brilliant emerald green sweater that has not faded. It was a color she liked to wear. It set off her olive skin and the shoulder-length dark hair that she wore pulled back to reveal a perfect widow's peak, a wide forehead, arching eyebrows, Oriental eyes, Lauren Bacall cheekbones. My mother does not look at the camera. She's scowling, at my brother or maybe my sister. She is turned away from me. She's angry. An angry beauty, her body tensed forward, like she's ready to spring.

Does this pantherlike mother and the blank-faced toddler, this mélange of immigrants all trying to be Americans together, constitute the perfect "family circle," 1956? I am haunted by Christmases past. I am haunted by the deception, violence, intemperance, and even hate lying just beneath the glossy surface of this picture. I am haunted by the pressure we felt to conform to an impossible standard, not unlike the Japanese students who lived in that enormous Western-style house for two weeks, pretending to be Americans. I, too, grew up in a Practice House and learned that much could be hidden with a few dessert forks and the silver-plated candlesticks.

The curtains in the photo are an awful fifties maroon, the

color of dried blood. The same ones hang in the Practice House on the hill just outside of Osaka, Japan, December 1990.

During the week I live in the Practice House by myself, I write and roam, flipping through the books and magazines in the small library alcove off the living room. It is filled with cookbooks, home entertainment guides, interior design magazines, books that come with audiocassettes, home ec textbooks with quizzes that have all been neatly filled in, and dozens and dozens of craft books with detailed instructions about charming gifts one can make for under five or ten dollars.

One day I open a cabinet to find a collection of *Family Circle* "Christmas issues" dating from the early fifties to the late sixties. They are all the same, only the hemlines on the models go up or down over the years. Even the crafts are interchangeable: pinecone wreaths you can spray paint (the colors change with time from pastel to psychedelic to gilt), accessories you can embroider or knit (always in red and green).

Each night I dream about the Practice House, especially the kitchen. There are eight of everything: eight wire whisks, eight cutting boards, eight sets of measuring cups and spoons, things I have never seen before and for which I have no name, but eight of them. Open a closet and there are eight brooms and dustpans. Open a drawer and eight *things* come popping out.

More and more I think of the students as prisoners of this house, like the women in Margaret Atwood's novel *The Handmaid's Tale.* And I find only one small sign of resistance. There's an inconspicuous bookshelf at the foot of the bunkbeds in one of the rooms. At the end of the bottom shelf, next to the wall, pushed to the back, hidden behind the home ec texts, are two surprising books: a 1970s edition of *Everything You Always Wanted to Know About Sex but Were Afraid to Ask* and a coverless old copy of *Lady Chatterley's Lover.*

"Guess what!" I tell an American friend who happens to call just then. "I finally found something *alive* in the Practice House."

I tell her how I uncovered the books by chance, how they were probably a secret that the students passed on, behind the teacher's back, year after year after year. The payoff. Living in this sterile Practice House, making all those soufflés by day, at night reading D. H. Lawrence—

"And practicing, practicing . . ." Geri jokes.

~~~

In my nightmares of the Practice House, I am often one of the KWU students, sewing madly, cooking up a storm, threading wire through interminable pinecones, sewing yarn strand-by-strand onto Raggedy Ann's head. The doll especially haunts me. One afternoon in my explorations through the house I open a trunk and find dozens of Raggedy Anns in various stages of completion. There are hundreds of black button eyes and a thick nest of yarn for the hair. The yarn is black, not the usual red, so Raggedy Ann can be Raggedy Akiko. There are also some flat head-shaped pillows without any features drawn on them. The blank faces send a chill up my spine, reminding me of the home economics class that I was required to take in seventh grade.

Once a week the boys went to shop and the girls to home economics. In home ec we did the usual cooking and sewing exercises but we also spent ten or fifteen minutes of each class period on something called "Personal Inventory." We were each given a cutout of a teenage girl at the beginning of the course. She was "developed," as the teacher said, and had a swingy ponytail, but she started out blank, with no color and with no features drawn in. Like Raggedy Ann, she was a tabula rasa.

For Personal Inventory, the teacher ran weekly checks on all of us. Were our shoes polished? (I don't remember ever polishing my shoes.) Did the hem of our skirt just skim the floor when we knelt? (Mine was always too short.) Were our nails neat? (I bit mine.) Did we have unfeminine personal habits? (I smoked.) Was our hair feminine and attractive? (I wore my flip ratted and hairsprayed.) The teacher regarded us dubiously, as if scrutinizing a Rolex she'd just been offered on a street corner, then drew a stingy mark on the cutout. The better we were groomed, the more we were allowed to color in. We began with the shoes, worked up to the bobby sox on her chubby cheerleader's legs, the box-pleated skirt, the wide belt, the blouse with the Peter Pan collar, and finally the face that we were supposed to draw to resemble our own.

My paper doll stayed blank, but defiantly so. I thought the whole exercise was juvenile and ridiculous, and I despised the teacher, a recent college graduate who loved to reminisce about her cheerleading days and who smirked with pleasure whenever she managed to reduce one of us to tears during Thursday home ec class. She was furious when, later that year, the boys raided our desks while we were at gym, carefully drew grotesque anatomical features on all the dolls, and then slipped them back into our home ec folders. She stomped around the room with a wastepaper basket, collecting the obscene dolls. I was glad to throw mine away.

For me, Personal Inventory represented the worst of the fifties, even though I took the class in 1962, just as everything was about to change. That's why I hate the Practice House. Here, it feels as if nothing has ever changed.

"It is pretty bad," Ted says when he joins me in the Practice House in December, after his classes are over. I've told him in expensive phone calls how the place is getting to me, that there's an unhappy aura here, an America past, the spirits of Japanese girls past, their failed soufflés and dropped stitches.

"And you should have seen it before," I joke.

I have rearranged the furniture. I have made *ikebana* flower arrangements for the rooms. I've pulled back the curtains to let in as much light as possible. I'm glad he's here.

"A VCR!" he says. We don't have one in America.

Ted, an incomparable sleuth, soon finds the best video store in the area, one that stocks hundreds of American movies, all sub-titled (rather than dubbed) in Japanese. He even finds a place where popcorn is sold, a rarity in Japan.

We have a ritual. We travel or visit our friends all day, return home on the last train, then nestle in front of the space heater in the living room of the Practice House watching some American movie and snacking on popcorn. By the end of our stint in the Practice House, I still cannot make a soufflé or a pinecone wreath or set a table family-style. But we've seen every movie Woody Allen has ever made. Pretty soon we don't even notice the Japanese subtitles running along the right side of the television screen.

"You know, this is the first time I've ever felt homesick when I was in Japan," Ted says one night, after *Hannah and Her Sisters.*

"It's this house, isn't it? Me, too."

"Ironic. Living here makes me miss our Japanese house back home."

We snuggle together on the sofa, blankets wrapped around us. It is Christmas break, the students have gone home, and the heat has been turned off at the college, which means no more central heating for the house. The few space heaters are no match for the chill of this enormous, high-ceilinged, drafty Western-style living room. It feels exactly like England.

"But the good news," Ted says, "is that I paid our rent today and they're only charging us a token rent, 4000 yen a day for *both* of us."

We had misunderstood and budgeted 4000 yen per person for our daily rent at the Practice House, a very reasonable rate by Japanese standards. When we find out about the actual rent, we have two simultaneous reactions. We are grateful once again for the generosity KWU has shown us; and we are excited to have 120,000 yen we hadn't counted on, almost a thousand dollars. We know exactly what to do with the extra money.

"Let's spend every penny on things for our own house!" Ted says.

We begin to buy and buy. A few days before Christmas, we

make our way through the throng of holiday shoppers, up the hill in Kobe to an enormous new store called, in an appropriate aggregate of Japanese and English, Tokyu Hands.

Christmas music blares over the loudspeaker. We don't see any other foreigners but the place is packed with Japanese buying reindeer, Santas, even mangers and plastic Jesuses. "Deck the harrs with bows of horry!" comes over the loudspeaker.

Ted finds the information desk. There is a sign, ENGLISH, in front of one of the men. We go to him.

"Where would we find *zabuton, chawan, hashioki,* and *washi*?" Ted asks loudly, in English, over the noise of the store.

The clerk gives him a blank stare, as though he's just said something in Croatian. Ted looks to me. He's better at grammar but I'm better at pronunciation and am usually better understood.

"Zabuton, chawan, hasioki to washi wa doko desu ka?" I inquire.

"Hhehhhhyh?"

When all else fails, fall back on pantomime.

I indicate the size and shape with my hands. "Pillow? *Zabuton?* For kneeling"—I pretend to drop into a Japanese posture—"in tatami room!"

"Ah, so!" The salesman starts to laugh. *"Mecha kucha, mecha kucha!"* (Topsy-turvy, everything's backward).

Then he switches into excellent English. "It makes no sense," he says, hitting the heel of his hand against his forehead like a Catskills comedian. "All these Japanese asking all day where to find Santas and finally two *gaijin* come in and they are looking for *zabuton!*"

He tells us exactly where we will find pillows, bowls, rice paper, and chopstick holders. Soon we head out of the store with all of these things and more—*chawan mushi* dishes for a kind of custard served hot in winter and chilled in summer; *udon* bowls for steaming Japanese noodles; sake pitchers and cups; *ikebana* vases and equipment.

One of the rooms of the Practice House begins to fill up with traditional Japanese items.

"What a haul!" Ted exclaims, as he surveys our booty one

day, spread out on the twin beds in one of the rooms. It looks like an all-Japanese issue of *Family Circle* magazine. At last we've caught the spirit of the Practice House!

Near the end of our stay, we decide to have a combination Christmas and *bōnen-kai* celebration, to mark the end of the year. We invite our friends—Japanese, American, French.

"Good evening. Please come see our house," I greet Maryvonne and Ichirō at the front door.

They know this story and appreciate the joke. Ichirō presents us with a nice French wine. Maryvonne brings a bottle of *umeshu*. I've warned them that I plan to mix things up as much as possible tonight. The whole house is strewn with *ikebana* arrangements I've made, delicately understated and asymmetrical, a Christmas ornament hanging from each one.

The dinner, too, is a mixture—*sushi* and *sashimi* served on Western-style plates, one of my grandmother's pasta recipes made with *soba* and served on little Japanese saucers. There are Christmas placemats and matching napkins as well as red-and-green chopsticks with Santas on them. Our boxes have all been packed up, ready to be shipped back to the Japanese house that awaits us in Cedar Grove. We don't know when we'll be returning to Japan again. Tonight is a night to share with friends.

We sit around, all of us, Japanese and *gaijin,* in the big Western-style dining room in the Practice House with its dark curtains and dimly lit hallways. We drink sake and wine. We eat pasta and raw fish. On the stereo Andy Williams croons, "I'm dreaming of a white Christmas."

15

HOUSE
GUEST

In September of 1991 my friend Kazue-san called from New York to say that she was traveling around the States for a month on an open-ended airline ticket. I immediately invited her to visit us in North Carolina.

What I did not say was that she would be our first Japanese houseguest since our return from Japan. Did the ghost of the Practice House haunt our Japanese house in North Carolina? I wanted Kazue-san to certify that our house wasn't just another Practice House, a stage set or a theme park, a construction of faulty memory and displaced desire.

Kazue-san is an instinctively kind person, with a delicate and nuanced sensibility. I've seen her, in a single sentence, run the gamut of emotions the way certain musical voices move up and down the scale. As I wait for her at the airport, I remember back to ten years ago, when we went together to Shirahama with the Japanese Women's Studies Society and encountered that irrepressible old lady in the communal bath. It struck me then as curious but perfectly understandable that Kazue-san could be a social activist, working for civil rights for women and for minority groups in Japan, but could also be versed in traditional Japanese culture, in particular tea ceremony and calligraphy. She is a strong woman who has mastered delicate arts. I've seen Kazue-san a number of times since then, but always too briefly. A lot has changed in our lives in the intervening years.

Her plane arrives around six. We go for a quiet dinner and then, well after dark, make the long drive on winding North Carolina back-country roads to the house. Outdoor lights illuminate the Japanese garden. The colorful *koi* rise to the surface of the small pond when they hear our footsteps on the wooden walkway. A frog even obliges by jumping in.

"Oh, yes, we must have a frog!" Kazue-san laughs. "It's a requirement."

She enters the house, automatically removing her shoes in the *genkan*. I pull Japanese slippers from the bottom drawer of the *tansu* (kimono chest) and she slips her feet into them. I feel a rush of nostalgia as Kazue-san walks across the floor: the swish of backless slippers sliding against smooth wood. A *Japanese* sound, I think to myself.

She walks around the house, appraising.

I wait for her to deliver a verdict.

"It's more Japanese than Japan!" my first Japanese houseguest exclaims.

While Kazue-san unpacks, I make us *sencha,* a fine-grade Japanese green tea, and serve it in the tatami room.

"*Itadakimasu,*" we both say automatically, the ritual utterance before one partakes of food or drink in Japan. We bow to one another and sip our *sencha.* We are kneeling close together in the tatami room. The room is 4 and ½ mats, the size of a tea ceremony room, and we observe the traditional rules for host and guest:

Kazue-san sits with her back to the *tokonoma* alcove. Looking at her, I also see the scroll, vase, and *ikebana* arrangement behind her in the *tokonoma*. I once read a poignant explanation of why Japanese sit this way, with the honored guest facing away from the most beautiful part of the room: it's so that the guest actually becomes part of the room's beauty. After she leaves, Kazue-san's image will linger there in my mind every time I look at the *tokonoma*. This is the essence of Japanese art, not only what's there but what's not, not just the object but its relationship to the people who have admired it.

"*Oishikatta!*" Kazue-san says after she finishes her tea (That was delicious). We bow again, "*gochisō sama deshita,*" the formal ending of any meal or refreshment.

I give Kazue-san a fresh *yukata* to wear around the house. While she bathes in our deep Japanese-style tub, I clear away the tea things and take the futon out of the closet in the tatami room to make up her bed for the night.

I've done the same before for American houseguests, but this time it seems different. False. I feel like a character in some schlocky play, a *gaijin* actress in geisha wig, pancake makeup, and thick liquid eyeliner designed to make the eyes go slant. I feel like an imposter.

I recall, with discomfort, a man I once saw at a flea market and antique sale held outdoors at Tōji Temple in Kyoto. He was a Western man wearing traditional Japanese clothes, the full regalia: a man's *haori* jacket, *hakama* culottes, and even the high, wooden *geta* sandals of another era. Well over six feet tall, he loomed imperiously over us all, his blue eyes resolutely refusing to make contact with any Westerners who looked as if they threatened to approach or even address him.

He fascinated me. I watched him slowly bend and pick up a delicate jade snuff bottle. He examined it carefully, turning it in his long, pale fingers; then he addressed the antique dealer in an elaborately refined and polite Japanese.

"Hyhehhh?" the antique man exclaimed in alarm.

When the *gaijin* started up again in his elegant Japanese, the merchant waved his hands in front of his face. "No Engrish, no Engrish," he said frantically.

The friends I was with could not contain themselves. They laughed out loud. The Westerner carefully set down the snuff bottle, pulled himself up to his full height, and strode past us, determined and long-legged, unmistakably American, Gary Cooper in *geta*.

At the time, the *gaijin* in his traditional Japanese costume seemed comical to me. I enjoyed telling the story of seeing him to various Japanese and Western friends. Now, waiting for Kazue-san to finish her bath, I'm overwhelmed by the pathos of it all. Did he enjoy dressing like that or was he on the lam, hiding from some other self? What would drive a person to such a relentless and futile quest for self-transformation (or was it self-erasure)? What are the rewards and costs of trying to leave one life to find another? Doesn't the thrill of cultural cross-dressing wear off sometime? What happens the day you look in the mirror and realize it's all just Halloween and the elaborate costume has done nothing to keep the ghosts at bay?

Fresh from her bath, Kazue-san's face is pink and glowing.

"You look sad, Cathy-san," she says.

I tell her about the guy at the temple sale and how I can't stop thinking about her phrase "more Japanese than Japan." I tell her I'm feeling like an imposter.

"In Japan, I hardly ever take time to appreciate my own culture—yet I call myself Japanese," she answers thoughtfully. "Maybe it's a delusion for us to think we are citizens of any country. Maybe it's too easy. Maybe that's what foreigners are for."

When we bow *"Oyasuminasai!"* to one another, the rough equivalent to "pleasant dreams," Kazue-san starts to giggle. She says my house makes her feel joy. Here, she's a child again. She tells me it's been years since she's slept in a tatami room, on the floor, snuggled between futon.

"What about at a *ryokan?*" I ask. Surely she's slept on tatami at a traditional Japanese inn.

"Yes," she nods thoughtfully. "But a *ryokan* is a kind of make-believe. That's the point. We visit temples or famous tea houses on vacations. We stay in a *ryokan* and it makes us feel good about our serene and beautiful Japanese life. But how many people really live like that anymore? We live in apartments, cement boxes, in cities that are noisy and huge."

Removing her slippers, she steps up into the tatami room, and sighs, *"Natsukashii!"* My house makes her feel nostalgia, the pleasant-sad longing for something that existed once before.

"Natsukashii!" I agree.

I tell her how sometimes my yearning for Japan is so intense I can hardly stand it. I tell her how I thought building a Japanese house would quell some of this desire, but it has had the opposite effect. Always, just beneath the surface of cognition, there's a longing for return.

"Of course," she says simply. "Anyone could have told you that. It's like the widow who keeps her husband's photograph on the piano. It's not there because she wants to forget him."

I hear a tenderness in her voice.

"I know," she adds softly, "because I also yearn for such a Japan."

The next day is hot and humid, more like early August than late September, but Kazue-san insists she likes it. The warmth, she says, feels good in her bones.

We go for a drive. I show her some favorite places in North Carolina, certain roads that make me feel the lyricalness of this landscape. There's one bend that opens onto a house framed by huge oaks and loblolly pines, on a ridge overlooking a rolling meadow with grazing horses. When our son, visiting from Canada, saw this scene for the first time, he said it should come with a label: "Countryside."

Kazue-san too is charmed. She is charmed by the landscape, the friendly people we meet in stores, the mosaic of North Carolina accents. I've been here only two years but already I'm growing accustomed to it all.

"Listen!" she says at a restaurant where we share a meal with our friends Lee and Edith, both native North Carolinians who have long been interested in Japan. Our waitress is a recent immigrant from Thailand. At the next table are some students, one with a midwestern accent, one with a lilt that might be Caribbean. "Listen to all the different English here. Amazing! My ears are very happy."

"Would you ever hear as many different accents in Japan?" Edith asks.

"Unusual," she says. "Very unusual. Even the country people who move to the cities try to adopt the accent so they don't stick out. For example, I'm from Kyushu, the southern part of Japan, but now I live in Osaka and I find myself sometimes falling into Osaka-ben, the dialect there. We like to think of ourselves as a homogeneous people. Not like in America."

"Is there pressure on you, to be the same?"

"Oh, yes. Especially on the children. Sometimes it's terrible."

We talk about a story that's been in the Japanese newspapers lately about a high school boy with a reddish tinge to his hair. Tired of being harassed, he began dyeing it black, but that got him into trouble at his public school, which has a rule against students dyeing their hair. Those are his choices, punishment at school for breaking a rule or punishment from bullies who beat him up because with that red hair he must have *gaijin* blood.

"Oh, we beat people up here too," Lee says wryly. "And our reasons don't have to be any better."

"But it's *not* like in Japan." Kazue-san is firm. "It's difficult for Americans to understand what it's like to live in a country that takes pride in its homogeneity. In Japan, it's very easy to be an outsider—and we live in fear that next time it will be us."

When we're back at the house, I bring up this subject again. I tell Kazue-san how sometimes my fascination for Japan reminds me that I'm always an outsider, in any country. Wherever I am, I seem to be aware of the things that don't quite fit. There are

things I like in both places but I also find myself profoundly critical of aspects of both countries; whichever one I'm in, the other
one runs like a counterargument in my head, in a way that always
makes me, somehow, *fidgety*. That's the word. My connection with
Japan makes me always anxious for the place I'm not.

"But don't you think that happens other ways too? Not just
from travel?"

We talk about this, about being a *gaijin* even in your own
country. Kazue-san is a single, professional woman who has chosen
not to marry. In Japan, she is outside of the mainstream. She says
she's content with her life. She likes living alone. She's not a person to expect more than life offers. But often, she suggests, she
feels as if it's her *job* to be different, it's her function to be seen by
those around her as someone who is happy and successful even
though she has chosen a different kind of life.

"It's tiring sometimes," she also admits.

"I know."

We are quiet for a while. We're comfortable letting this silence last. No need for small talk. It's been four years since we last
saw each other and, without having to say it, we feel grateful that
our friendship has been taken up again as if it's been four days.

"Your life is very nice," Kazue-san says matter-of-factly.

She's never really seen me and Ted together on a daily, domestic basis. She'd met him before, but this is the first time she's
gotten to know him. He makes breakfast for all of us one morning. He joins us at night for tea. He makes his voice soft when he
joins in the conversation, purposely staying in the background, letting us have these days together. He knows how important this
time is for me and how rare a break this is in Kazue-san's hectic
Japanese life and my frenetic American life. He leaves us time
alone.

Kazue-san notices these things. She's impressed. She observes
again that I'm lucky to have such a kind husband, someone who
doesn't seem to mind that I have a career of my own.

"In Japan, that's rare," she says.

She tells me about the man who lives across the hall from her in her apartment complex. He was always kind and considerate to her. Then one day he, his wife, and Kazue-san all went to look together for their dog that had escaped from the apartment. Kazue-san was shocked at the harsh and disrespectful way he kept snapping at his wife.

"Like *she* was a dog," Kazue-san says, then pauses. "No, I've seen him hug the dog and scratch under its chin and talk to it in baby talk. He treated his wife worse than a dog. I couldn't live like that. In America, perhaps you don't have to make such a choice."

"Sometimes yes, sometimes no," I say. "It's not always easy here either."

"Ah, don't disillusion me!" she exclaims. "I like to think you *all* live like this."

"I like to think you *all* live like this!" I gesture to our Japanese house.

Again we find ourselves laughing together.

"Remember this?" I point to a *shikishi,* a poem-paper mounted on a small scroll and hanging in our hallway. The haiku is in her beautiful grass-style calligraphy, flowing lines like wind through a wheat field. She gave it to me as a *sayonara* present at the end of my first visit to Japan. She said then, simply, that she had no words to express her sense of sadness that I was leaving Japan. I don't know if she wrote the poem herself or if it's a famous poem that someone familiar with Japanese literature would know. On the back is Kazue-san's translation in neatly printed English:

> *When looking at the frost on the small bridge,*
> *I know it is the real midnight (the air is quite cold).*

Kazue-san doesn't recognize it at first. When I say it's hers, she exclaims, "I'm embarrassed by my poor calligraphy!" Very Japanese. Then, without a pause, she says something that takes me by surprise.

"You know, you shouldn't miss Japan too much." She is smiling. "You are a very lucky person. Very lucky and very rich."

"I *am* a lucky person," I say.

"And rich."

"Well, hardly rich!" The word sets off all of my alarm bells. I begin my tiresome litany about how I grew up with debt and resolved to live my adult life owning nothing and owing nothing; now I have a mortgage and it's frightening. Besides, the house isn't as expensive as it looks; land and building costs are lower here than other places. In Tokyo, you couldn't make even a down payment on a *tsubo* (six square feet) for what our five-acre lot cost here.

She listens quietly to my rant. She waits for me to finish.

"Five acres?"

"Yes."

"My *university* in Japan is built on half that much land."

We watch the sun set from the small breakfast nook, facing the lake. A heron flies low over our cove. The sky is turning from Carolina blue to a rich gold, a harbinger of the coming autumn. There's a coolness in the early evening breeze.

"Look!" Kazue-san says. "Look!"

She makes me *feel* all of this, the rarity of such simple beauty, my everyday life.

"You are very lucky and very rich," she says again, definitively.

This is not something to argue with. I hear the urgency in her voice. It is *immoral* to sit here, on this day, amid so much beauty, and fret about a mortgage. To have so much and to worry, to complain, is to invite punishment from the *kami,* the ever-watchful Japanese gods, more vengeful than Jehovah.

"You're right," I concede. "I'm very lucky."

"And very rich," she adds. She is being so utterly insistent—so un-Japanese—that I'm shamed into an admission.

"And very rich," I repeat.

Oh god. I could be in therapy twenty years and not bring myself to say those words.

Kazue-san knows enough of my history to know what that phrase costs me. But right now she's not interested in personal psychology. There's something else.

"You Americans," she begins, "it's what I'm noticing while I'm here this month, even on the news every night. Americans hate to admit what a rich country they have."

"But there's lots of poverty. Every time we drop garbage at the dump, there's some poor person picking through it—"

"Of course. Partly that's *because* most middle-class Americans don't appreciate how rich they are. It's interesting: Americans are the nicest, friendliest people on earth, but I heard someone say once that their biggest fault is that they regard their own privileges as rights and everyone else's as entitlements. I don't know if that's true but, as a Japanese, I see what an abundant country you have, so much space, so much beauty, so many resources. We Japanese feel very *urayamashii,* envious. It's hard for Americans to understand this. You feel angry with Japan, all the trade imbalance and so forth. When I was growing up, it was the other way around. America was mad at Japan because we were importing everything. We were dependent and weak. Everything we made was cheap, no good. Now it's hard for us to hear it when you complain because you owe us too much money. I don't mean the government—I don't care about that."

She points to her heart. "I mean in here, *individuals,* ordinary people, we Japanese *feel* this. We worked so hard for Western approval, we have pride, we didn't like being cheap, dependent. But now it's the opposite. The other night on the news in New York I even heard how Japan is taking over America and there was worry about too many Japanese restaurants and Toyotas and so forth. But no one here wears kimono! Look at us! Everything we do is Western. We live in Western-style apartment buildings in Western-style cities. We dress in Western clothes. We eat McDonald's, we watch *Batman.* It doesn't feel to us like we are taking over America. And it's hard for us to see your rich country and understand why you have such a big debt and no one has savings and there's poverty and unemployment. We live in tiny apartments—they'd be slums here, even the middle-class ones. We work and work and work, seventy or eighty hours a week, to live in poor conditions. It's hard for us to hear about how we are so unfair, how we are exploiting America."

"You sound angry."

"Not at *you,* Cathy-san. You've been to Japan. You know. You've seen it. And Japan is not perfect. I'm not saying so. You know about the racism, you know the problems. But sometimes I feel as if Americans *envy* us, especially when they see Japanese tourists buying up Cartier watches or Armani clothes. Americans don't understand how *hard* life is in Japan, how cramped and poorly we live."

She's right of course, both about the bad and about the good. It would be inconceivable to most middle-class Americans to work fifteen hours a day in order to live in a minuscule apartment—two nine-by-twelve-foot rooms, an hour's commute from work. When I drove Kazue-san around North Carolina, she thought even the smallest, poorest rural houses looked affluent.

"Look at all the land they have!" she exclaimed as we drove past a tiny bungalow with a plastic deer teetering on the front lawn.

When we passed a large, suburban tract development, Kazue-san described the houses as "real mansions" and asked if this was where North Carolina's millionaires lived. She's traveled in Asia, Africa, but she has no category for what we consider to be American middle-class life. What most Americans don't realize, she says, is that Japan's economic success has also brought hardships—life is so expensive in Japan. Since she was a child, in the mid-fifties, land prices in the largest cities have gone up sixteen *thousand* percent. She points again to the tract houses. "Americans think we're all millionaires—but even millionaires couldn't live this well in Japan."

I am surprised that Kazue-san has been willing to speak with such candor. I wonder if we would have had this conversation in

Japan. The codes of politeness would have made it more difficult, even with our friendship. Something is happening here, in this Japanese house in North Carolina. I want her to know I've heard her.

"You know," I say, "that we thought about living permanently in Japan. We decided against it—the language was too difficult for us, we didn't like being *gaijin* all the time. There are many things we don't like about Japan, but other things we love. It's why we built this house. It's our substitute for the real thing."

"Listen, Cathy-san," Kazue-san says as she gives me a gift. "This is *better* for you than Japan. It happens sometimes—that the imitation is better than the original." She laughs again. "We know all about that in Japan."

That night we once again have tea in the tatami room before she goes to sleep. Together we spread out her futon.

"*Oyasuminasai.*" I bow "good-night" to her, hoping this deep bow can convey the psychic equivalent of the hug I would like to give her.

"*Oyasuminasai,*" she whispers quietly, then turns out the light in the tatami room.

I putter around the kitchen for a while, then tiptoe past the tatami room on the way up to my own Western-style bed. I see her sleeping on the futon and realize that whoever designed the first tatami room did so with the compact Japanese body in mind. Kazue-san's futon is exactly the same size as one of the full rectangular mats in the tatami room. Her body fits it perfectly. She sleeps on her back, Japanese-style, in the center of her futon, her arms at her sides beneath the covers. Her thick black hair, the roundness of her Japanese head, is in counterpoint to the black-edged straw mats arranged asymmetrically in the room. Her body is the touch that completes the tatami room's austere art, like a Japanese version of a Mondrian painting.

I imagine what I look like curling long-limbed and auburn-haired between the futon. I realize again that Japan can never be my home. Kazue-san is right. We've created an imitation, an American version of Japan. This house is a replica and, like every replica, a fantasy. A moment captured under glass. Turn it upside down. Shake it. Little snowflakes come tumbling down.

16

CLIMBING
THE
MOUNTAIN

For the first-time *gaijin*, Japan is an underachiever's fantasy of success, a place where you can have recognition without effort. If you are young, tall, or blond, you are treated as if you are a movie star. It can easily go to your head. I've seen numerous Westerners come to believe they are as glamorous, brilliant, and important as the Japanese pretend they are. Conversely, long-term residents of Japan are often made to feel as if they will never measure up. I've heard the very same person who has complimented me on my Japanese make a point of correcting the pronunciation or usage of a friend who is a professional translator. Whether you are applauded or criticized, as a foreigner in Japan you're never invisible.

   In Japan, the *gaijin* body becomes a kind of repository for the Japanese idea of "the West." Japanese television is filled with commercials featuring Western movie stars, athletes, or rock singers, many of whom wouldn't dream of peddling goods on American television—Paul Newman, Mickey Rourke, even Brando. Sylvester Stallone sells ham. David Bowie used to hawk whiskey in a super-cool, almost silent commercial, the whiskey swishing around in his glass.

One hot June day, on my first visit to Japan, I wore a sleeveless fuchsia dress with a round open neck to a faculty meeting. Sporting big dark sunglasses, my hair twirled in a casual French twist up off the back of my neck, I walked through the back streets of Nigawa. Cars swerved when they passed me; young boys hung out the windows. A couple of elderly women on a street corner gaped at me. A garbage truck almost went into one of the open ditches that line the roads, the driver was so intent on following me with his eyes.

"What in the world was going on?" I asked a Japanese friend when I arrived at the meeting.

"It's because people thought you were Audrey Hepburn!" she said without a second's hesitation.

"What would Audrey Hepburn be doing in Nigawa?" I protested. "Besides, she's about sixty years old now."

"Never mind," she said. "You look like our *idea* of Audrey Hepburn. You know we love her here. That's why everyone was so excited."

The foreigners who live in Japan are as diverse a group of people as one would find anywhere in the world. There's no generic type of "expatriate" that sums up all of the *gaijin* I know in Japan, and I only know twenty or thirty. There are *gaijin* who are totally committed to Japan, who never associate with other foreigners, and who preserve some kind of shining nostalgic Japanese presence. An admired *shakuhachi* (Japanese flute) teacher in Japan once remarked that if it weren't for foreigners, he'd probably have to give up his family's ancestral occupation. Only about half of his students are Japanese. Most young Japanese, he lamented, would rather play electric guitar than *shakuhachi*.

At the other extreme are those Americans in Japan on business or in the military who manage to live there for years without learning the language and who hate their posting more and more all the time.

In between is a range of people, every one in Japan for a different reason. More important, each foreigner holds dear some image of the country left behind, a recollected "home" that can have little to do with everyday life in that country but that can exert a powerful hold over the imagination. This may be the ultimate paradox of the expatriate. Leaving can sometimes be the best way to never go away.

Our friend Kōichi Takeguchi is a Japanologist who has lived in the United States since he was a junior in college. He came here for a year and never left. In Japan, he wanted to be an English teacher. He realized quickly that there was no way he could stay in the United States and teach English, so he earned first an M.B.A. and then an M.A. in Japanese Studies. He now works as a consultant on Japanese relations for a large, multinational firm based in New York.

"I make my living as an authority on the country I fled from as fast as I could," he likes to joke. Now, he says, in the current climate of Japan-bashing, he's not only an authority but a defender.

"I don't believe everything we have done or do now is right, not at all," he says. "But I do believe actions have a history, and it's the history most Americans know nothing about."

At one point, he thought of becoming an American citizen but when the Japan-bashing began, he decided he'd better stay Japanese.

Ours is an interesting friendship based partly on the symmetry of our lives as foreigners. He teaches Americans about Japan from the point of view of a Japanese man who left his country. I find myself telling Americans about Japan from the point of view of an American woman who learned she could not live in Japan but who admires aspects of it. We find ourselves alternately defending and criticizing both countries. If he condemns Japan—trade practices or racism or sexual discrimination—and I agree with him, he gets defensive and trots out numerous examples of parallel offenses in America. If I'm discussing some aspect of my country that I'd like to see changed and he becomes critical of the United States, I find myself responding with examples of worse shortcomings in Japanese life.

Once, after he had corrected my Japanese pronunciation for the sixth or seventh time, I asked if he was feeling competitive with me.

"Sure," he acknowledged. "You can write these things in English. What language do I have?"

His American wife corrects his English for him, he says, but there's always the frustration of knowing exactly the right *kanji* character to express an idea and then having to translate that *kanji* laboriously into an English word that cannot begin to approximate its nuances, its flow. Worse, he says, he knows he forgets more and more *kanji* every day. Whenever he meets a "real" Japanese associate, he finds he is no longer fluent in the language of indirection and nuance that characterizes the high-level business and social negotiations at which he is supposed to be adept.

"For example, *giri*," he says. "In the West there's barely even a concept for reciprocal responsibilities, the way you have to anticipate someone else's needs, the way every favor requires a return favor. In Japan that's the basis for the whole society, all business and personal dealings, everything. I spend my life trying to explain these things to American executives and they just look at me like I'm crazy. Then I'm with some Japanese businessmen and they'll feel compelled to explain *giri* to me. From their point of view, I'm not Japanese anymore."

When I tell him that I admire his ability to function in both languages, he protests.

"No, no, I envy your ignorance of Japanese!" he jokes. "If I were a *gaijin*, it would make my job lots easier!"

When we first moved into our house, we realized we had made a passage to another life. The Japanese house was a way of finding some peace in our busy schedules, a retreat, but it has also been a mediation between our attraction for Japan and our acute awareness that there are aspects of Japanese society we will never be able to accept and ways in which we would never be accepted. This house is the connection between our American and Japanese lives.

The embarrassment we used to feel when a Japanese visitor came into the house has passed. Yes, the *tokonoma* alcove is in the wrong place and, yes, it is too brightly lit for the shadowy effect that novelist Tanizaki says is its hallmark. We cannot invite our guests to *agaru* (literally, step up from the *genkan* into the house), because the house is built into a hillside and one must step down into the main part of our house. It's against housing codes here to have a drain in the bathroom floor and so one cannot scrub thoroughly outside the tub, Japanese-style, and then soak long in the clean hot water. Our guests (horrors!) must take their soap into the bath itself.

Maybe that's the whole point. Kyoto is a long, long way from Cedar Grove, although sometimes it feels next door.

When Kōichi visits us in North Carolina, I tell him that I'm writing a memoir about my time in Japan, what I've learned about the country, what I've incorporated into my American life.

"Why did you decide to call it *Thirty-Six Views of Mount Fuji?*" he asks.

I say that I liked the idea that I wasn't presenting the whole picture. I liked being able to offer different perspectives on Japan, but all told from my very personal point of view. It is the same with Hokusai's prints; each view of Mount Fuji is intimate, particular, and no one picture is presumed to be the whole.

"They're all different," Kōchi says, "even though Mount Fuji is always the center."

"That, too. My feelings for Japan are contradictory. In the West, there's an impulse to resolve it, to sum it all up, to come up with one and only one conclusion. For me, Hokusai's way is more accurate."

"Which one of Hokusai's prints is your favorite?" he asks.

"It changes. Right now, I like one where you can't see Mount Fuji because the pilgrims are actually *on* the mountain. I like the concept. How you can never really see what you're in the midst of, what you're closest to."

"I see," he laughs.

Suddenly Kōichi jumps up from the couch and hurries to the window.

"What is it?" I say.

He doesn't answer. He is staring out the window, up and down the lake. His head moves back and forth, as if he's straining to see something.

I join him and ask again, "What are you looking at?"

He turns toward me, his eyes twinkling slyly.

"Ah," he smiles. "From here I cannot see Mount Fuji."

GLOSSARY OF
JAPANESE WORDS
AND EXPRESSIONS

aoi: blue, azure, green, pale

awamori: distilled, brandy-like liquor native to Okinawa

bentō: traditional boxed lunch

burakumin: Japan's untouchable caste; descendents of butchers, leather tanners, or morticians and therefore "unclean" according to Buddhist and Shinto proscriptions and caste hierarchies

daijōbu: safe, secure, sure, all right

denki: electricity, light

fusuma: sliding paper doors

gaijin: someone who is not Japanese (equivalent to *goy* or *gringo*); foreigner or outsider (*gai* means "outside"; *jin* is "person"). In common usage, *gaijin* is a problematic term since it is typically used by the Japanese to connote Westerners (especially Caucasians). Non-Western foreigners (including East and Southeast Asians) are typically designated by country of origin: Firipin-jin, Kankokujin (Korean), etc.

gaman: perseverance, endurance

Gambatte kudasai!: Persevere! Do your best! Good luck! Hang in there!

genkan: entry, the place where shoes are removed in a Japanese dwelling

genki: vigor, energy, vitality, high spirits, pluck

geta: raised wooden sandals

giri: obligation, a debt of gratitude, a sense of honor

gomen nasai: form of apology ("I'm deeply sorry")

haori: traditional coat worn over kimono

hazukashii: ashamed, abashed, embarrassed

hiragana: one of the two phonetic systems for writing Japanese

Honma!: Osaka dialect for *"Hontō!"*

honne: "reality," what lies beneath the surface, the private self, one's "true" intention or motive (cf. *tatemae*)

Hontō!: Really! Is that true? (rough equivalent of "Wow!")

ikebana: the art of flower arrangement

ishin denshin: wordless, heart-to-heart communication

Japa-yuki: non-Japanese women, primarily from other parts of East and Southeast Asia, brought to Japan and forced into prostitution

jiko: accident, the unpreventable and unpredictable

juku: after-hours cram school

kanji: Chinese characters (the primary form of written Japanese)

karōshi: death from overwork

katakana: one of the two phonetic systems for writing Japanese, now used primarily for transcribing foreign words

kawaisō: pitiful, pathetic, sad

koi: carp

kotatsu: a heating device in a Japanese home, now typically a low table with a heating element underneath

koto: a harp-like instrument with movable frets; it rests on the floor and is played from a kneeling position

kura: storehouse where family antiques might be kept

kyōiku mama: "education mom," who works to make sure her children succeed in school, stereotypically in a pushy or driven manner

mama-san: woman who runs a bar, restaurant, or nightclub

meido: region of the dead, spirit world, Hades

mon: family crest

muzukashii: difficult, complicated, troublesome

natsukashisa: nostalgia, homesickness, a pleasant-sad feeling (one of the most valued emotions in Japan)

nengajō: New Year's cards

nomiya: small bar, drinking establishment

nūru: priestess, shaman (Okinawan dialect)

obāsan: grandmother, old woman

obi: long, broad sash wound around the waist of a kimono

Obon: Buddhist Festival of the Dead, usually held in mid-August

okāsan: mother

OL: Office Lady; typically a young, unmarried woman who holds a low-level office job such as receptionist or secretary after she has graduated from secondary school or college and until she gets married or has children

Omedetō!: Congratulations!

omiai: the formal matchmaking meeting between the couples, parents, and go-between preparatory to arranged marriage

Oshōgatsu: New Year

rakugo: traditional art of story telling, often involving puns and wordplay

rōmaji: a system for phonetically transcribing Japanese into the Roman alphabet

rōnin: a masterless samurai; sometimes used to describe a student who has failed a college entrance exam and is adrift while waiting to take it again the following year

ryokan: a traditional Japanese inn

samisen: three-stringed lutelike instrument

-san: genderless suffix appended to names as a token of respect (roughly equivalent to "Mr." or "Ms.")

sanshin: Okinawan three-stringed instrument, ancestor of the Japanese *samisen*

sarariiman: "salary man" or businessman, typically used to describe male white-collar workers in a Japanese company

sensei: teacher, mentor; a description as well as a term of respect, sometimes addressed more generally to someone in authority (such as one's doctor)

sharabune: Oki dialect for "spirit boat"; a symbolic boat made of straw that carries food and goods to the spirits of the dead during *Obon*

shikataganai: common phrase, meaning "it can't be helped," and denoting resignation or acquiescence to the inexplicable

shinkansen: the "bullet train" that traverses Japan at speeds up to 150 miles per hour

shukusha: inexpensive, modest inn

soba: buckwheat noodles

subarashii: spectacular, wonderful, splendid, magnificent

sumimasen: an apology ("I'm sorry" but can also mean "Excuse me" or "Thank you")

tatemae: appearances, the proper or appropriate part of the social self, and the expected way of communicating in social situations (cf. *honne*)

tatami: straw mats, approximately two inches thick and three feet by six feet wide, used as flooring in traditional Japanese rooms

tōkō kyohi: resistance to school; a recent social syndrome of students who refuse to go to school

tokonoma: alcove, the most important place in a traditional Japanese room; it typically holds a scroll and a vase with a flower arrangement

tomodachi: friend

torii: gate (usually plain wood or painted vermillion) marking the entrance to a Shinto shrine

tsubo: the six-by-six-foot measure by which land is sold, approximately the size of two tatami mats

Uchināguchi: the Okinawan dialect of the Japanese spoken on mainland Japan

umeshu: sweet liquor made from distilled spirits and Japanese plums

utaki: sacred grove of Okinawan Religion

wakaru: to understand, comprehend, follow, grasp, take in, accept

yakitori-ya: restaurant specializing in grilled chicken

yakuza: gangster, mobster (literally: coarse, worthless, good-for-nothing)

yukata: casual, cotton summer kimono

zabuton: floor cushion or pillow (on which one kneels or sits)

Plume   **Dutton**

AMERICA IS READING ABOUT—

☐ **EARTH IN THE BALANCE** *Ecology and the Human Spirit* **by Vice President Al Gore.** An urgent call to action to save our seriously threatened climate, our water, our soil, our diversity of plant and animal life, indeed our entire living space. "A powerful summons for the politics of life and hope."—Bill Moyers
(269350—$13.00)

☐ **BEYOND BEEF** *The Rise and Fall of the Cattle Culture* **by Jeremy Rifkin.** This persuasive and passionate book illumines the international intrigue, political give-aways, and sheer avarice that transformed the great American frontier into a huge cattle breeding ground. "Should be compared with *Silent Spring, The Fate of the Earth*, or *Diet for a Small Planet*. . . . Draws our attention to a threat to what we most value."—*New York Review of Books*   (269520—$11.00)

☐ **REINVENTING GOVERNMENT** *How the Entrepreneurial Spirit is Transforming the Public Sector* **by David Osborne and Ted Gaebler.** "This book should be read by every elected official in America. Those who want to revitalize government in the 1990s are going to have to reinvent it. This book gives us the blueprint."—Bill Clinton   (269423—$13.95)

☐ **REINVENTING EDUCATION** *Entrepreneurship in America's Public Schools.* **by Louis V. Gerstner, Jr. with Roger D. Semerad, Denis Philip Doyle, William B. Johnson.** This book pulls no punches; it tells how much remains to be done, while it offers a compelling argument for entrepreneurship in education. This detailed and convincing blueprint for change, makes it clear how vital change is to our nation's future as we move into the 21st century.   (937498—$20.95)

☐ **SCHOOLS THAT WORK by George H. Wood, Ph.D.** This groundbreaking book proves that schools *can* shape students not only to master reading, writing, and math skills, but to develop the confidence and ability to take on the world. "This is an exciting book designed to explode myths about the death of education in this country . . . Buy this book."—*Booklist*   (269598—$11.00)

Prices slightly higher in Canada.

Buy them at your local bookstore or use this convenient coupon for ordering.

PENGUIN USA
P.O. Box 999, Dept. #17109
Bergenfield, New Jersey 07621

Please send me the books I have checked above.
I am enclosing $＿＿＿＿＿＿＿＿＿＿＿＿＿ (please add $2.00 to cover postage and handling).
Send check or money order (no cash or C.O.D.'s) or charge by Mastercard or VISA (with a $15.00 minimum). Prices and numbers are subject to change without notice.

Card # ＿＿＿＿＿＿＿＿＿＿＿＿＿＿＿＿ Exp. Date ＿＿＿＿＿＿＿＿＿
Signature＿＿＿＿＿＿＿＿＿＿＿＿＿＿＿＿＿＿＿＿＿＿＿＿＿＿＿
Name ＿＿＿＿＿＿＿＿＿＿＿＿＿＿＿＿＿＿＿＿＿＿＿＿＿＿＿＿＿
Address ＿＿＿＿＿＿＿＿＿＿＿＿＿＿＿＿＿＿＿＿＿＿＿＿＿＿＿＿
City ＿＿＿＿＿＿＿＿＿＿＿＿＿＿ State ＿＿＿＿＿ Zip Code ＿＿＿＿＿

For faster service when ordering by credit card call **1-800-253-6476**

Allow a minimum of 4-6 weeks for delivery. This offer is subject to change without notice

There's an epidemic with 27 million victims. And no visible symptoms.

It's an epidemic of people who can't read.

Believe it *or* not, 27 million Americans are functionally illiterate, about one adult in five.

The solution to this problem is you... when you join the fight against illiteracy. So call the Coalition for Literacy at toll-free **1-800-228-8813** and volunteer.

Volunteer Against Illiteracy. The only degree you need is a degree of caring.